# ADVANCE PRAISE FOR *POINTING IS RUDE*

"Not a simple or predictable inspirational story. Instead, it recounts the complications and nuances, both logistical and emotional, of living in a family with a special needs child…But the book also includes good measures of joy and revelation, showing the family's rocky journey to acceptance."
—*Kirkus Reviews*

"As a father, grandfather and sporting icon who has always tried to use my fame to help children all over the world, I can appreciate *Pointing Is Rude* and the lessons it offers people everywhere. All children are a gift from God. I celebrate this family as they fully embrace their life journey by welcoming a young boy from Africa—a part of the world that has always been close to my heart—to take their journey with them. I encourage everyone to read this wonderful story."
—Pelé, Soccer's only 3-time World Cup winner, FIFA's "Football Player of the Century, Time Magazine's "Top 20 Most Important People of the 20th Century"

"*Pointing Is Rude* reads like a Hollywood script, with more laughs than most comedies and a better ending than most dramas."
—Rob Riggle, Actor/Comedian/Marine

"In his work as an Emmy Award winning producer at NFL Films, Digger O'Brien regularly celebrated the teamwork and sacrifice that defines the game of professional football. In *Pointing Is Rude*, he tells a different kind of story about teamwork and sacrifice, the story of a family raising a child with autism. The O'Brien family—and especially Frederick—will touch your heart."
—Ray Didinger, Pro Football Hall of Fame Writer

"With the eye of a trained documentarian, Digger captures all of his family's trials and triumphs in a way that makes the book seem somehow visual. This captivating story comes to life like a great film, making you feel like you're witnessing everything he is living."
—Patrick Creadon, Award-Winning Filmmaker, 30 for 30's *Catholics vs Convicts*, and *Wordplay*

"The intro will make your heart race and the rest of the book will break it, as Digger shares the cold facts and raw emotion of how autism strains his family and, ultimately, strengthens it."
—Kim Rossi Stagliano, author of *All I Can Handle: I'm No Mother Teresa—A Life Raising Three Daughters with Autism*

# Pointing Is Rude

# Pointing Is Rude:

*One Father's Story of
Autism, Adoption,
and Acceptance*

## DIGGER O'BRIEN

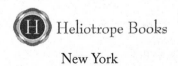

Heliotrope Books

New York

Cover Photography by Jesse O'Brien
Cover Design by Shandon Melvin
Interior photgraphs by Digger O'Brien and family

*This book is dedicated to all Special Dads and Special Moms;
none of our stories are the same, but the feelings are universal.*

# TABLE OF CONTENTS

# PROLOGUE:
## 02/03/04

It was windy and cold, one of those February days where you can never get warm and the rain feels like it's one degree away from turning into ice. My wife drove as I sat in the passenger seat of our Toyota minivan writing a list of questions to ask at the appointment.

How can we get him to communicate more?

Any strategies for coping with his tantrums?

Why have the delays persisted if we've done everything that was recommended?

Bernadette didn't talk much on the ride. Later, she told me she was quiet because she knew what the doctors would say.

After checking in at this suburban satellite office of the Children's Hospital of Philadelphia, we were led into an examining room that had a kiddy-size circular table and four tiny chairs. The woman who greeted us looked like a caricature of a librarian, with large, black circular glasses that stood out against her pale complexion, and dark hair pinned back in a bun. She introduced herself as Paula, the Occupational Therapist who had examined our son.

Two weeks earlier, with me "too busy at work" to make it, Bernadette had taken our two-year-old son Frederick to Children's Hospital for a developmental assessment. We were concerned because he didn't have much of a vocabulary, and didn't play with toys like a typical two-year-old. Friends and relatives said, "He's just a boy, he'll grow out of it." But we'd been hearing that for six months, and the only thing he was growing out of was his size 2T pajamas.

During that examination, Frederick was placed in a cavernous room with shelves full of toys. Paula observed what he played with and how he played with it. Not exactly high-tech stuff. She occasionally tried to interact with him but he wasn't in the mood. To me, it sounded more like a playdate than a medical exam, and I couldn't understand how it related to his speech delay.

Now, two weeks later, I was about to find out.

Paula asked us to sit at the table that came up to our knees but never acknowledged we were in chairs meant for little tikes. No one spoke as she organized her papers. Ten seconds passed and it felt like ten minutes. The tiny chairs were already uncomfortable. With my chin resting on my knee I broke the ice by raising my hand. "Teacher, when's recess?" Bernadette gave me a "That's not funny!" look for about the millionth time in our marriage. Paula didn't take the bait—she was all business.

"Frederick was observed by myself and the speech pathologist two weeks ago. We administered the A.D.O.S. test, which stands for the Autistic Diagnostic Observation Schedule. It's a test that helps us determine whether a child fits within a range of Autism or PDD-NOS, which is Pervasive Developmental—"

I cut her off. "I've been doing some internet research. It stands for 'Pervasive Developmental Disorder-Not Otherwise Specified.' I'm an informed consumer."

Paula looked at me with the same death-stare I used to get from the Nuns. The combination of her stop sign-sized glasses and the foot-high chairs made me feel like I was back at St. Ignatius Grammar School. The only thing missing was my old clip-on tie.

"Let me finish, Mr. O'Brien."

"I'm sorry for interrupting," I said, not really all that sorry, "but before Christmas we took him to a neurologist and that guy ruled out Autism."

"I read the other doctor's report, but we are specialists," Paula continued. "We have specific training in this diagnosis, and you need an expert because there's no blood test. There's no X-ray. Developmental diagnoses are made by observation and inference. We have specific scripts, such as presenting plastic tea-party pieces to see if the child will pour an imaginary drink. We're looking for a certain performance. It's a standard score."

At that moment, six months of frustration and worry and fear finally settled in. Maybe, just maybe, my only son had some serious problems. I began drifting away. The rest of Paula's review seemed like it was off in the distance, like hearing people talk when you're coming out of anesthesia.

*It takes a lot of input to get him to react; he has low registration; zero joint attention; he doesn't point, and pointing is the common currency of communication; no pretend play; he never pulled us into his world.*

Paula continued on for another few minutes and then concluded: "These results point to a conclusion, but I'd like Dr. Landau to come in and discuss that with you."

She left the room and returned with Dr. Beth Landau, the Head of Developmental Pediatrics at C.H.O.P. And then it hit me—Dr. Landau was the closer. Paula had given us eight strong innings of tests results and analysis. And now Dr. Landau was coming out of the bullpen for the ninth inning to deliver the diagnosis.

She introduced herself then said, "Sorry about the chairs. We're used to little people." I looked at Paula—she was reading her notes.

Dr. Landau explained that her job was to interpret what the data meant. She summarized some of what Paula had said, using terminology even more convoluted than what we had just heard. As Dr. Landau was getting more clinical, I was starting to get emotional. I wasn't angry or sad—just desperate. She had yet to say the "A" word, but after this torrent of negatives that pounded like the rain outside, I knew it was coming. After a minute or two she paused, and I jumped in to stall her.

"Dr. Landau, I know he has a lack of speech, and sensory difficulties, but he's a good kid."

He's a good kid. It was all I could think of. No medical relevance, just a last-ditch courtroom plea before the judge hands down a life sentence.

Dr. Landau paused and looked down, as if to compose herself. It was the first hint of compassion I felt all morning.

"He is a sweet boy, but his other issues can't be looked at individually. They're all branches of the same tree. Something is driving all them. The engine driving it is Autism."

She kept talking, something about blood tests for chromosomal disorders and a large percentage of diagnosed children having mental retardation. My wife's eyes were red, and she was clutching a balled-up tissue. Near the end of our session they handed us a ready-made packet with photocopied sheets about special schools and future prognoses. Our parting gift was an offer from C.H.O.P. to participate in a study that would help determine why husbands and wives often have diametrically-opposed assessments of their child's strengths and weaknesses. We declined.

On the A.D.O.S. test, Frederick's score placed him between moderate and severe Autism. We were now officially part of the Autism Community. And to paraphrase Groucho Marx, I didn't want to join any community that would have us as members.

On the way home Bernadette cried while I drove and tried to process it all. It was a quiet ride except for the sound of the windshield wipers barely keeping up with the downpour. I remember saying, "It's a good thing. At least we have a diagnosis now. We have something to attack." Bernadette's contribution to the discussion was an occasional, "Not my baby. Not my baby," in between sobs.

And as we drove back from C.H.O.P. that day, I remembered an incident that occurred a long time ago. I hadn't thought about it for many years but on this day, driving home from a doctor who told me my son had Autism, I remembered it in vivid detail.

In the mid 1970's, *The Six Million Dollar Man* was a TV hit, one of the most popular shows for kids my age. Lee Majors played a character named Steve Austin, who was rebuilt into a "Bionic Man" with more power and speed than any other human. We would often play in the back yard and pretend we were that character, running in slow motion and making the mechanical sounds that Steve Austin emitted when using his bionic powers.

On school days, my brother and I and a few other kids would wait on the corner for the bus. And there was always a kid across the street waiting for a different bus.

A short bus.

He was maybe 10 or 12 years old, never spoke, and never really looked at us. We would yell across the street to him, but he never responded. And I guess it was because the Bionic Man was so popular, and because the word "retard" to a grade-schooler in those days wasn't yet a demeaning slur but rather a catch-all word for someone different, we started calling him the "Bionic Retard." We would yell "Hey Bionic Retard, what are you doing?" "Hey Bionic Retard, say something."

One particular day it had been snowing, and the plows made piles of snow so big they seemed over our heads. We were having a snowball fight on our side and when we got tired of that we started throwing them across the street. I don't remember the kid throwing any back. He just did his best to dodge them while remaining at his bus stop. Eventually, someone on my side of the street connected hard with the kid we called the Bionic Retard.

The snowball hit him right in the face. He dropped to his knees and screamed. But it wasn't really a scream; in fact, it didn't seem human. It was a bleating, animal sound and when he made it we all froze. He got to his feet and took off up the street, running awkwardly, the way a foal runs just after being born. He kept running as our bus pulled up.

The next morning we arrived at our bus stop. Across the street, the Bionic Retard was back, and behind him, hands firmly on his shoulders, was his dad. The man never said a word; he didn't have to. Just looked at us. We tried not to make eye contact.

And now as we drove home from the hospital, almost thirty years after that incident, I couldn't shake the image: a father standing defiantly behind his disabled son. I wondered if I'd be that father someday. Or if I was that father now? Growing up, I was always the class clown, the one who invented derogatory nicknames for classmates. What would Frederick's nickname be? "Freakrick?" "Freaky Freddy?" Would he go to college? Get married? Would life be a constant struggle for him? The only thing I knew for sure was that I wanted to find the Bionic Retard's dad and hug him. I wanted to tell him I didn't realize, that I didn't understand. I wanted to know his son's name. I wanted to say I was sorry.

And I prayed I'd always be there for my son when the snowballs started flying.

# 1 TEN FINGERS, TEN TOES

Frederick O'Brien was born in November of 2001. The labor and delivery was a complicated, nerve-wracking affair. As it turned out, those few hours ended up being a perfect sneak preview of the next several years of his life.

And it wasn't just the delivery—getting pregnant was no picnic, either. It takes a while to get things going in my wife's uterus, but when they finally do get started it's like she's got Velcro in there. But I'm getting ahead of myself.

Bernadette and I met in 1992 at the wedding of my college roommate. Three years later, almost to the day, we got married. Back in 1995, I worked at NBA Entertainment, the film company of the National Basketball Association but then took a job at NFL Films, which is located in southern New Jersey. I was a Producer, which meant it was my job (along with about 50 other Producers) to make football shows by selecting the shots, editing them together into a segment, and then writing the voiceover script. For a guy who grew up living and dying with the Philly teams—the Eagles, Sixers, Flyers and Phillies—it was a dream job in my own backyard.

Back then, Bernadette worked as an assistant teacher in a deaf and multiply-handicapped classroom for the Gloucester County Special Services School District in New Jersey. It was a pre-school class with a diverse group of kids; all the students had some form of disability, ranging from mild hearing loss to cerebral palsy. She loved them like they were her own, which was easy to do since we didn't have any of our own.

Our first child, Anna, was born in 1997. She was a treat, a godsend—everything I hoped parenting would be. So a year later we tried to have another baby. And kept trying. After six months of trying without conceiving, Bernadette started to get bummed out.

The problem is, once you decide to get pregnant, the only thing that counts is the result. It also didn't help that Bernadette had been born into a family full of Fertile Myrtles. Her mom bore six children before the age of 30. Her four sisters churned out kids the way Henry Ford produced cars. So this was foreign territory for my wife and her side of the family. Everyone said "Just relax" or "What's the rush?" and they were probably right. But by the eighth month of trying Bernadette was in full panic mode. Her sisters were on eggshells around her, dreading that time of the month when Bernadette would find out we failed again. Things got so bad that two of her sisters got pregnant while we were trying and they attempted to keep theirs a secret.

We went to a fertility doctor who tried several different approaches including an In Vitro Fertilization, but none were successful. They told us, "We think you should find a different doctor. We're just not equipped for your level of need." The frustration mounted, and Bernadette and I began talking about the alternative—adoption. Talking became research, research became action, and we ended up deciding to pursue an International Adoption through Cambodia (if we didn't get pregnant.) We even had a Home Study done, which is an interview at your home conducted by a social worker who tries to determine if you and your wife are qualified to be adoptive parents. It's kind of like taking a test where you're given the questions beforehand.

But we didn't take any chances. On the day of the Home Study we dusted, vacuumed, dressed in our Sunday best, and when the social worker showed up we acted like Ozzie and Harriett. When Anna asked for a snack, we gave her strawberries. "What about Frito's?" our precocious little three-year-old asked. "I always get Frito's."

"Oh, you are so funny Anna," Bernadette said, then turned to the social worker. "I don't know where she comes up with these things." The woman complimented us on our commitment to healthy eating and then on cue, Anna started choking on a strawberry. After a few seconds of gasping, coughing, and terror, she spit it out.

But we had decided to go the distance with at least one more round of IVF, and went looking for a new doctor.

It was time for an all-star, a big gun, and we found our man in Dr. Rock Star. He practiced out of a town in North Jersey that was two hours from our home, but we would have driven five times as far for someone who could deliver results, and from the moment we walked into his office we knew we were in the right place. His waiting room looked like a Lexus Dealership. He had up-to-date magazines. He had a huge fish tank. And his IVF clinic had a staggering success rate with a long list of patients (including, it was rumored, several celebrities and an NBA player.)

After a few weeks of at-home injections we drove back up to the hospital in North Jersey, where they retrieved eight eggs from Bernadette. We returned four days later and received shockingly good news. "You have three viable fertilized eggs," the doctor said, showing us a picture. "These two are very good quality." He pointed with his pen. "The third one here, see these spots—that's only a four-cell. That's right on the border of what we consider viable. I'm not optimistic about that one." He shoved his pen back into his pocket. "Anyway, I'll be back in a few minutes to ask you how many you want to put back."

Thanks, doc. Thanks for giving us a "few minutes" to discuss the fate of the rest of our lives.

I didn't have much confidence in Bern's eggs (talk about the soft bigotry of low expectations.) Our first IVF attempt resulted in no viable eggs; we would have been happy with one this time. But we had three, and that was a major dilemma for two reasons.

On the one hand, we were scared to death of triplets. Scared of carrying them, scared of raising them. On the other hand, Bernadette and I were raised Catholic and were taught that life begins at conception. So if we requested they implant only two, what would we do with the third fertilized egg? Most fertility clinics will freeze fertilized eggs in case you want to get pregnant again down the road, but ours wouldn't if you only had one left over. So would we allow the clinic to "dispose" of it, or would we toss it back into Bernadette and see what happened?

It wasn't much of a discussion; both of us knew we had to keep it, triplets be damned. Before you nominate us for "Catholics of the Year," realize this—just being in the Clinic was a violation of Church rules.

Yes, my Church had a rule against artificial insemination. But ever since I was a little kid, I've had a penchant for doing the opposite of what I was told then rationalizing it afterward in my mind. My thinking went like this: if I'm not allowed to create life, why am I allowed to preserve it? If I'm sick, I can go to the doctor. If I'm really sick, I can get an operation. So what is the difference between IVF and, say, chemo? If I can use technology to prevent death, why can't I use it to create life?

I won the debate, of course. In fact, I'm undefeated when arguing with myself. We did the in-vitro procedure and used all three embryos. And we ended up pregnant with twins.

Fast-forward to 40 weeks and two days later: Bern's uterus hadn't given up, but the OBGYN had. We went into the hospital for an induced labor that lasted a crisp eight hours.

All day, the delivery room had been bright and airy and tension-free, with nurses and doctors coming and going, looking at monitors, making small talk. Then around 5 pm, Bernadette hit the magic dilation number and bang—it was showtime. Without a word, the nurses put their game faces on. Tables were moved, monitors adjusted, BP cuffs tightened, trays set up. They had everything but yellow police tape, which would have come in handy when her mom and my mom (who had somehow wrangled invitations to this auspicious moment) began pushing in like gawkers at a crime scene.

We didn't know the sex of either twin; Bernadette had been adamant about that. I accompanied her to many doctor visits during the pregnancy and at every ultrasound she'd tell the technician, "Don't tell me. If I don't know, that's added incentive to push." So here we were in the pushing phase with a head coming out and three heads—the doctor, her mom and my mom—pushing in to see how it would all turn out.

And then all of a sudden the doctor was holding up something slimy and pinkish-gray. "It's a boy," the doctor shouted.

The moment was followed by a ten-second pause, where nothing seemed to be happening. Soon I got a strange feeling, and then it hit me—Frederick wasn't crying.

Two nurses descended on him, working him over like corner men massaging a boxer. They shook him, twisted him, pushed and prodded him, but no sound. I got scared, then looked at the nurse's faces to see if I could read panic. It's the same thing I do on airplanes during turbulence—if the flight attendants are calm, then I'm calm. If they look like they're scribbling out a will on a napkin then I panic. But the nurses were cool and professional, the type of people you'd want to avoid in a poker game. After thirty seconds of rubber tubes and pumped oxygen, Frederick sputtered like an old motor cranking up and started wailing.

My relief was short-lived as his twin sister decided to use the birth canal as a sliding board. The doctor yanked her out feet-first and held her up; she dangled there with her head pointed at the floor, and for a moment it looked like a dockside photo of a fisherman holding his prized catch by the tail.

We had always envisioned naming our first son after her father, but his name is Fred. Don't get me wrong, he's a great guy, one of the best people I've ever met—plus he jokingly offered free college tuition for any grandson named after him. But Fred...that's a big load to carry around for a kid. So we had settled on an unusual and complicated fix: we would name him Frederick Thomas Macklin O'Brien, after her dad, my dad (Thomas), plus Macklin, a name we discovered when Bernadette was pregnant with Anna. It means "red-haired boy" in Gaelic. Of course, Frederick didn't have red hair, but that wasn't relevant since it was his third name, the backup to his backup name. And the name "Macklin" had one big plus—it would make me the "Mack Daddy" or the "Daddy Mack." Win-win.

At that moment, with my family rounded out as two girls and a boy, I allowed myself to dream about my only son. I imagined us a few years down the road; we're sitting on the front porch and he's got a worry on his mind.

"Dad, I really don't like my name. I'm the only Fred in class and, well, I don't like it."

I nod my head sympathetically and say, "You know son, that's why parents sometimes have to think ahead. Most dads do irrelevant stuff like set-up college funds or take out life insurance on themselves to protect their children's future. But since I'm too cheap to do the former, and my congenital heart defect makes me ineligible for the latter, I'm glad I was able to do something important for you when you were born. I gave you a third name, son."

"What?" He looks up into my eyes with awe and wonder.

"That's right buddy. You only know your name as Frederick Thomas. We never told you about the third name. I've kept in my hip pocket, waiting for the right moment, knowing a day like this would come." Then I wink and tousle his hair. "That day is here. You have a third name. And it's not a dorky name like Eugene or Abner. You can call yourself... (I pause for dramatic effect)...Mack."

His eyes fill with tears of joy, and also pride in his forward-thinking father.

"I can call myself Mack?"

And I cement our male bonding with a semi-curse. "Damn right you can."

They let Bernadette hold Frederick for a few minutes, and then the nurses took him to the Neo-Natal Intensive Care Unit. They said it was standard operating procedure— Frederick seemed fine but any kid who has a low Apgar score has to spend the night in NICU. (An Apgar Test is given to every newborn at one minute and five minutes after birth, and it's simply an observation of the child's breathing, reflexes, pulse and skin color. The scale goes from one to ten, with seven or above being normal. Frederick scored a two.)

When we were discharged I asked the doctor if he thought Frederick would have any permanent damage. He said no, not if the child only spends four hours in the NICU then feeds well with mom the next day. The next few days were a blur of making and fielding phone calls. And at least half the people I spoke with used the old cliché: "Did they have ten fingers and ten toes?" I said yes, even though it was technically twenty fingers and twenty toes, but the question they were asking was this: Are they healthy? And I could answer, "Yes." But knowing what I know now, the correct answer would have been: "Yep. Ten finger and ten toes. They're both healthy—barring any unforeseen neurological issues that may or may not become apparent during the first 12 to 24 months of their lives."

## 2  FROM DAD TO DETECTIVE

That first year with the twins in 2002 might have been the best year of our lives. We had three healthy kids. I had a job at NFL Films that was the envy of all my high school and college friends. We bought the house that Bernadette grew up in, and the paper arrived every morning in the driveway. Life was good. We had officially made it.

But there were signs. Subtle signs, the kind of things that are obvious now through the lens of hindsight. Years later, when people asked the question, "How did you know Frederick had a problem?" the best answer I could give them was to paraphrase the character in *The Sun Also Rises* who, when asked how he lost his fortune, answered "Gradually, and then suddenly."

There was no definitive moment or incident where we said, "I'll be damned, look at that—Frederick has Autism!" It's not an easy thing to diagnose in the first year. According to Autism Speaks, the charity founded by former NBC President Bob Wright and his wife Susan, there are certain warning signs to look for:

No big smiles or other warm, joyful expressions by six months or thereafter.

No back-and-forth sharing of sounds, smiles, or other facial expressions by nine months or thereafter.

No babbling by 12 months.

No back-and-forth gestures, such as pointing, showing, reaching, or waving by 12 months.

Seems pretty straightforward, right? Well it's not.

For starters, we're talking about a baby. They don't do much. The list says "no big smiles" by six months. Frederick smiled, but were they "big smiles?" I didn't whip out a tape measure to check. Were we doing "back and forth sharing" by nine months? Not sure, but I know we didn't play charades or do improvisational acting camps in our living room at that age.

The late Jim Valvano once described his mentality during the NCAA basketball tournament as "survive and advance," and that's what we were trying to do. It was hard to know where Frederick fell on the Autism Speaks rating scale because by the time the twins hit their first birthday our home was pure chaos and our only goal was to make it through the day without one of our three children visiting the ER. Maybe Frederick didn't have any "warm, joyful expressions" but honestly, I can't blame him. I didn't have any either.

Frederick was a late walker, and then he was a late talker. He had a terrible case of eczema, and seemed allergic to certain baby foods. But we weren't overly concerned. And even when we did voice concern, we got shot down by older and presumably wiser family members.

"He's a boy, boys are always slow."

"This always happens with twins."

"Your Aunt Betty's neighbor has a sister whose nephew didn't talk till he was four. The kid's at Cornell now."

Of course, I now know the proper response to those assertions should have been, in order: "No they're not." "Not always." And "Aunt Betty's neighbor's sister's nephew has no friends, still plays Dungeons & Dragons, and recites the Magna Carta under his breath as he walks around campus."

But at the time, I took those reassurances from family members as if they came from Moses on the mountain. They were coming from people older than me, and they had children. They must know. Frederick would be fine.

He had ten fingers and ten toes, right? What could be wrong?

**Our team photo: Frederick, Anna, and Grace.**

The first time I ever remember thinking something wasn't right, Frederick was maybe a year old. On the nights I would put him to bed, I had this ritual of cooing in his ear while carrying him up the stairs, saying over and over "Who's my big buddy? You're my big buddy. Frederick's my big buddy." And then I would put him in the crib where he'd stand up, hold the railing, and hop—not really jumping, just flexing his knees up and down.

And one night, I decided to hang with him for a little while. I hate to admit it, but that was unusual for me. I had always spent a lot of time with Anna, practically devouring her every waking moment. But the twins were different. You're obviously going to spend less time with twins who are your second and third children than you would with a single baby, but there was something else, something that I only realized in retrospect: Frederick was like an ATM machine that never had any money. If you had an ATM like that, you'd eventually stop going back. I never got the kind of back-and-forth emotional attachment from him because he simply wasn't capable of giving it.

It's a hard concept to explain. Frederick wasn't a block of wood; he smiled, he laughed, he reacted to funny things. But he never plumbed the depths, never seemed to fully soak-in the emotion of being alive.

I wasn't fully aware of that until the night in question. It was the end of another busy day but I didn't want to just toss him in the crib and walk away. When he stood there bouncing I held his shoulders to make him stop, then I put my hands on either side of his face and peered directly into his eyes. I said, "You're my big buddy, and I'll always protect you." He snorted a little laugh and tried to turn away. Odd, I thought, he doesn't want to look at me. So I held his head in place and said, "I love you buddy." He couldn't turn his head so he flicked his eyes away from my stare. I let go, but I kept my face inches from his. I guess removing my hands from his face made him more comfortable because he looked right back into my eyes for several seconds. Wonderful, I thought. This is a wonderful moment. And then my heart sank. Frederick was looking at me but his face and his eyes didn't react like they were seeing something that was particularly meaningful, or gave him any joy. In other words, he wasn't looking at me, he was looking through me. That's the only phrase I could muster in my brain, and still the only accurate label today. He's looking through me. I got the feeling that there was no connection.

I told Bernadette about it, and she dismissed it. "He's a one-year-old, what do you want him to do?" I moved on from it as well.

Soon it was springtime. The birds were singing, the weather was warming— everything was blossoming except my son.

We had a concrete slab at the far end of our backyard where a shed once stood. It was maybe 10 foot by 10 foot and three inches high—a small island of stone in a quarter-acre of grass. One day I looked over and saw Frederick standing on the edge of the concrete, looking down. My first urge was to run over and engage him, start playing with him, but there was something weird going on, so I waited. I watched as he looked down to the grass and moved his right leg to step down, but then stopped. He brought his leg back to a standing position, and kept staring down at the grass. After five seconds, he tried again. This time, his leg quivered as he inched it forward, but then he brought it back again. It seemed like he was scared, but of what? I held out my hand; he took it and leaned his weight on my arm as he stepped three inches down to the grass, and it reminded me of how I used to help my 85-year-old Grandmother out of our S.U.V.

He walked across the grass as I looked back at the concrete, trying to imagine in my mind what he was thinking in his mind. I finally concluded that Frederick knew what he wanted to do—get off the concrete—but his body wouldn't obey. And then I thought no, that's not it. He just doesn't know how to ask his body to respond. He was staring down at this three-inch drop as if it was the Grand Canyon. It seemed like Frederick's body had all the parts, but no one gave him an owner's manual.

And then I noticed him wandering in the yard and for some reason I ran in to get my video camera. I shot him walking past a kiddie bike, then a tree, then our sliding board. None of these got his attention, although he was definitely concentrating on something.

Later that night I couldn't stop thinking about how aimless and disengaged Frederick had been outside. After the kids went to bed, I grabbed the video camera and watched the clip.

I watched it once, then again, and it wasn't until the fourth or fifth viewing that I figured it out, like Bruce Willis finally hearing voices on the cassette tape in *The Sixth Sense*. Frederick wasn't wandering aimlessly. He was doing something, but it wasn't something you or I would do. On the tape, he wanders, but every time the leaves started rustling and the tree branches started swaying he would stop. And I concentrated on his face—every time the wind kicked up he stood motionless, and then narrowed his eyes, as if concentrating. When the wind died down he moved on. When it kicked up, he stopped. And the only conclusion that made sense was that he was simultaneously enjoying the feel of the wind on his face while trying to make sense of it. It was as if he was trying to understand and interpret the breeze on his skin. I didn't know what it meant, and I couldn't stop thinking about it.

If there was any big, eye-opening moment, that was it. After that day, in the spring of 2003, I became two people: the father who loved Frederick and some CSI detective who was trying to solve a mystery.

# 3  WHAT IT IS

Picture the fuel gauge on your car. It arcs from Empty to Full, with little notches in between. The needle rests somewhere between the two.

That's a good way to picture Autism.

Autism is a "spectrum" disease, meaning that a person diagnosed with Autism can be so severely affected that he's completely nonverbal (down near the "E" on the gauge) or so mildly affected it's hardly noticeable to an untrained eye (the needle is up near "F"), or be anywhere in between.

Depending on whose numbers you believe, the current estimates are as many as one child in every 68 will be diagnosed with Autism. It affects boys far more than girls— more than 75% of children diagnosed on the Autism spectrum are male.

If blindness can be defined as a compromised ability to see and deafness as a compromised ability to hear, then Autism can be defined as a compromised ability to interact with other human beings. That's the heart of it. High-functioning kids on the spectrum have difficulties with social transactions. Low-functioning kids may not differentiate between a parent and a stranger, and can't communicate with either.

If your child is closer to "E" on the metaphorical fuel gauge, he may be self-injurious, rocking by himself in his own little world with a vocabulary that consists of a few distinct grunts or high-pitched screams. He might twiddle his fingers and stare intently at them, not because he thinks it's cool but because light and sounds and everyday living overwhelm his sensory system and staring at his fingers or flapping his hands has a calming effect. The parents might do everything they can to make him part of the family, but if their other children are like planets, he is a moon, circling around the periphery. There—and not there—at the same time.

If your child is in the middle of the spectrum you can make connections with her, but it's limited. She might have favorite TV shows, but they will likely remain her favorite shows well past the point where her peers have moved past *Blue's Clues* and *Sesame Street*. She can say words, maybe even say "I love you Dad," but it's never spontaneous, only parroted. If anything breaks her routine, or if a favorite toy is not where it's supposed to be, chaos ensues. A child like this can be more integrated into a family but day-trips and excursions to restaurants can be an adventure. A meltdown is never far off. As for vacation involving airplanes, don't kid yourself. Maybe when she hits 15 or 16. Maybe.

If your child is in the high end, up near "Full," he is classified with what was commonly called Asperger Syndrome. He goes to a regular school and most likely attends regular classrooms. He has very narrow interests. He might have an encyclopedic knowledge of the local train schedule or the Latin names of all tropical fish. Social situations are his biggest challenge. Making friends or talking to a girl is like being dropped off in a strange city at 3 a.m. with no map, no vehicle, and no flashlight. As a parent, you revel in his accomplishments and marvel at his progress but your heart breaks every day knowing he was so damn close, this close, to being like everybody else. You love him as he is, and you wouldn't trade him for the world, but you know things are harder for him. Not a tragedy, just harder.

All of us over the age of 30, in retrospect, probably knew someone with Asperger's. I knew a kid in grade school who was, to be kind, quirky. He invited me over to his house to watch the inauguration of Jimmy Carter. He knew everything about the ceremony, including what book the Bible was open to for the swearing-in; I was barely aware that we had a new president. While I was there, he kept telling me Nixon was misunderstood.

I knew a kid in high school who we all thought was brilliant, but in actuality his grades were far from genius-level. He could recite the Popes in order and astound us with arcane facts and figures, usually without prompting. My buddies and I would be talking about girls or sports and he'd wander up and say something like, "Did you know that the Battle of Gettysburg had approximately the same number of casualties as the entire Korean War?"

I had an uncle who was a bit of an odd duck. He lived with my grandparents until he was well past the age of 40 and his subsequent apartments looked like shipping warehouses because of all the boxes and clutter. He was into computers before most people had heard of them, and he could never keep a job for very long.

I lost touch with the kid from high school, so I don't know how things turned out for him. But my grade school friend was killed by a mugger in New York City. And at the age of 70 my uncle was killed in a robbery while working the overnight shift at a dinky hotel chain. Coincidence? Maybe. Small sample size? Definitely. But were they on the Autism spectrum? And if so, did their inability to read people's intentions and emotions play a part in their deaths? Who knows?

But there's more to the puzzle than just the interpersonal piece. The National

Institute of Mental Health (N.I.M.H.) website says:

"Without meaningful gestures or the language to ask for things, people with Autism Spectrum Disorder are at a loss to let others know what they need. As a result, they may simply scream or grab what they want. Until they are taught better ways to express their needs, ASD children do whatever they can to get through to others"

Maybe the best way to understand why kids on the spectrum have these difficulties is to wrap your head around something called Theory of Mind. Scientists, doctors and educators have attempted to explain this phenomenon in layman's terms, but it's hard to do.

Before their first birthday, typically-developing children already understand a simple premise: what they are seeing and thinking may be different than what others are seeing and thinking. That's why they point at things, like an airplane in the sky. They're saying, "Look Mommy, up there. Not sure you noticed that. Isn't it cool?" They want to jointly share the experience. Or if they want a toy up on the shelf, they point to it in order to say "I know you can't read my mind so I'm telling you I want that toy. Now!"

Children with Autism can't grasp that concept. They believe what they see is what the world sees, and everyone thinks what they think. So why bother to interact when the thoughts and feelings in your mind are thought and felt by everyone else? Why bother to point out a car, or a dog, or a tree? If you know you want to play with the red toy, everyone knows that. Case closed.

Autism has so many different levels and nuances that, in many ways, it's fascinating—unless, of course, you are a parent of a child on the spectrum. If you are, then this stuff isn't clinical, it's your life. But as my wife likes to say, "We'll sleep when we die."

# 4  POINTING IS RUDE

It started with a phone call. And before we get into the details of that call, here's some advice: when you have bad news—I mean really, really bad news—and your significant other is about to board an eight-hour flight, wait until the plane lands before letting him or her know.

It was June of 2003. At this point, Frederick had delays but no diagnosis. Because of a lucky one-off assignment for work, I had spent the week in London and was now frantically packing for the flight back to the States.

At that moment, the highlights of the trip had been seeing Boy George in the lobby of our hotel and having dinner at a restaurant where we sat one table over from Sir Richard Branson and Rachel Hunter (we couldn't think of her name right then, so we said "Isn't that Richard Branson and the model who used to be married to Rod Stewart?") That would have been plenty of memories for one trip. Unfortunately, I had one more to come: I was about to get The Call That Started It All.

My turn-of-the-millennium international cell phone (roughly the size of a 16oz beer can) began vibrating on the bed. Bernadette was on the other end.

"How you doing honey?" she asked.

"I'm fine, dear." I was also fine ten minutes earlier, when I hung up after a 30-minute conversation with her. I stuffed the last of my socks into the corner of the suitcase. "I'm packing so I'll call you when we get to the airport."

I was hoping she'd say "Ok, call me later." I certainly wasn't expecting her actual response: "I took the kids to the doctors yesterday."

Ah-ha—something was up. And whatever it was, it was taking a second phone call to spit out. Not good. Bernadette was talking fast—not panicked, but a bit breathless. "The doctor asked me a bunch of questions, he asked me about Frederick pointing, and what he points for and—"

I rolled my eyes. "Pointing? Is he a doctor or a mime?"

"Dig, I'm serious. He wants us to call for Early Intervention."

"What the hell is that?" I said.

"It's the County sending people out to work with kids who are a little delayed. But he mentioned something else."

Silence. Was I supposed to ask what something else was? After an awkward gap in the conversation I jumped in—not with the soothing, understanding "husband voice" but with the hurried, sarcastic tone I'd been perfecting since my teen years.

"Bernadette, you need to tell me because if I don't get a cab in the next five minutes I'm sleeping over again. And just to remind you, I'm in LONDON!"

More silence. I then shifted into the soothing, understanding "husband voice." One of these days, I'll lead with that.

"Honey, it's ok," I said. "Trust me. It's nothing we can't handle. What did the doctor say?"

Bernadette swallowed. "He mentioned...Autism."

Autism. The pediatrician mentioned Autism.

Immediately, relief spread over me like a wave.

"Oh, come on honey," I said. "Autism? Autism? Are you joking?"

"Dig, it's not a joke, he asked me all these questions..."

I cut her off. This wasn't even worth discussing. I had seen the movie Rain Man.

"Bernadette, every doctor today wants to be the first one to slap a kid with a label. ADD, ADHD, ABCDEFG, it's all crap. Let me ask you something: have you ever seen Frederick spin like a top, or bang his head against the wall? No? I didn't think so. In college I knew guys who had an off-campus house, and they lived next-door to a family who had an autistic kid. The kid wore a hockey helmet—and he didn't even play hockey! He needed it because he whacked his head all day. Does that sound like Frederick to you?"

More silence.

"Seriously, does that sound like our son?" I demanded. "Does it?"

She let out a long sigh. "I guess you're right."

"Of course I'm right, honey. Frederick's a little behind, but we're going to work our butts off and he'll catch up. Remember, he's a twin. And a boy! And who cares if he's a little delayed. When he's 36 do you think anyone would notice if he started acting 35?"

Flying from Europe back to the U.S. takes at least an hour longer than the way over because of the headwinds. But that flight home seemed a day longer. I tried to work, tried to sleep, tried to watch movies, and then just tried staring straight ahead, but I couldn't shake the conversation. The doctor said Frederick doesn't point. I thought pointing was rude? Why did it even matter?

I've learned a lot about Autism in the last few years, but the most important thing I learned is this: if your kid doesn't point, you've got some problems. Simple. Done. It goes back to the idea of Theory of Mind. Why would a child point at something if he thought you were thinking the same exact thing?

But I didn't know all that in the summer of 2003. I just knew my son, who was 20 months old, was a little delayed, and that the pediatrician was suggesting we call Early Intervention and get him evaluated. And as it turned out, Frederick's twin, Grace, was a little behind in speech as well. What the hell, I figured—why not recoup some of the insanely high New Jersey property taxes and get the state working for me?

In case you're lucky enough to be unfamiliar with New Jersey Early Intervention, it's a program that identifies children aged newborn-to-three who have at least a 25% deficit in development and sends professionals into the home to work with the child. Kids with less severe issues like a minor speech delay (i.e. Grace) get a smattering of services like a weekly visit from a speech teacher; kids who have "global" delays (i.e. Frederick) can get 10 or 12 hours of therapy a week.

An easier way to think about it is this: basically, your kid has a warranty until age three and the government will send out a technician (i.e. a Special Ed teacher) to repair things. The purpose is to get your kid back on track and hopefully erase the developmental delays. It's a win-win for the state—if they can get your kid up to age-appropriate behaviors early enough then they don't have to do it in a school setting; the quicker they deal with it, the less it will cost them.

Our first appointment, the "get-to-know-you" visit by a social worker, was scheduled for a few weeks later. When the big day arrived, Bernadette and I greeted the woman at the door and she introduced herself as Jane, and then inexplicably said, "You two look like you're handling this well. A lot of times when I come to the door the parents are crying." Before we could digest that nugget, Frederick ran into the room, looked at her, and then wandered away. Jane smiled. "Oh, is that your son? He's not what I expected."

As Bernadette and I stared at each other, mouths agape, Jane walked past us and put her things on the table.

She had a short, Joan Baez-type haircut straight out of the social worker manual, accompanied by long, dangling earrings that seemed like wind chimes and a voice so soft and reassuring she sounded like Julie Haggerty on Xanax. We sat down at the table, and Jane pulled out an enormous folder. I immediately hoped it contained paperwork from every client she had ever had, or maybe every case the state had ever processed. But I was wrong. It was all for us.

Over the next half hour, I supplied my social security number several times, signed my name at least a dozen times, listed some previous addresses, produced a W-2 and gave everything but a DNA sample. I kept looking over at Bernadette; her face had a numb look, as if she was using all her powers of concentration to robotically sign her name instead of jumping up and yelling, "My son is in the other room, and he can't say 'Mommy,' can't clap his hands, and likes playing with the safety lock on the toy chest more than the toys inside. Can we get him some freakin' help please?"

Having a kid who needs Early Intervention is hard enough, but when the first official state of New Jersey attempt to help your kid involves more paperwork than a mortgage re-fi, it gets a little disconcerting. Actually, looking back in hindsight, I wish I could have refinanced Frederick's condition. He would eventually get an Autism diagnosis, but why not haggle?

"So, right now this is a 30-year Autism diagnosis, but can I opt for a 15-year and take it all the way down to Asperger's by paying points and having a bigger down payment?"

"No," Jane might respond, "but we do have a nice new product. It's a 5-year adjustable, with no points, and anytime within that five years you can lock into a less debilitating neurological condition, but you have to remember the balloon payment down the line—when that comes due you revert back to Autism and have to enroll him in a group home."

When we finished signing, Jane explained that we were now part of the Early Intervention "team," which consisted of her, the therapists that would be coming to our house, and a representative from the local school district.

A few days later, the next step of Early Intervention took place: the evaluation. A physical therapist came to the house to observe Frederick and interact with him so that she could grade his level in seven categories: Cognitive, Communication, Social-Emotional, Gross Motor, Fine Motor, Self Help and Sensory. The summary we received a week later read, in part:

| Strengths | Needs |
|---|---|
| -likes to watch Teletubbies | -not talking |
| -likes to look at books | -not pointing |
| -loves to be in the stroller | -clumsy |
| -likes music | -gets upset easily |
| -likes to go outside and play | -attention span |

In Cognitive, Communication, Social-Emotional, Fine-Motor and Sensory he scored below 12 months. On Gross Motor and Self Help he was graded above 12 months because he could walk without falling down and was able to finger-feed himself. It wasn't a high bar.

But if the report had been written in the most forthright manner possible, it would have read:

*Frederick does not interact with children, preferring to play by himself. Not that you can really call it "play"—his preferred activities include pulling all the books out of bookshelves, fiddling with door hardware and latches, and putting anything he sees into his mouth. He dislikes loud noises. He has no fear of strangers. He's a terrible sleeper. He communicates a desire to get out of the double stroller by yanking on his twin sister's hair. He doesn't like the feel of poop in his diaper and often tries to manually remove it, resulting in a Feces Fresco on our TV room paneling. Oh, and if that wasn't enough, he has really bad eczema, which doesn't help the tantrums. And when we try to put the skin cream on he reacts like he's being rubbed with battery acid.*

I kept coming back to an old saying of mine—"We'll just hit it hard." I think I came up with it in college as a way of blowing things off until the last possible minute, as in "Sure I have this paper due in two days, but I can go out and party tonight and then hit it hard tomorrow and it'll get done." There was nothing in my life I couldn't fix with a little extra work. If congenital procrastination had me falling behind on producing a show at work, I'd just hit it hard. If I had gained a few pounds, I'd just hit it hard with a month of calorie-counting. And if Frederick was delayed, we'd just hit it (not him) hard.

And I had reason for optimism. Frederick was not the type of kid where you could tell there was something wrong from a mile away. He wasn't in a wheelchair. He didn't have "stims," a classic sign of Autism where the child flaps his hands or rocks back and forth or does some other repetitive behavior. Frederick didn't do any strange stuff; he just didn't do much of anything. And since he wasn't even two years old yet, it's not like we noticed he wasn't reading yet or was having trouble with subtraction. Our family and friends constantly reassured us. "Oh, Cousin Jack was a real handful too" or "Cousin Laura would scream for twenty minutes sometimes; we actually considered an Exorcism." That's the thing—unless your child has two heads or consistently tries to jam silverware up his nostrils, you can always rationalize the behavior of a 20-month-old.

**Always excited to chow down.**

A good example of his sudden changes in demeanor was diaper changing, which should be a fairly unremarkable event for a kid his age. But if Frederick was sitting in the TV room and saw Bernadette coming with a diaper, and if for whatever reason he didn't want to be changed at that particular time, he would throw himself backward and scream. Now, we've all seen kids do something similar to this, but they usually do it with some sense of their own safety in mind. They throw themselves down in a delicate way that will get their point across without causing any pain. But Frederick would throw himself backward from a seated position in a way reminiscent of someone jerking the 'recline' lever while leaning back in the passenger seat of a car—he just snapped backward at a very high speed, the back of his skull crashing into the floor and making a sound similar to a cantaloupe hitting the pavement after being dropped from a third floor window. That's how he let us know he didn't want his diaper changed.

On July 21, 2003, the formal part of Early Intervention started. As if to fulfill the social worker's earlier prophecy, Bernadette was crying when a freckle-faced girl fresh out of college knocked at our door. Megan, the young therapist, must have assumed the tears were from Bernadette admitting that Frederick had a problem. Instead, she was crying because our beloved Beagle, Flanders, had died the day before.

Seriously. A day before Early Intervention starts, the dog dies. This was not our year.

After a get-to-know-us discussion, Megan stated that our first goal should be to limit Frederick's tantrums, because a kid can't learn the skills necessary to shed his delays when he's rolling around on the floor. She suggested the best way to extinguish negative behavior was to ignore it. Frederick's tantrums were a way to get attention and sympathy and "It's ok buddy" cuddles from us. Megan instructed us to turn our back during these meltdowns, and when he stopped crying we should turn back to face him and ask, "Done?"

That led to a few hilarious scenes, like the time he and I went shopping at Home Depot. We were walking hand in hand through the aisles when something must have caught his eye. He stopped, but I gently pulled him forward and said "C'mon Frederick, let's keep walking." In a nanosecond, he was flat on his back, flailing his arms and legs on a floor so dusty you could write your name on it. A few burly guys with work boots gave me The Stare (something I'd get used to over the years.) The Stare is a mixture of bewilderment and anger; equal parts "I've never seen a kid do that before" and "If that was my kid I'd whip his ass." But Megan told us to ignore tantrums, so there I was, paying no attention to my son doing snow angels while tattooed guys in overalls were stepping over him. Problem was, Frederick had the endurance of a marathon runner. He could wait us out better than we could wait him out.

Grace was getting her one or two sessions of speech per week, and doing great; in fact, both Bernadette and I wondered if Grace's slight delays had anything to do with being around Frederick all the time and modeling his behavior. Whatever the cause, we just weren't that worried about Grace. All of our worrying was reserved for Frederick.

At that time, our biggest concern was language. He didn't talk, or talk much, and we needed him to so we could understand his tantrums. And when he did talk, he had this way of articulating that was similar to the victim of a minor stroke but more like an over-emphasis of sounds—every syllable was harder, and every long sound was drawn out.

Megan told us the best way to build his language was to make him work for everything. If you know your child wants something really bad, and if he knows that words are the only way to get that desired item, he's more likely to talk. This philosophy led to a phrase we repeated seemingly hundreds of times a day: "Use your words." I remember once when Bernadette was in the kitchen holding Frederick's binky just out of his reach. "Use your words: binky." Frederick really wanted it, but he was getting frustrated, reaching for it, thinking he didn't have to use his words because it was right there in front of him.

We had a gate in the doorway that separated the kitchen from the kids' playroom. We installed it when we started early intervention, thinking it would be best for the therapy sessions if Frederick knew he was a "captive" audience.

So I watched Frederick get close to meltdown mode as Bernadette repeated "Use your words: binky" over and over again. And then I had an idea. I grabbed the binky from her hand and tossed it over the gate and into the playroom.

Bernadette said, "What are you doing? I was trying to get him to talk."

Frederick's tantrum stopped as he walked to the gate and rattled it in frustration. I removed his hands and replaced them with my hand, squeezing the latch. "Frederick, what do you want?"

"Binky!" was the response, clear as day. I opened the gate and he retrieved his precious binky.

Another way we encouraged speech was to leave out parts of songs. I would sing a line and then stop, hoping he would finish it. Our favorite was:

Twinkle, twinkle little...SHAR

How I...WUNYA

What you...ARE

Up above the clouds so...HI

Like a...DI-NUN

In the...SHHKY

So now, with Frederick at 20 months old and me chucking pacifiers around the house, our situation was slowly outgrowing the "delayed" label and graduating to "things are starting to get weird around here." He still lacked the building blocks of communication. He couldn't sit in one place for more than 30 seconds. He had no imaginative play, and had tantrums of such visible fury that he looked like he was being electrocuted.

But he smiled, oh lord could he smile. It was a great smile, a giant smile, the kind that made everyone in a room notice and made them smile too. And he had a loud, low belly laugh that would go on for a good five seconds longer than you thought it would. He liked playing peek-a-boo games. His face lit up when he saw me or Bernadette or his sisters. I was probably overreacting.

# 5  LET'S HAVE A C.H.A.T.

By the fall of 2003 we had three different Early Intervention people coming to the house: an Occupational Therapist (works on motor skills), a D.I. Teacher (Differentiated Instruction—a therapist who tailors instruction to a child's unique way of learning) and an ABA therapist (Applied Behavioral Analysis—heavy emphasis on following directions through rewarding task completion.) At the end of each session, which usually lasted an hour, the therapist filled out a one-page report that explained what they worked on and how the child responded. Each report had a white top copy and a yellow bottom copy. After it was filled out, the therapist kept the white copy and the yellow stayed with the family. Thankfully, it didn't say "customer copy."

I kept every yellow sheet they ever gave us. Still have them. Many times while cleaning out filing cabinets or straightening up, I thought about tossing them, but I never did. I imagined that when Frederick got older, and everything was fine, they were going to be mementos from our harrowing days when we thought he had a problem, the equivalent of a Niagara Falls magnet on the fridge—a reminder of some long-ago family adventure.

Some of the most telling comments from the first few months of yellow sheets were:

August 5: "Frederick waved bye today; this is a new thing for him."

September 23: "Went outside today. Frederick had no interest in paints set up on table."

October 1: "Mom concerned that Frederick still does not clap his hands."

October 14: "Ten minute tantrum when Frederick didn't get his cup immediately."

One of the therapists recommended a book on "Sensory Integration," a term that encompasses how the body receives messages from the nerves and then reacts to them. The book was a primer on the sensory system, and I learned cool new words like Vestibular (how the brain processes information about movement) and Proprioceptive (processing information about body position). I spouted them as often as I could when people asked about Frederick. I'd say, "Sure, he has delayed speech and poor eye contact and is a loner but the real problem is he can't synchronize his sensory system."

I completely bought in, and followed the book's recommendations to the letter. We put a blow-up kiddy swimming pool in the basement and filled it with chunks of foam so Frederick could safely work off his pent-up energy by going down a little sliding board and crashing into the foam. We bought beanbag chairs to smoosh him in, and a 'snuggly vest" to wrap him in several times a day for the purpose of soothing and calming him. Another recommendation was to take empty two-liter bottles and fill them with sand so your child could hold them while walking around, thereby helping him feel the sensation in his arms and help the sensory system "communicate." (Unfortunately, his sensory system told him to drop them and wander away each time.) And since Frederick only seemed to talk when he was moving or swinging, we bought an Ikea swing and hung it on the archway that separated our living room from the TV room. Not only was it helpful to Frederick, it was a great conversation stopper for people visiting for the first time. "Wow, love the kitchen…the paneling's so cool in the TV room and…what's that thing hanging over there?"

**Re-creating their time in the womb.**

What I didn't realize about this book was that the subtitle should have been "1001 Ways to Work on Your Child's Autism Without Actually Using the Word Autism." It was like having a book that suggested activities to "work around your child's issues with the spinal cord, nerves, and lack of motor function" but never mentioned paralysis.

Here's a simpler way to look at it: if it's even remotely possible that your kid might benefit from carrying around two-liter bottles of sand, then you might have some bigger fish to fry than "sensory integration."

Maybe I was too busy, maybe I was naive, maybe I was just a moron, but I wasn't really, really worried—yet. Impatient is a better word. Some days I would call Bernadette from work a half-dozen times a day, asking for updates on his progress after every session. And most of the time I felt better after I hung up. I would think, "Ok, Frederick is delayed, but this magical thing known as Early Intervention can get kids up-to-speed before school-age. My kid's in it, and that sucks, but we're just gonna have to deal with therapists coming to the house and it's gonna cost Bernadette a few playdates in the park, but we'll look back on it and laugh someday."

Ha.

(That was me laughing someday.)

Looking back, I wonder if I had a "Kick Me" sign taped to the back of my shirt, or if I was wearing one of those "I'm With Stupid" t-shirts with the finger pointing up, because I can't believe how dumb I was. Leave it to your friends to set you straight.

Two instances that summer stick in my mind. The first was when my best friend Dave was down to show us pictures from his wedding album. Actually, his wife was showing the wedding album to Bernadette, and Dave and I were in the other room shooting the breeze. He asked how Frederick's therapy was going, and I went into one of my canned Sensory Integration speeches. "If you think about it, the brain is really just a sensory processing machine. We respond appropriately when the brain is processing properly. But it's almost like Frederick has A.D.D. of the senses. He's not sure which of the thousands of sensory inputs each day are meaningful."

At that moment, Frederick entered the room and walked over to the computer desk. He jiggled the latch that held the printer door until it opened, pulled all the paper out of the printer, then walked away.

Dave and I sat for a moment, looking at the white sheets of paper covering the area rug, and then he looked at me and said, "You sure that's all that's wrong with him?"

The other time was when my college-buddy Gary was over; like Dave, he could comfortably say anything to me. We were having an outdoor get-together and I was giving him a similar Sensory Integration speech as we looked out over my backyard. Anna and the cousins were playing a game that seemed to involve running around and screaming; Grace was frantically trying to catch up. And Frederick was all by himself, meandering in the corner of the yard. At first glance, he seemed to be purposefully walking, but if you were really paying attention you realized he was doing nothing— noticing nothing, engaging nothing.

As I got to the end of my explanation of Sensory Integration Disorder, Gary looked at me and had the same word-for-word response as Dave: "You sure that's all that's wrong with him?"

Apparently, my friends weren't the only ones who had concerns about Frederick. On a chilly Saturday in November, Bernadette announced we were going to drive the kids to Duffield's, a family farm with a market, hayrides, and a little petting zoo. With the temperature hovering around 40 degrees it seemed like a strange thing to do, but I had a flight to catch the next morning and since I'd be gone all day Sunday I decided to go along with the idea and not complain.

At the farm, and especially at the animal feeding area, I noticed it was hard to keep Frederick's attention. You would think that feeding sheep and goats by hand would be interesting to a child on the cusp of his second birthday, but not Frederick; after a few seconds he would dart and twist and pull away, always on to something else. At one point Grace was feeding a goat by hand and Frederick was five feet away, poking each individual letter on the "No Smoking" sign.

Next, we went on a hayride. I held Frederick, talked to him and pointed out things he might enjoy, but he didn't seem interested. And then I would tickle him. That always brought something out in Frederick—an infectious belly laugh and broad smile. And it would also make him engage; he would lock his eyes on mine and implore me, without words, for another tickle. A few times during the hayride I noticed Bernadette looking at Frederick, and then at me. It wasn't the usual loving smile or frown of disapproval (always at me, never at him.) These were quick, furtive glances, like she didn't want me to notice. And there was no emotion to her face. She wasn't just watching; she was trying to learn something.

The yellow sheet from that week had a classic line:

"Mom discussed that Frederick wasn't interested in looking at animals at farm; mostly interested in No Smoking sign."

The next day, I got on a plane for Denver. ESPN was putting a microphone on Broncos linebacker Al Wilson for use in the broadcast, and it was my job to be the NFL representative and "filter" what ESPN could put on the air. Cursing was obviously out, but so was reference to referees, derogatory comments about teammates or opponents, etc. During the game I tried to concentrate as best I could, but it was hard because the truck parked in the bowels of the stadium was about 20 degrees, and I couldn't get Frederick off my mind.

I had my radar up constantly—any nugget of information on Autism that would have previously passed unnoticed was something that I now paid attention to and stored. My emotions and moods waxed and waned depending on the latest piece of information. I might read something that said any kid with speech delays past 18 months had a 90% chance of being on the Autism spectrum, and I'd immediately get this low-flame feeling in my gut and then go into a 48-hour funk. But on other occasions I might find something on the internet that said most children with Autism don't differentiate between loved ones and strangers, and I'd think of how Frederick would light up if Bern's sister Margie came over, or if he saw one of the older cousins like Mary Kate or Laura, and I'd feel great for a few days because I was sure my son didn't have Autism.

So during the Broncos-Patriots game I listened to the sound from the player microphones while also paying attention to the ESPN play-by-play and commentary in case they mentioned New England offensive coordinator Charlie Weis, whose daughter Hannah had Autism. Would they say something about his daughter and her behaviors that reminded me of Frederick, igniting the fire in the pit in my stomach? Or would they mention something about her that was different than Frederick, which would make me breathe a ten-second sigh of relief, like exhaling after a long drag on a cigarette?

They didn't mention Hannah at all, and the next morning I was at the airport, content in the belief that I had a child with sensory issues, not a special needs child. I had a plan for the flight—watch a movie on my laptop, read a new article I found on Sensory Integration and make notes on how to implement it at home, and then grab an hour or two of sleep. But I did not have an enjoyable flight home from Denver because Bernadette still suffered from her affliction. The medical journals might call it Aeromiserabilis—the urge to tell people bad news right before they board a plane.

It was early Monday morning, and because of the two-hour time difference I waited until I got to the gate to call home.

"Did I wake you?"

"No," she said, "Frederick got up at 5."

"Ouch, sorry. Maybe you can put the TV on and take a nap later."

"I'll be fine."

"Ok," I said, trying to wrap up. "I'm sitting at the gate. The plane isn't here yet, but the board still says On Time. Anyway, I'll call you when we land. Love you."

"Dig...."

Oh god, I thought. Here we go.

I waited for her to say something. Nothing.

I finally said, "What's the matter honey?" Notice it wasn't "What's up" or "Do you have anything more to say?" Anytime I get a 'Dig' followed by ten seconds of silence, it's not good news. The only thing I knew was that no one died, because she probably would have led with that.

After an additional five second pause, she blurted it out. "Megan thinks there's something wrong."

Aware of my London hotel room-attitude, I skipped the sarcasm, but also sped past the soothing/nurturing mode and went directly into condescending right-brain "guy" mode. "Of course there's something wrong sweetie. Frederick is delayed. That's not news. But he's getting help and we're doing everything we can. In fact, I just skimmed that sensory book again and I have some notes on more things we can do, like every morning when he wakes up we should..."

"She thinks it's more than that."

The fire returned. It was a low flame, warming my innards. This time I paused for a few seconds.

"Like what?"

Bernadette audibly swallowed, then exhaled. "Like if it was just a sensory issue he'd communicate more. She thinks we need to take him to a developmental pediatrician."

She didn't mention the A-word, but she didn't have to. Autism was always lurking just around the corner; we just preferred to not venture down that alley to take a peek.

I could sense Bernadette was using all of her powers to keep it together, to not cry like a baby. "Megan was the one who made the suggestion that we take Frederick to go to the farm last week, to see the animals. She told me to really pay attention to how Frederick reacted. I told her how it went. She wants to go over stuff with you and me together. She can come next Saturday morning and talk to both of us."

I was searching for a funny one-liner to end the conversation. I couldn't find one.

"We're going to get through this honey. I love you."

"Love you too," she said.

What normally would have been a four-hour flight home turned into an all-day affair. My flight was cancelled and the next one didn't leave till noon, so I killed time by stuffing myself full of comfort food that did nothing to comfort me.

Back at work the next day, I couldn't concentrate. There was a big party that night for the launch of the NFL Network. I was involved in a lot of the preparation and had helped create some of the shows that filled those first few months on the air. I should have been celebrating. The Commissioner was there. The hors d' oeuvres were hot. But I just stood apart, avoiding people, then left after a half-hour.

The following Saturday, the wait for Megan was interminable. Because we wanted to give our full attention to her, we sent all three kids and the dog to my mother-in-law's house. Our house was quiet. And cold.

When Megan got there, we sat down at the kitchen table. She began with a preamble, and I could tell she rehearsed it on the car ride over. Here was this 22-year-old kid, sitting at the table with two adult parents, and she was faced with the task of delicately but forcefully telling them that it was time to wake up and smell the coffee. Her goal was to get us to take Frederick to a developmental pediatrician.

She began softly, her voice barely above a whisper, telling us that Frederick had made some nice progress over the past few months, but some things were still lagging behind…he doesn't initiate interactions…his eye contact could be better…his speech is still delayed.

She pulled out a typed-up, formal looking page from her bag and asked if she could read from a pediatrician-approved quiz, and then the three of us would discuss each question and come to a consensus on the answer. He didn't know it, but Frederick was taking his first standardized test.

### M-CHAT: Modified Checklist for Autism in Toddlers

Please fill out the following about how your child usually is. Please try to answer every question. If the behavior is rare (e.g., you've seen it once or twice), please answer as if the child does not do it.

1. Does your child enjoy being swung, bounced on your knee, etc?
2. Does your child take an interest in other children?
3. Does your child like climbing on things, such as stairs?
4. Does your child enjoy playing peek-a-boo/hide-and-seek?
5. Does your child ever pretend, for example, to talk on the phone or take care of dolls, or pretend other things?
6. Does your child ever use his/her index finger to point, to ask for something?
7. Does your child ever use his/her index finger to point, to indicate interest in something?
8. Can your child play properly with small toys (e.g., cars or bricks) without just mouthing, fiddling, or dropping them?
9. Does your child ever bring objects over to you (parent) to show you something?
10. Does your child look you in the eye for more than a second or two?
11. Does your child ever seem oversensitive to noise? (e.g., plugging ears)
12. Does your child smile in response to your face or smile?
13. Does your child imitate you? (e.g., you make a face-will your child imitate it?)
14. Does your child respond to his/her name when you call?
15. If you point at a toy across the room, does your child look at it?
16. Does your child walk?
17. Does your child look at things you are looking at?
18. Does your child make unusual finger movements near his/her face?

19. Does your child try to attract your attention to his/her own activity?

20. Have you ever wondered if your child is deaf?

21. Does your child understand what people say?

22. Does your child sometimes stare at nothing or wander with no purpose?

23. Does your child look at your face to check your reaction when faced with something unfamiliar?

The authors of the M-CHAT recommend conservative scoring rules in order to miss as few children on the Autism spectrum as possible. Any child who fails three or more items on the entire M-CHAT, or two or more of the critical items should receive a comprehensive evaluation.

We did the test together, with Megan reading and the three of us discussing the appropriate answer to each question, and we agreed on almost everything. I fought her on #22—I agreed Frederick wandered, but I believed he had a purpose: to get away from people. She gave me that one. I also argued #8, saying that although he doesn't play properly with toys, he has never played with an actual brick, since we didn't live at the Little House on the Prairie.

But as we slowly went through the "Modified Checklist for Autism in Toddlers," you didn't need a medical degree to know which way the answer was supposed to go, and by my unofficial mental tally, Frederick was getting crushed. On more than half the questions, he was on the wrong side of the ledger.

When we got done, Megan didn't even take a minute to add anything up. She just pushed the paper to the center of the table, as if it spoke for itself, like a bloody knife in a courtroom.

We sat there in silence, until I broke it.

"So you're saying he has Autism."

It was a statement, a challenge, as if I wanted to start a fistfight. She was fresh out of college, but mature enough not to take the bait.

"I'm not qualified to make a diagnosis, and I could be wrong, but I think it's possible, and you should take him to a doctor who is qualified to make that call."

Again, more silence. For once, Bernadette wasn't crying, she was just staring at the oven. Maybe she was thinking about climbing in. Maybe there was room for two.

Megan continued. "At the bottom it says if the child fails three or more, or two or more of the critical questions, he should get evaluated."

I grabbed the paper. "Which are the critical ones?"

"They're the ones I circled."

I adjusted the page so it was directly in front of me, square and level. The circled items were 2,7,9,13,14,15. I slowly moved my finger across the page, from question to answer, not wanting to confuse or transpose anything.

# 2- Take an interest in other children? No.
# 7- Does he point? No.
# 9- Does he bring objects to you? No.
I took a deep breath. 0 for 3, with 3 strikeouts. Not good.
#13- Does your child imitate? No.
#14- Does your child respond to his or her name? No.
#15- If you point at a toy, does he look? No.

"Wait a minute," I argued. "Number 14. Frederick responds to his name. That should be a 'yes.'"

Megan's eyes began to well up. The first person to cry at the table and she wasn't even the Mom or Dad. Were we that emotionally spent?

Megan chose her words carefully. "No, he really doesn't. Not specifically to his name. He responds more to the way you say it...like you could say any word in a calling voice and...what I'm saying is...if it was just a sensory problem, he'd be able to communicate..." Her voice trailed off.

I routinely went 0 for 6 in Little League, mainly because I was a terrible athlete and mortally afraid of a pitched ball. But at least I was able to overcome a deficit in one area with the ability to talk, make friends, and occasionally wrangle a date from a girl. Frederick went 0 for 6 on the Modified Checklist for Autism in Toddlers. What was in store for him?

After some hot tea and small talk, we hugged at the door, and now everyone's eyes were a little moist. We thanked Megan for coming out on a Saturday, and we went about our business as best we could. Bernadette vacuumed, I went outside and did some lawn work. I made a mental note to call C.H.O.P. for an appointment. I also remembered thinking that tomorrow was Sunday and I could watch some football and get my mind off it. And then I realized the Eagles were playing on Monday night that week. It was a big game, in a season that would ultimately find them one game shy of making the Super Bowl, but suddenly I realized I didn't care. And then I wondered how I could ever enjoy watching sports again if I had a handicapped child.

My thoughts kept returning to that word. Handicapped. My son was handicapped. These days, the proper term is "Disabled," but handicapped just stayed in my head.

Back before we had kids, when we were talking about starting a family, Bernadette and I used to discuss made-up scenarios. How many children did we want? What if we couldn't get pregnant—would we adopt? What if we had a handicapped child?

I remember my answer to that one. "You know what? I think I'd be really good with a handicapped child."

Besides being a little bit condescending, the answer was also a little vague. What did that mean, "I'd be good?" And what constituted "handicapped?" One thing for sure: back in 1996, before we had children, handicapped didn't mean Autism to me. I think I was imagining a physical handicap, maybe a little girl in a wheelchair, and we'd be coming home from a big family gathering, and it would be a struggle to get the chair out of our Toyota Corolla (I guess I hadn't upgraded to a minivan in my musings.) As I banged up the wheelchair and scratched up my car, I'd laugh it off. And when I put her in the chair, with a nice comforter over her lap that my Nan had knitted, I could see in her little face that she was embarrassed, or more accurately sheepish, because she couldn't do this by herself; but I'd see that and make a quick joke, maybe about the wheelchair needing shock absorbers when Dad's pulling it, and that would lighten the mood and put a smile on her face. And later I'd carry her body up the stairs to bed and kneel down next to her like my Dad used to, and I'd kiss her and tell her that she was soooo loved, and somehow I'd let her know that even though all this was a struggle, and it may not have been the way she imagined her life, and even though she got jealous from seeing her friends running and playing, I loved her the way she was and wouldn't trade her for anyone in the world.

Could I do that now?

# 6 THE NEUROLOGIST BEHIND CHICK-FIL-A

I attended the University of Notre Dame and in my Junior year I took a Statistics class. One day I was completely spacing out until I heard the professor say, "If I flip a coin 49 times and it comes up 'heads' 49 straight times, what are the odds that it comes up 'heads' on the 50$^{th}$ flip?"

I perked up. "Is this guy a moron?" I thought.

I didn't raise my hand because this was one of those big lecture classes, maybe 100 people in an auditorium, but I answered the question in my head. "Duh, like, zero chance. Like no chance at all. There's no way you're gonna get a 'heads' again after 49 heads in a row."

I bring up that embarrassing mathematical faux pas not to denigrate my high school education but to give a little background on my thoughts about Autism relative to my own health. I was born with a heart anomaly in which a membrane in my upper heart chamber made it appear like I had three atriums instead of two, plus a gaping hole between the two lower chambers which made it seem like one big ventricle. If you want to stay in math-class mode and count them up, I had a four-chambered heart like everyone else. Of course, the doctors didn't see it that way but after two surgeries, a big scar on my chest, and lots of little procedures and medications here and there, I'm fine now. The relevancy to Frederick's developmental issues was simple: in my mind, there was no way someone who had a heart problem that maybe 1 in 10,000 people are born with is going to have a special needs child. Seriously, what are the odds of that happening? A guy with a heart operation having a kid with Autism? That's like lightning striking twice, right? If Michael Jordan went 0 for 49, he was probably going to make his next shot. Right? Help me out here.

The answer to the professor's question was obvious to everyone in that auditorium except me. "You have a 50% chance of getting 'heads' on the next flip," the professor continued. "Every random flip of a coin has a 50% chance. All the previous flips have no bearing on the next flip. Doesn't matter what happened prior, you have the same chance going forward."

Despite the pronouncements in that Statistics class I still believed in the law of averages or karma or something, so I was still reasonably confident Frederick didn't have the "Big A," even after Megan gave us the C.H.A.T. test.

But we took her advice and called Children's Hospital of Philadelphia. Their first available developmental pediatrician appointment was four months away, in February 2004. I booked it just in case, but then searched for other doctors who could see us sooner. I got a recommendation from a guy at work whose son had been diagnosed with Asperger Syndrome (the type of Autism that sits at the mildest end of the spectrum; kids with Asperger's typically can communicate and are usually placed in a mainstream classroom, but have impairments in social interaction.) Dr. Malarchuk's earliest available appointment wasn't until after the New Year. But as his secretary was taking information over the phone about Frederick and his symptoms, she asked me if there were any birth complications. I told her Frederick's Apgar scores were 2 and 3. She immediately perked up. "Oh, let's get him in soon. How about December 10?"

It's never a good sign when a receptionist tells you there's no opening for two months, and then suddenly says, "How soon can you come in?"

We pulled into a sprawling suburban office campus containing a dozen buildings, all with the same one-story architecture, bland beige color, and big directory board that you stopped your car in front of to find the locations of the suites. The medical-snob hair rose on the back of my neck as I noticed that this doctor shared a building with an insurance company, a dentist, and a ReMax agent. You would think a really good neurodevelopmental doctor wouldn't be a stone's throw from the Chick-fil-A, but here we were. To make matters worse, the doctor's name was misspelled on the directory.

We invited Megan to the appointment, hoping her dispassionate therapist opinion would give the doctor a more accurate picture of Frederick's day-to-day abilities. After she arrived we walked across the parking lot; Megan and Bernadette made small talk while I carried Frederick and whispered a pep talk in his ear.

That's right—a pep talk for a two-year-old who had trouble understanding language and communicating. But I was desperate, and Frederick had what you could call "on" days and "off days." Some days he was better behaved than others, and on this day, I was begging him for one of his better performances. I gave him my best Knute Rockne speech.

"I need you to come through, buddy," I told him. "Show this guy what you got. You need to be clutch—Jerry West clutch, Adam Vinatieri clutch—we need it today. Do it buddy, do it."

The doctor began by asking boilerplate questions—Was there any birth trauma? Have any skills regressed? Did he lose any language? Does he have stranger anxiety? Can he perform any basic tasks like brushing teeth or getting dressed? What services is he currently receiving? Bernadette, Megan and I elaborated on our answers as best we could. We talked about how Frederick was two years old but spoke less than our daughter Anna did at 13 months. We talked about his hyperactivity and how he didn't play with toys properly. We told him Frederick said "da" for "dad" at a year old but hadn't progressed much since, how he didn't like being in a stroller unless it was moving, and how he flipped through the pages of a book without looking at the contents. All the while, the doctor would sneak glances at Frederick, or simply nod his head at our answers as he kept his gaze on Frederick.

Maybe my pep talk in the parking lot worked, because Frederick was about as calm and lucid as he'd ever been. When the interview portion was over, Dr. Malarchuck examined Frederick fully—head size, muscle tone, and a simple follow-the-pen eye test. He gave Frederick toys to play with then gauged his level of frustration as he re-directed him to a different toy. When he was finished, the doctor asked for and received a high-five from Frederick, then excused himself to go into his office to organize his thoughts.

So here we were: me, Frederick, Bernadette, and Megan, the "team member" who definitely earned that status by showing up (I probably should have named her captain.) We just kind of looked at each other for a solid minute until Bernadette stood up and said, "I can't take this." Then she paced a lap around the room and sat back down.

I walked over to Frederick, who was rearranging the magnets on a file cabinet, and got my own high-five. "You were on fire, buddy!" That's the term we always used when he behaved well or acted close to typical. If we went to a family function and he was noticing people and interacting we'd say, "He's on fire." And he really was on fire this day.

Five minutes turned into ten. It was starting to feel like some sick game show where the contestants sat in a sound proof room and waited for the results: Did we win the million dollar diagnosis or a set of steak knives?

Finally, after 15 minutes of pure unadulterated nauseating anxiety, the doctor returned.

"I looked over my notes and tried to come up with a clinical impression. But first things first: he needs speech therapy, with the amount and intensity to be determined by the therapist. But I think that's a first thing that should be done. Language is his big issue—he doesn't respond consistently to language cues, and most kids with a significant speech delay have some form of Pervasive Developmental Disorder, the umbrella term for the Autism Spectrum. It's difficult to know what, if anything, Frederick's issues will be over time. What's important is that you not avoid any issues, and the good thing is you're not avoiding anything. You're doing everything you can as parents right now."

He smiled, and we lapped up the compliment like a thirsty dog at his bowl.

"You had some concerns about his motor skills and clumsiness. I don't believe that will be a problem for him over the long-term. I think skills like getting dressed without a fight will come along. What's going to be important isn't what does emerge; it's what doesn't emerge. What doesn't emerge will lead us to a diagnosis. This field of science is more about what you become than what you are. We need to keep a broad-based score of how he progresses. But it's important not to be overly concerned with little things; focus on the big picture and just see if he is improving. Don't judge him on his highs and lows. Judge his average.

"As a doctor, I have to ask myself: what diagnosis does this child seem most like? To me, Frederick seems like a diagnosis of speech delay and developmental delay, but not PDD. He does have a few autistic features, but he does not give the impression that he is an autistic child. He's in the world of the people around him, and you can engage him. I wouldn't be able to engage him if it was Autism. So from that standpoint, he needs a language therapy program, not an autistic program."

A casual observer, someone with no emotional investment in Frederick, might have listened to Dr. Malarchuck and been concerned by some of his remarks:

Most kids with significant speech delay have Pervasive Developmental Disorder.

We don't yet know what his long-term issues will be.

He does have a few autistic features.

Bernadette and I had a different point of view. This is what we heard: "It's not Autism."

Yay !!!!!

We sprinted out of that office before the doctor could change his mind; I was carrying Frederick, taking little leaps every few steps, jumping in the air yelling "You did it buddy, you did it!" I was never a great athlete, and I wasn't on any championship-winning teams, but the feeling I had running across that parking lot had to be the same feeling ballplayers have when the final out of the World Series is recorded and the whole team races for the pitcher's mound and jumps all over everybody. I carried Frederick to the car, kissing him the whole way, and kept saying "You did it, you did it." I hugged Bernadette, I hugged Megan, then strapped Frederick into his car seat and grabbed his shirt and shook him, "You did it, you did it, you did it."

Now, when I re-read my notes from that day, I always chuckle at the doctor's line "He's in the same world with the people around him." It was partly true—that doctor was in the same world as Frederick, but it was some alternate universe where black was white and peanut butter was jelly and Autism meant neurotypical. In the real world, Frederick had Autism, and Dr. Malarchuck missed it. He told us that Frederick presented with everything you need for an Autism diagnosis, but he was in "our world" and therefore didn't have it. But if it walks like a duck and quacks like a duck, it's usually Autism.

So a 22-year-old Occupational Therapist who was six months out of college said there was a problem, and then a neurologist with four years of med school and probably eight more years honing his craft before hanging out his own shingle said it wasn't a problem. Granted, he didn't give a glowing review, but this doctor visit was pass/fail to us. If we heard the "A-word," Frederick failed. If we didn't, he passed, and the Doctor specifically said, "I don't think it's Autism."

Frederick was back to being a kid with some delays and a short attention span but a great laugh and a great smile. We thought we had our son back.

The rest of that day was spent spreading the good news. Bernadette rushed to tell her parents and all her siblings, and I called my buddy Dave who also had good news—his wife was pregnant. The next day was the Christmas pageant at our parish. We arrived a little late and sat behind Bernadette's sister Margie and she turned around with tears in her eyes and gave me an awkward, leaning-over-the-pew hug and said "That's great news. That's the best news."

And during the show, Frederick wasn't very attentive; in fact, he was his usual disruptive self, but there was a moment where Pop Pop Fred was holding him, and I saw maybe a hint of a tear in Pop Pop's eyes. He's an old school grandfather who never tells you what's on his mind and doesn't really say much at all. But this was the man who gave Frederick his looks and his height and his name. Frederick was his 'special guy.' Pop Pop's eyes said it all: My little guy's ok. He's ok.

# 7 THE REPORT

Despite the good news we received right before Christmas 2003, we never canceled the appointment we made at Children's Hospital in Philadelphia, scheduled for 02-03-04. A few weeks after that terrible drive home in the rain, when I was wracked with guilt about pelting a special needs child with snowballs when I was a kid myself, this report arrived in the mail from Dr. Landau.

```
DOE:        02/03/04
NAME:       Frederick O'Brien
AGE:        2 years, 2 months
CHIEF COMPLAINT:
Frederick is a 2 year, 2 month old male and
his parents are here to receive our impression and
guidelines for Frederick's future development. Frederick
has a history of global developmental delays and
some difficult behaviors such as tantrumming during
transitions and a short attention span and high activity
level. He received a comprehensive evaluation on 1/20/04
which included the ADOS, Autism Diagnostic Observation
Schedule, Module I, and an occupational therapy
evaluation along with a sensory profile.
    The ADOS, Autism Diagnostic Observation
Schedule Module I, was completed. In language and
communication, Frederick had no words. He had an
occasional vocalization directed toward his caregivers.
Frederick had no pointing during the ADOS. He had
no spontaneous gestures. He had poor eye contact to
regulate communication. Frederick did have some facial
```

expressions directed towards his mother with a nice social smile. To the observers he had no response to his name and mother reports that this is variable. We did not find Frederick directly requesting. He did show balls to his mother in an inconsistent manner and the play telephone. Frederick had no spontaneous joint attention and no interest in a response to joint attention by targeting the bunny rabbit. Frederick's social overtures lack integration with eye contact, gesturing and vocalization. Frederick does not have pretend play.

ADOS Module I Score:

Communication: Total score was 6.

Qualitative impairments and reciprocal social interaction: His total score was 11.

Composite Score: 17 for communication and social. The Autism cutoff is 12. The Autism Spectrum cutoff is 7. A higher score is consistent with more difficulties. The ADOS classification is Autism and his overall diagnosis is Autism.

DIAGNOSES:

1.   Autism

2.   Moderate range of developmental delay.

RECOMMENDATIONS:

1.   We recommend a behavioral intervention program using principles of Applied Behavioral Analysis, Functional Analysis and Principles of Reinforcement. This program can also include some ideas from the Floortime program or TEACCH and provide an eclectic approach and be carried out in the home and educational environment. The behavior program should focus on enhancing verbal and nonverbal communication. Hours of service should be increased as tolerated.

2.   When Frederick turns 3 we recommend a specialized preschool with small class size with frequent opportunity for one-on-one instruction. Curriculum should focus on language and social skills throughout the day. The behavioral intervention program

should be integrated into the program. It should be full-time, extended year.

3. Intensive individual speech language therapy with exploration of alternative communication systems such as the Picture Exchange Communication System or sign language.

4. Continue intensive occupational therapy weekly with sensory integration.

5. Continue developmental teacher weekly.

6. Medical investigation for the etiology (cause) of PDD/Autism: Fragile X (molecular DNA probe) and karyotype (chromosome analysis) with telomere screen of all chromosomes by FISH and 22q11.2 FISH analysis. Head MRI and EEG not necessary at present.

7. Close communication and carry over of educational and behavioral interventions in the school and home settings.

8. Before embarking on alternative treatments read as much as possible and discuss with physicians caring for your child.

9. Follow-up in six months.

# 8   BANG OUT THE DENTS

Autism.

There it was. The dreaded "A-word." Someone with a medical degree finally said it.

And just in case we thought they were kidding, they had also used the word nine times in a three-page report, printed it in Courier font to make it look serious and official, then mailed it to our house.

The words Dr. Landau spoke, and the words in the report, were like a sledgehammer driving a spike. No spontaneous gestures…no response to his name… a higher score is consistent with more difficulties…score of 17…the Autism cutoff is 12…

Frederick took nine months to gestate in the womb, and then 26 months after he was born his delays developed into a full-blown diagnosis.

It happened on February 3, 2004, a date which will forever be the line of demarcation in our lives, the before and after point, a fault line where the earth gave way and left us staring down into a hole where once had been something solid. I'm sure we would have always remembered the date of his diagnosis, but on the off-chance that in 20 years down the road things were going really well and we'd almost put it behind us, the convenient numerical transcription of the date—02-03-04—would snap us out of our amnesia. 02-03-04 is a tough one to forget.

When Frederick finally got the diagnosis I figured that was it. Ball game. Sayonara. Thanks for playing, we have some lovely parting gifts for you. I assumed I'd be walking around in a stupor, mailing-in every single day for the rest of my life. And that was certainly how I felt for awhile. I started projecting about what would happen to him, to my wife, to us. Would ours become one of the countless marriages with an autistic child that failed? Would we become "those people"—the ones you see in Church with the adult child with special needs, the ones whose house always looks older than it is, curtains always drawn, moss growing on the bricks?

But then the weirdest thing happened—after a few weeks of CAT-5 depression, Frederick's diagnosis became the equivalent of sniffing an ammonia capsule or taking a hubcap-sized Ritalin. It woke me up. It focused me. We now had a diagnosis, and from that we could make a plan and get to work.

But what were we working toward? Improvement? A fix? A full cure?

From what I had read, kids with Autism could not be "cured" but they could "lose their diagnosis." I didn't know exactly what that meant, and I was wary because the term had the whiff of a marketing ploy or political spin. It was as if a kid could reach a certain age and shed his issues the way a snake sheds its skin. Regardless of the word-choice gymnastics involved, it was clear that a parent didn't just have to throw up his hands; the situation could be improved.

In keeping with the buffet-style approach I'd perfected, I ignored some of Dr. Landau's dire pronouncements about mental retardation and genetic abnormalities and concentrated on one thing she told us: "A good goal to shoot for would be for him to be indistinguishable from his peers by grade school." And I also kept telling myself that in the grand scheme of things, an Autism diagnosis is a good one to get. It's one of the few maladies that could be worked on by the parents and made better through sheer hard work. I came up with yet another analogy for Bernadette. "See, we're lucky. If Frederick had leukemia, that's like your car being totaled. But he has Autism, which is more like a fender bender. We just have to take him to a body shop and bang out the dents."

My career as a mechanic began by reading the manuals.

I researched and read any book I could get my hands on. I read *Peer Play and the Autism Spectrum. The Late-Talking Child. More Than Words. The Affect-Based Language Curriculum.*

I tackled *Biomedical Assessment Options for Children with Autism and Related Problems, Children With Starving Brains, Enzymes for Autism,* and *The Biology of the Autistic Syndromes.*

I bought *Raising a Child With Autism,* then I bought *Educating a Child With Autism,* just in case I wanted to both raise and educate Frederick. I also got *Helping Children With Autism Learn* which, although unrelated to the previous two, seemed to form a sort of Tolkienesque trilogy. And I'm sure if I had seen a book called Raising and Educating a Child With Autism to Learn I would have grabbed it as well.

It was like I was back in college. I highlighted passages in the books and typed them into a word document. I created a 25-page handout for my parents, Bernadette's parents, and her sisters that lived in the area. In it, I explained what Autism was, the six developmental skills that were most important for Frederick to work on, and strategies for helping him advance.

One book stood out above the others: *The Child With Special Needs.* It was written by Dr. Stanley Greenspan, one of America's leading Developmental Pediatricians and a former director at the National Institute of Mental Health. In the book, Greenspan took a radical turn from the popular view of educating children with Autism.

Most educational programs used Advanced Behavior Analysis, or ABA, which involves rewarding good behavior (completing a task) and withholding rewards for negative behavior (use your imagination.) Greenspan's theory was called the "Floortime" philosophy because implementing it meant getting down on the floor with your child, watching what he did, then trying to interact with him—whether he was playing with toy cars, Sesame characters, or the lint in the carpet. You attempted to insert yourself into everything he did in order to get him to respond to you, and you'd do it over and over until you had several minutes (or hours) of interactions between the two of you.

It was the first book I read that gave me hope for Frederick. Greenspan didn't wallow in what these children lacked; instead, he asked, "How high can they climb?" And he found the answer to that question by attacking Autism's core deficit—emotional interaction.

Floortime became a 24-hour, seven-day-a-week lifestyle change.

Before Floortime, when Frederick wanted something he would pull us toward it and just stand there. If he wanted fruit, which was kept on top of the refrigerator, he would push us into the kitchen and up against the fridge. And we usually knew what he wanted, so we gave it to him. No more. Now, he had to use some vocalization. If we knew he wanted a cup, we'd hold it above his head. "Frederick, say cup." He'd make a sound that wasn't even in the ballpark of "cup" but because he made a sound, we'd get him some juice—but then only a sip. That way, he'd finish it quickly and have to ask for more, thereby forcing more interaction.

Even before we started with Early Intervention I had created games to play with Frederick that were task-oriented. When the pediatrician asked if Frederick could clap, and we said no, and he said he should be able to clap by now, I invented the "Clap-Tickle" game. If he clapped, I tickled him. He liked being tickled, so he learned how to clap. Pretty simple.

Now, with Floortime, our games had matured into silly things. When getting him dressed we might put his socks on his hands so he could vocalize a protest. If he wanted his binky, we'd play "Hide the Binky" and I'd run away with it and shove it under a sofa cushion. He'd have to follow my instructions and hints in order to find it. If he wanted the TV on he'd try to pull me out of my chair to turn it on. I'd look at him and play dumb.

"Frederick, what do you want?"

I'd wait till he pushed my hand toward the TV and I'd say "Oh, TV? Do you want TV on?"

As he progressed, I began to throw in a twist. Every time he wanted it on, I'd oblige, but put on C-Span. Then I'd set the remote down and walk away. He'd protest, I'd return, and he'd point to the TV to indicate he wanted something else on. He was interacting with me. Mission accomplished.

After a few months of this, I was drinking the Floortime Kool-Aid and asking for a re-fill. I joined the Yahoo! Floortime User Group and listened to Dr. Greenspan's weekly podcasts. Then I attended Greenspan's Floortime Conference outside Washington, DC.

I spent most of the drive down from South Jersey on my cell phone, calling people who were not yet aware of Frederick's diagnosis. Obviously my extended family and my closest friends knew, but people from my old job at NBA Entertainment and some college buddies didn't know the full extent or weren't aware at all. Although I've never had to make one, it was probably similar to calls people make when they get diagnosed with a terrible disease. But instead of "Yeah, they caught it early so I'm optimistic" it was, "Yeah, we thought there was a problem for a while and he got the formal diagnosis a few months ago, but we're working hard and doing everything right so we're optimistic." A few of them added their own experiences: "That's funny you say that. I know a guy at work, his son had Autism. But they did a lot of stuff and he outgrew it."

I was surprised by my desire—or maybe 'need' would be the right word—to discuss it with anyone and everyone. It was as if I was walking around with a black eye and felt I had to bring it up before someone else did. "Craziest thing. I'm down on one knee, tying my shoes, my wife barges in and—Whack!—the doorknob gets me right in the eye." On the way to the conference I stopped at a mostly-empty Dunkin Donuts and chatted up the guy behind the counter while waiting for my coffee. "Yeah, headed to a conference. Autism Conference. Yeah, my son just got diagnosed." Mr. Paper Hat didn't ask any questions or even feign interest, just gave me my large coffee and chocolate chip muffin.

I took a lot of notes at the conference, but the most memorable and daunting note concerned how you were supposed to implement the Floortime philosophy:

Recommended Intensity for Optimum Outcomes:

Floortime: 8 sessions per day; 30m each

Sensory Work: 2 sessions per day

Peer Play: 4 sessions per week

To recap: not two months after my only son was diagnosed with Autism, a former director at the National Institute of Mental Health—a guy who wrote a groundbreaking book on my son's disease, a guy who was influential enough to get a few thousand people to hear him speak in a hotel ballroom—was telling me and my wife that we had to drop everything, including our two other kids, and go into the Frederick business 24/7.

In the ensuing months I became friendly with a guy who was very active in the 'Floortime Community.' He asked me how much Floortime we did with Frederick and I said, "I don't know, maybe an hour or two a day." After a long pause, during which time I was afraid he might punch me, he contorted his face into a half-horrified, half-enraged mask, then responded "No, no, no, no. You have to do more. Hire a live-in, do whatever you have to do, but you're gonna need to do at least seven hours a day."

So because I didn't take out a second mortgage to hire a nanny and because my wife occasionally liked to play with Grace every now and then or volunteer at Anna's school, we were bad people. For me, this was the hardest part of being a special needs parent. You have doctors and therapists and teachers and holistic healers telling you your kid won't get better unless you do a certain thing, take a certain supplement, turn your life upside down. And the implication is simple: these things work, and if your kid doesn't improve it's your fault. That's the overwhelming guilt and pressure that's put on you, pressure that would crush a normal parent.

Are we doing enough...could we do more? Those were the thoughts, the echoing mantra that never left my brain. Are we doing enough...could we do more...maybe you missed something...maybe there's a new thing out there...you have to find it...

I was his dad, and I loved him, and it didn't seem right or fair that Frederick had to endure this, so no stone was left unturned. At the Floortime Conference, one of the presenters was a woman who was considered the guru of Floortime-based speech therapy. Naturally, I had to make an appointment with her. A few weeks later, Bernadette, Frederick and I took a three-and-a-half hour car ride—not to Six Flags, not to some awesome zoo or aquarium—but to spend 90 minutes getting speech therapy in this stranger's basement.

Donna Leonard looked like the kind of person who ate massive quantities of dried fruit and nuts. She was in her 50's, maybe even pushing 60, but sinewy, like a graying yoga instructor, and everything about her screamed healthy aging.

I videotaped the entire session so I could consult the tape in case I forgot some of the things we were taught. Looking at it now, years later, it's so wonderful to see Frederick frozen in time. He has some redness to his cheeks from eczema, but the eyes twinkle and the blonde hair poofs up at the forehead like the angel in my favorite childhood Christmas book, *Touselhead*. It's easy to see why Bernadette and I weren't convinced of the accuracy of his Autism diagnosis. Frederick didn't seem much like a child with a behavioral disorder; instead, he 'presented' (as the doctors say) like someone rehabilitating from a brain injury, as if he was in a car accident and had to re-learn everything. He knows what he's doing and what he wants, but he's frustrated because it's not coming out right. That's the thought when you watch the video: this is a kid who has a blockage somewhere between thought and expression.

In one priceless moment, Frederick says "Mommy" as clearly and crisply as polar ice. Off camera, you can hear Bernadette explode, repeating "Oh my gosh, oh my gosh" over and over in a wonderful combination of laughter and tears.

One other memorable item from the video that I'd nearly forgotten about was the presence of a blue cast on Frederick's right forearm. A few weeks before we visited the speech therapist, I came home from work to find Grace and Frederick in their normal positions on the floor and couch, respectively, watching Teletubbies. I kissed both then noticed something odd about Frederick; upon further inspection, his arm looked a little strange.

After a few more seconds of observation I yelled into the kitchen. "Bern—why is Frederick's arm shaped like a U?"

As it turned out, Bernadette had heard a loud bang a few hours earlier and surmised that Frederick had jumped off the radiator (something we discouraged but found hard to prevent.) When she checked on him, he was standing up, pointing at the TV, hopping up and down—in a word, normal. Then he walked upstairs to take a nap, and Bernadette checked on him several times. He was sleeping soundly. But when we took him to the doctor, they found a complete fracture.

Later, I searched the internet for pain threshold and Autism. Indeed, insensitivity to pain is on the long list of complications. Who knew?

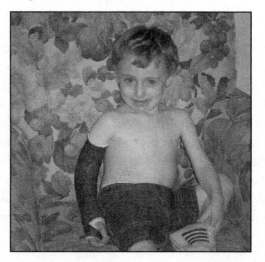

**High pain tolerance… just add it to the list.**

Not that anything surprised me anymore. Near the end of our speech therapy session Donna abruptly stopped and announced, "We need to get in his mouth." Then she picked up two boxes of rubber gloves. "Frederick, do you want grape or bubble gum?" She turned to us. "They're flavored, you know."

"I'm going to rub his gums and at the same time have him lick my finger," Donna said, explaining that it was somehow the mouth's equivalent of stretching before running. She stuck a finger in but Frederick screamed and recoiled. She shook her head, disappointed. "Well clearly, nobody's going in his mouth."

She said that like it was a bad thing.

Undaunted, Donna sat down next to Bernadette. "I'll demonstrate on Bernadette so you can understand what we need to do on Frederick. You want to run your finger along the gum line and make sure you don't cross over this midpoint here. Take your finger out and skip over the midpoint then run it along the gum again. Now Bernadette, lick my finger as I'm doing this, roll your tongue around." Bernadette did as commanded, making the same guttural moan you hear in a dentist's office.

At this point, something should have happened to me. I should have been intrigued or freaked out or something. But nothing happened. I had no reaction. It was just another day. Flavored latex gloves, a woman rubbing her finger in my wife's mouth, and it barely registered. We had jumped the parenting shark.

The session with Donna Leonard ended with her saying we needed to help Frederick "find his mouth" in the same way that New Age people speak of finding yourself. And, of course, she was quick to point out that her method was better than anything we previously attempted. "He's a great kid. He went up five levels because we engineered things properly today."

"Engineered things." That was a new term. Frederick was now a building to construct, or some massive Department of Public Works project.

So we decided to capitalize on that analogy. Any massive construction project needs massive amounts of workers, and now that we had a real Autism diagnosis, we pushed the Early Intervention people for more services.

It started with a letter to the Early Intervention director, another "team meeting" and a few weeks of teeth-pulling, but we eventually got it done. It wasn't everything I requested but we had taken our Early Intervention hours, plus private therapy and a formal playdate with Bern's friend's kid, from two hours to over ten hours per week.

Ten hours a week may not seem like a lot—most people work 40 hours, kids watch TV an average of 30 hours per week according to a recent survey—so ten hours a week seems like no big deal. But it is a big deal when you consider those ten hours mean no answering the phone, no computer surfing, no playdates, and a state-licensed therapist coming to your house.

Early Intervention had taken over our lives. It was how we arranged our day. It was how we got our bearings. It was our North Star. We knew what day of the week it was by which therapist was in our house. They would come nearly every day, sometimes two or three hours in a day. To borrow Donna Leonard's "engineering things" analogy, the Early Intervention specialists were trying to build Frederick into a child who could compete—or at least survive—in a classroom setting. If you think about it, before a kid can sit at a preschool table and learn he must be able to sit at the table for more than a few seconds without getting up and walking away. Quite often during a session, the therapist would say "sit in chair" as if she was a teacher saying "Ok, let's move on to two-digit subtraction." For Frederick, "sit-in-chair" was not a command but a subject he had to master—and we were running out of time. In New Jersey, a child could begin special schooling at age three, so we only had a few months left to get him ready.

As the summer turned into fall, we saw minor improvements in Frederick's behavior, but no game-changing metamorphosis. We passed the one-year anniversary of our involvement with Early Intervention, and those yellow sheets they gave us after every visit kept piling up. I stored them in a huge three-ring binders and after 16 months of accumulation that binder looked like the Manhattan yellow pages.

The last day of Early Intervention was November 24, 2004, five days before Frederick and Grace's third birthday. We had all the therapists over for a Margarita party, and Bernadette played a game where she read from various yellow sheets and the therapists had to guess who wrote what line.

March 29: Do not give Frederick banana if he is saying cracker. (Good call!)

June 15: Frederick is demonstrating age-appropriate skills, except in the areas of cognition, communication, fine motor and self-help. (So what was he doing well? Seriously—what else is there?)

August 4: Frederick has been getting into his diaper lately and making a mess. This is a stress for the family. (Ya think?)

November 8: Frederick has been out-of-sync this past week. He has been breaking objects and furniture.

Yes, we endured some broken furniture. And our family, our life, our world and our marriage had been out-of-sync since this had all started. I had many days when I felt a real appreciation for the work we did and the improvements that Frederick made. But more often, I had days when I was bitter and resentful. I wanted what (most) everyone else had: walks to the park, enjoyable family outings, and control of my life. Maybe that was the worst thing—we couldn't control this disease, and it took control of our family. We couldn't enjoy a day at the beach or an hour at Chuck E Cheese. And I don't even enjoy Chuck E Cheese, but the only thing worse than going was knowing you couldn't go.

I thought Early Intervention was going to be like smelling salts. We'd pop the capsule and wave them under Frederick's nose and he'd snap out of it. I was wrong.

As the good-bye party for the therapists drew to a close, I raised a glass in toast, thanking them for everything they had done. I ended with this: "I'm not sure how far Frederick will go in life..." pause, sniffle, wipe tear... "but however far he goes, I know you will be the ones responsible for getting him there."

# 9  DOCTOR DIXIE

When I was in third or fourth grade my friends and I played Doorbell Dixie, the game where kids would sneak up to a house, ring the doorbell, then scamper away to a hiding place and watch the owner open the door, look around, and find nothing.

Now, imagine playing that game with a screaming kid in your arms, replace suburban homes with doctor's offices, and you'll get a good idea of how Bernadette and I spent most of our free time. We played Doctor Dixie (or Doorbell Dixie with a co-pay.)

For months we'd been asking ourselves "Which therapists and what methods would get the most out of Frederick?" And in the tiny pockets of time we had between Early Intervention visits we were also asking "Was there anything out there—some doctor or test or medicine—that could improve or even undo this developmental delay?"

We began where you're supposed to begin: with a second opinion.

I was hoping that Dr. Landau was wrong. Or at least overstating things. The Early Intervention therapists were always much more bullish on Frederick's prognosis and they were the people who spent the most time with him. They would say things like, "Oh, his eye contact is really good; he wouldn't be looking to you for a reaction if he was as severe as they say he is."

So we set up another appointment at C.H.O.P. with a different doctor.

At our first meeting with Dr. Mark Joplin, I was blunt. "We're not saying he doesn't have some problems, but we are saying that Dr. Landau's evaluation in February might be overly pessimistic."

"Let me start with this chart," he said, pulling out a piece of paper with a printed image that looked like a gyroscope.

"The first thing to understand is that a child can have any degree of atypicality, right to left, and any degree of IQ level, the up and down line. We all have a few of these atypicality traits. But when they rise to a level of interfering with day-to-day activities, that's when we need to be concerned."

His proprietary drawing was an interesting way of describing Autism, one that

I had never heard before. He was saying that behavior and intelligence were both measurable, and understanding your child's blend gave you a picture of where he was on the Autism spectrum. He also used another easy-to-grasp analogy. "Think of atypicality like an iceberg, and intelligence as water temperature. The higher a child's intelligence, the higher the water temperature, and the more his atypicality will melt away."

I liked this guy. He was right up my alley. I always thought in metaphors, and he spoke in them. I figured it was the beginning of a beautiful friendship.

As always, I heard what I wanted to hear. Dr. Joplin didn't say Dr. Landau was wrong. He didn't say the diagnosis was incorrect. But I thought I heard him say that things weren't as bleak as they seemed. His report read, in part:

"When comfortable with examiner, Frederick gave eye contact to examiner and looked up frequently for affirmation."

"Has expressive facial features—disappointment, happiness."

"High activity level—discussed possible need for stimulants in 1-2 years."

"Needs individual discrete speech therapy program on a weekly basis."

But I wanted more than just a re-evaluation. What I most wanted was revenge. Dr. Landau had said my kid was hopeless, a goner, and I wanted to scream at her, "How dare you?" but I couldn't. The only way to get back at her was to go to a different doctor to prove her wrong, go to a peer who had the same medical degrees and leave with a different outcome. I'm not sure that's what Joplin did, but that's what I wanted and that's how I took it.

Dr. Joplin's evaluation may have seemed more optimistic, but parenting Frederick was still much more challenging than we allowed ourselves to admit.

We were thrilled when he made eye contact or tickled his sister. We also got over-excited when he did something that a typical kid his age would do without a request. For instance, if he was lying on his bed and we were dressing him, we thought it was a major accomplishment if he guided his leg into his pants without us having to shove it in there. Honestly, if a session of dressing Frederick didn't seem like calf-roping then we were over the moon. And if Bernadette came home from a doctor visit without a bloody lip from Frederick throwing his head back and hitting her in the face, then we considered it a successful trip.

It seemed that the key to everything was speech. Every doctor we had seen was unanimous in this regard—Frederick needed intensive speech therapy, pronto.

But during our time with Early Intervention, the powers-that-be said he wasn't ready for it. He could get Occupational Therapy, Physical Therapy and even Applied Behavior Analysis therapy, but not speech. Their theory was that Frederick needed the ability to sit still for a full session in order to benefit from formal speech therapy. I had a theory on their theory—that they had a backlog of kids in the district who needed speech therapy and not enough speech teachers to go around.

Luckily, there were plenty of qualified therapists around if you were willing to go out of pocket.

We found a therapist with a great reputation who worked out of a massive Victorian house in one of Philadelphia's toniest suburbs. When I pulled up for the evaluation there was only one other car there—a Mercedes convertible—and it occurred to me that I made the appointment and forgot to ask what it would cost. The therapist was smartly dressed and perky—imagine a host of one of those fashion reality shows, but with a master's degree. During the evaluation, she held up objects and asked Frederick if he could identify them. It was pure chaos.

"Frederick say ball. Say ballll. Ballll" She held up a ball, which Frederick took and put in his mouth.

She held up a spoon. "Frederick, say spoon." Frederick ran to the other side of the room and stood on a chair.

The therapist grew frustrated. She turned to me. "Dad, maybe you can hold him." I chased him down and brought him back to the table. She held up a toy dog. "Frederick, say dog." He thrashed in my arms. "Frederick, say doooog." He thrashed more. Then she held up her keychain—her Mercedes keychain—and dangled them. "K-K-K-Key. Say key." But he was gone, somehow managing to corkscrew out of my arms and under the table.

The therapist charged us $850. Seems a bit pricey, doesn't it? In her defense, it wasn't just an office session. A few weeks later, we received a nine-page document in a handsome leather folio that told us our son couldn't talk.

Some of the gems in the report included "Try to make him vocalize his needs."

Good call.

After writing the check, I think I would have been happier if the therapist had just come clean and let me know that I was about to get royally hosed. Or maybe she could have let me know through her evaluation techniques. "Frederick, repeat after me: Vay-ka-shun Hohm. In-In-In-ground Pooool. Now let's work on the alphabet—B....M....W."

We wanted to do everything possible for Frederick, but also wanted to keep a roof over our heads, so we found a more reasonably-priced therapist at the bargain price of "only" $90 an hour.

At our first visit Becky, the new therapist, pulled out an old-school Sesame Street pop-up toy. It was the one with Big Bird, Oscar, Ernie and Bert popping out when you pushed the button, flicked the switch or turned the rotary dial. After Frederick played with it for a minute, Becky said "Where's Big Bird" and then waited to see if he popped the right one. She was quick to point out how Frederick looked to her for a reaction, and then even more quickly pointed out that joint attention is not a characteristic you saw in children with Autism.

In that first visit I learned something important—the therapist had to give you hope or else you're not coming back.

Becky knew from our opening conversation that Frederick's diagnosis was Autism and that I didn't believe it or didn't want to believe it. So she fed that. In just our first session, she managed to drop some verbal chum that I swam after: "He's doing great. He's very smart. You wouldn't see this eye contact if he had full-blown Autism. Oh, I can tell he's going to do very well. He reminds me of a kid I used to work with; the kid's an honor student in high school now." Little nuggets, little treats that I ate up, a few compliments here and there to keep me coming back.

I was hooked.

But after 10 weeks of speech therapy with Becky and no discernible improvement we decided to pull the plug. Money was a big factor. With weekly sessions, the bill was $360 a month. Financially, this therapy was a knife that had cut through flesh and was hitting bone. Schedule was also a factor, since we could only schedule Saturday mornings. But the main thing that made me stop going was an incident in the car one morning as we were heading to an appointment. A few blocks from Becky's office, I was stopped at a light and looked into the minivan next to me. A woman, about my age, was having an animated conversation but no one was in the passenger seat. Weird, I thought. Maybe she has one of those Bluetooth phone things in her other ear.

And then she suddenly laughed and turned in her seat, and then laughed even harder.

I saw a kid in a car seat, roughly Frederick's age, in the row behind her.

Oh—that's who she's talking to.

And then it hit me—nearly three months of driving to this therapist's office, just me and Frederick, and I never once had a conversation with him. I had even given up on saying things out loud to him. What was the point? He never answered.

But I needed answers.

I scoured the internet looking for anything that might help. One day I stumbled across something called the Gluten Free/Casein Free diet. "Anecdotal evidence" suggested it could help kids on the Autism spectrum improve in a variety of ways. It's based on the theory that the proteins found in wheat, rye, oats, barley and dairy products (gluten and casein) are not completely broken down in some autistic children.

The unbroken peptides enter the bloodstream and cause an opiate-like effect, which would manifest itself as an aloof, un-connected personality.

In order to stick with the diet, you had to eliminate all dairy and wheat products, which essentially meant you eliminate all food. Or at least all enjoyment in eating food. Frederick already had allergies to egg and peanut, so attempting this diet meant feeding him fruits, vegetables, and a variety of home-cooked baked goods, including a gluten-free bread that looked and tasted like pale cardboard. Around our house the gluten-free diet was known as the "taste-free" diet. We tried it for six months but it didn't help at all, although it did help me understand that the term "anecdotal evidence" is a synonym for "wasting money."

It was also roughly the heyday of the vaccine controversy. At its root, the premise of the anti-vaccine crowd is that an outside-of-the-body "insult" (vaccination) triggers Autism. By extension, people of that ilk believe that Autism is reversible if you attack it properly.

I took Frederick to two separate "homeopathic healers." Both were legitimate MD's, and both claimed that Autism was curable. The one doctor suggested a battery of tests, including one from a mail-order company that for the bargain price of $280 would send you a kit to collect stool in order to test how a child's body broke down chemicals. So for a while there I was spooning Frederick's poop, dropping bits of it into small vials, "shaking well," then sending it back for testing.

We received a 12-page report that was color coded, very analytical-looking, almost a power point presentation, with each page having headings at the top of three columns: Sensitive (green), Intermediate (white) and Resistant (peach, mauve, or light orange, not sure.) They tested over twenty items, many of which seemed kind of pointless. For instance, I found out Frederick is sensitive to oregano, which I guess I needed to remember the next time he ate a Hoagie. He was also sensitive to black walnuts.

I wondered why they didn't test for raspberry vinaigrette.

On another page, the list of "Nutrient Elements" that were tested included Chromium, Cobalt, Molybdenum, Boron, Strontium, Sulfur and Vanadium. His Vanadium count was 0.0636, and of course the reference range you're looking for is between 0.0254 and 0.0574. The report stated "Excessive vanadium in blood and hair is clinically associated with melancholia, depression, and manic depression."

So is having a special needs child.

It also noted his Cadmium levels were above the referenced range, and in children, elevated Cadmium has been correlated with lower IQ.

I suspect that paying a few hundred dollars for a mail-order poop test is also associated with a lower IQ.

The doctor also suggested we do a heavy metal detox, which I thought was unnecessary because Frederick didn't listen to Def Leppard or Metallica. But then he explained it was a procedure in which we would insert rectal suppositories that were made up of a compound that would bind with the mercury (presumably from the vaccinations) and then expel it through bowel movements.

Frederick was not a big fan.

The other homeopathic healer we visited suggested rubbing emu oil on him every night (on my son, not the doctor.) An emu is the second-largest bird native to Australia, has a nail on its toe that can be wielded like a knife and a nine-foot stride at full gallop but, alas, no medicinal benefits for kids with Autism. Not that that stopped us. Soon the bizarre, expensive, and ineffective list of creams and drink powders we gave Frederick on a daily basis included Calcium, Zinc, Cod Liver Oil, Nystatin, Authia Cream, Primrose Oil, Glutathione, Capryllic Acid and Ultra Flora Plus Powder.

Next, I came across an internet article on a doctor in Canada who claimed that "Cranial Misalignment" was responsible for most Autism, because the child's brain was pressing up against the skull. It said that if the cranial bones were misaligned then the blood supply to the frontal lobes would be compromised and that could affect the behavior centers of the brain.

I figured, what the hell. Why not?

I made an appointment with C.H.O.P.'s best cranial guy. To make a short story shorter, his evaluation lasted 30 seconds.

"This kid?" the doctor said, staring at Frederick. "You think his skull is misaligned?" Sheepishly, I said yes. "Did a doctor refer you?" I shook my head no. He turned to me. "Do you realize I work on kids whose skulls are malformed—I mean visibly and obviously misaligned. Noticeable stuff." He looked downright pissed off and ready to walk out, so I brought up the Canadian doctor.

"Cranial misalignment causing Autism?" the C.H.O.P. doctor said, furrowing his brow. "Can't say I've seen that in any journals." Apparently he didn't subscribe to The New England Journal of Snake Oil Salesmen.

I paid the co-pay and slouched home.

But none of these dead-ends dissuaded me.

I probably should have been asking myself some important questions: Did I need to subject my son to every test and screening imaginable while bankrupting my family in the process? Was it somehow written in stone that I had to take him to every physician, homeopathic healer, herbalist, shaman and horse-whisperer I could find?

The experience with the cranial doctor was like getting caught playing Doorbell Dixie. He gave me a tongue-lashing, but it didn't deter me. I was already moving on to the next door.

One of Frederick's ex-speech teachers had a child with some challenges, and she told me about a psychiatrist in Princeton who was supposedly a real miracle worker. But her recommendation came with a caveat. "Be careful," she said. "He's different."

It didn't take long to understand the warning. I called his office and after two rings I heard a loud voice. "Dr. Warner"

I hung up.

What kind of doctor answers his own phone? Was it a home number? I double-checked the number and called back a few minutes later.

"Dr. Warner!" he barked.

"Yes, hello doctor. My son Frederick was diagnosed with Autism and I was wondering..."

"No he wasn't," Warner interrupted.

Silence. I wasn't sure how to proceed. I was ready to hang up and move on but I was a little miffed about a Doctor I had never met dismissing the worst day of my life.

"Actually, he _was_ diagnosed with Autism," I snapped. "I remember because it kinda sucked. I was there."

His tone changed almost imperceptibly, from crotchety to know-it-all, which was somehow more palatable.

"He could not have been diagnosed with Autism because Autism is not a diagnosis. It's an aggregation of symptoms."

Wasn't sure where to go from here. I figured I'd wait a second and he'd keep talking. I was right.

"Five hundred years ago, fever was a diagnosis. But now we know fevers are a result of an infection. Autism is just a list of symptoms, you have to find out what's causing it."

"Well, how do we..."

"Anyone checked his brain?"

"I'm pretty sure he has one."

"No, dummy. Anyone order a SPECT Scan?" he growled.

"No, I don't think—"

"Well why the hell not? If your car's running like crap you gonna look under the hood? Damn right you are."

"Well what do you recommend?" I asked.

"I have a free seminar at my office on Fridays at 5:00. Come up for that."

"Where are you located?"

"I'm in the book." Click.

All I can say is, for your kid, you'll try anything. It was an hour drive to his office that sat on the edge of the Princeton University campus. It was in a tiny corporate park with three buildings that had roofs with pointy-triangle tops which made them look like churches. His suite was on the ground floor.

I was a few minutes late, so I burst through his door without breaking stride. It wasn't until I was halfway through his massive waiting room that I noticed the people. Lots of them.

The room was the size of a racquetball court. About twenty-five people sat in folding chair along all the walls, and all manner of men and women were represented. A punk girl in her late teens. A 50-ish businessman. A hardcore biker. And a man with a beard that looked like Tom Hanks' after four years on the island in *Castaway*, except this guy had rubber bands in his.

"You Obie?"

The sound came from the top left corner of the room. Dr. Warner was in his 70's, with a big potbelly popping between his suspenders, a little like St. Nick without the beard. He wore a rumpled pink-and-white striped dress shirt and tie. Although seated, he seemed in a hurry.

"Find a spot." Warner said.

The only available chair was three down from the Doctor. I muttered an apology for being late then sat down.

The first thing I noticed about Dr. Warner was his eyebrows. Giant caterpillars. Pierre Salinger eyebrows. Just raising them as he talked must have been an exhausting effort.

"Now, where were we?" Warner boomed.

Across the room was a couple in their sixties. The man continued.

"I was telling you about my diet. It's that Atkins thing and it hasn't worked." A woman put her hand on his, for comfort. She was holding a teacup Poodle with a bow in its hair. The dog licked her hand, then his.

Warner bellowed. "Diets don't work, period. Within two years 98% of all dieters return to within 5% of their original weight. Next."

A man in his 30's spoke up from the other side of the room. "The Lamictal has really helped my hallucinations. I wake up less at night. And the hand-washing is way down."

"That's why we diagnose before we treat. How long had your previous doctor prescribed that crap that didn't work?" Warner asked.

"Six years."

"There it is," Warner said. "Diagnose then treat. That's what Obie here has to learn." He gestured toward me; I put my head down.

"Let's get to him," Dr. Warner continued. "Obie, why are you here?" He gestured out toward the room where two-dozen complete strangers were sitting. I cleared my throat.

I mumbled, "Well, uh, a few months ago…"

"Louder!" Warner boomed.

"Ok, uh, a few months ago my son was diagnosed with Autism. And I came here to find out what your course of treatment would be."

Warner's eyebrows went up until they merged with his helmet of silver hair. "And what would my course of treatment be?"

At least 10 hands shot up. Warner pointed to one.

"Don't treat the symptoms, treat the problem."

I stopped listening for a moment and gathered my thoughts. Apparently I had stumbled into a cult where people from all walks of life—young, old, business people and college kids—came to see Dr. Warner on a weekly basis. He seemed like Marlin Brando in Apocalypse Now, which I guess made me Martin Sheen. But I wasn't trying to kill Dr. Warner; I just wanted to get the information that would save my son.

The hands stayed up as Warner called on them one at a time. His "patients" were suggesting tests for my son.

"Did he have a contrast MRI yet?"

"Have you ruled out epilepsy?"

"You're sure it's not a hearing problem?"

A young man in his early twenties was two seats to my left. He raised his hand. "Do you think he has a plate in is head?"

I finally jumped in. "Why would he have a plate in his head?" I said.

"I don't know," the guy said matter-of-factly. "I do."

After about 30 minutes, the meeting broke up. On his way out, a disheveled man in his 40's stopped me. He looked like Nick Nolte's mug shot.

"Don't mind the Doctor. He always acts like that. When he gets going it's like he wants to get his ass kicked. I'd like to kick his ass. Probably would have a few months ago before the treatment."

He reached out to shake my hand.

"What's your name? Where you from?"

I just shook my head no and moved away.

For the next few minutes I loitered, looking at brochures, until the room cleared out. Dr. Warner headed for the door and I matched strides with him as he walked outside.

"Dr. Warner," I said, "What's the next step?"

"Call me to make an appointment. And bring your son." As we hit the sidewalk outside the office he made a sharp turn to his right and walked to his car.

I couldn't wait to tell Bernadette. I called from the cell while driving home and described the whole scene. When I finished she was flabbergasted. "Do you think it's a self-help group?" she asked.

"Not sure. But I think Dr. Warner is the only crazy one." I said.

"Well, at least it's over with," she said.

I paused. "Actually, I'm taking Frederick next week."

Silence.

More silence.

"Who's the crazy one?" she asked.

When I arrived at Dr. Warner's the following week he told me to wait in his back-room office. While Frederick knocked over nearly every plant and knick-knack, I studied the diplomas and pictures that adorned his walls. There was one picture taken a few years back, where Warner and his Princeton classmates posed for a 50th Reunion picture. They wore straw bowlers and pink-striped jackets. The men on either side of him were leaning away to avoid the eyebrows.

Warner barged into the room.

"Ok, Obie, what's the story?" He sat behind his desk and watched as I tried to control Frederick, who was squirming and clawing his way out of my grasp.

"As I told you my son was diagnosed with Autism and they said...."

"Bullshit," he roared. "He's not autistic. I can see that. How did they diagnose him?"

"Well, they put him in a big room and watched what he played with and how he interacted with the Occupational Therapist. I remember they mentioned how he picked up a ball and never put it down the whole time. They said it was perseverative and a sure sign of—"

"Bullshit! I play with my balls and I'm not autistic."

He reached into his drawer and pulled out a pill. "Give him this." I wouldn't take it.

"Are you out of your mind? What is it?" I said.

"Lamictal. Helps blood flow through the cerebral cortex. He had low Apgar scores and hypoxia at birth. If I'm right about what's wrong we'll know in ten minutes."

I was tempted. "What are the side effects?"

He eyed me, taken aback by my temerity. Who was I to refuse treatment from him? With a combination of venom and arrogance, he flatly stated: "The side effects are he'll go to college."

The visit went downhill from there. I left without giving Frederick the pill. I did follow one recommendation and took Frederick for a SPECT scan. But the only thing we had to show for that was an outstanding $2,000 bill that my insurance refused to cover. It should have occurred to me that Warner would recommend a test that mainstream neurologists and the insurance companies don't recognize as valid.

Luckily, his cantankerous side came in handy. In the months that followed, we fought with our insurance company. I asked Dr. Warner for a letter of medical necessity. It was handwritten.

> *To Whom It May Concern:*
>
> *Frederick T. M. O'Brien was seen by me due to language and fine motor problems. He had been mistakenly diagnosed as "autistic" and no treatment had been recommended. On examination he showed none of the usual autistic signs or symptoms, related well, and was quite appropriate socially. In lieu of his birth history of anoxia and low Apgar, I recommended a brain SPECT scan as the best and cheapest brain function study (under anesthesia.) This was ABNORMAL- indicating a right inferior medial temporal lobe focus. This then gave this little boy hope for treatment: anti-epileptic medication.*
>
> *There is no reason this test has not been paid for. Not only does it offer this boy and his family hope, it also will save his insurance company thousands of dollars in bogus psychiatric "autistic" treatment. Let's not have to go to lawyers now. I am a good expert witness.*
>
> *Sincerely,*
> *Dr. J. Warner*

The insurance company paid the bill promptly.

# **10** SCHOOL DAZE

Our war against Autism had three fronts: in addition to Early Intervention and our quixotic medical crusade, we were also trying to figure out which school Frederick should attend. In New Jersey, when children hit their third birthday they leave the Early Intervention system and become the responsibility of the local school district. From April of 2004 through the Early Intervention goodbye party in November of that same year, we were involved in a school-selection process that was known as the "Transition" phase—yet another capitalized, proper noun vocabulary word in the ever-growing lexicon of fixing Frederick.

On April 29, around the same time as the Floortime Conference, I attended a formal seminar on Transition, hosted by COSAC—the Center for Outreach and Services for the Autism Community—in a large common room at a local hospital in South Jersey. There were maybe thirty people in attendance, all parents with children having various disabilities, all scared to death because the Early Intervention process they had grown to love and depend on was about to end. Rhonda, the woman leading the seminar, welcomed us and said that the purpose of the meeting was to get us ready for "one of the most important times and decisions of our lives."

Well, at least there wasn't any pressure.

She started with some basic facts: our children were legally entitled to a "Free, Appropriate, Public" education according to the Rehabilitation Act of 1973. Kids with disabilities had a right to be educated in the "Least Restrictive Environment," which means they had to be placed in a regular classroom with typical kids unless it could be demonstrated that the student with disabilities was not able to have his educational needs met in that type of classroom.

So that meant a typical kid would obviously attend his local school, and a kid with moderate disabilities might also be in the same class. But if you could prove that it was necessary, a kid with more challenges might attend a school outside of your home school district if it was deemed the most appropriate place for him or her. According to Rhonda, school districts would always want to put a disabled kid in a typical class because it's cheaper.

I listened to her tell me that a "Child Study Team" would collectively determine where Frederick would embark on his education. (Hooray—another team! Who's bringing the snacks this week for halftime?) The "team" would consist of Bernadette and I plus a social worker, psychologist, speech teacher, and developmental readiness consultant from the Haddon Heights school district where we lived at the time.

Rhonda also tutored us on our vocabulary. She told us not to use the term "best" as in "this is the best school for my kid" because the law didn't say you were entitled to the "best" education, only an "appropriate" one. She said we needed to write down the goals for our child in a way that they could only be met by the one school you wanted him to attend. She also told us we had to make the Child Study Team think we were heavily involved and invested, and wouldn't go away. And then she mentioned that she once sued her district on behalf of her son but the district settled right before the case was to be heard. In her words, "I played chicken with them and won."

As I sat there in that conference room, just scribbling notes and nodding my head, I couldn't be sure what was true or false or undersold or exaggerated. And I don't recall if I had any preconceived notions about the Transition Process when I stepped into that room, but by the end of the presentation I was feeling adversarial, feeling that the Child Study Team and my local school district were the enemy, and that everyone at the meeting was applying war paint and donning body armor.

And then things got weird.

Rhonda ended the seminar by stressing how important it was, no matter how severe your child's disability, to incorporate him or her back into the school district before it was too late. Apparently, her son was at a specialized school for disabilities and she had worked him back into a mainstream school. I guess the kid was in high school at that point, and her voice began to quiver a little as she told the story of him working at a balloon store after school. One day he was at the store when a kid from his class came in and said "hi." She paused, collected herself, but it was getting harder; the tears weren't rolling down her face yet, but they were gathering in her eyes. She pressed on. "It's the most important thing you'll ever do. Get them back out into the world and into the community. Because you never know…" Then the spigot was turned and the tears flowed. "You never know when your child is going to see someone, or need a friend, and you have to know that someone out there cares about him…"

Her voice trailed off but she stood there, defiant, in front of thirty strangers, tears on her face but bravely holding off on a full collapse. This was my first up-close look at the face of a parent who had a child with a lifelong disability. For the entire 90-minute session she seemed to vibrate like a tuning fork, as if she was "this close" to losing it at any second. It scared me.

But then I quickly put those thoughts out of my head, and replaced them with more palatable thoughts, however delusional they were—I reminded myself that Dr. Joplin seemed more optimistic and even Dr. Landau said with hard work he could eventually be indistinguishable from his typical peers, so if we picked the right school this whole nightmare would be over someday.

In order for the Child Study Team to help determine the most "appropriate" school, each of the disciplines—psychologist, speech teacher, and developmental readiness— had to evaluate Frederick.

All the evaluations ended up being on separate days, so there was no way for me to take off from work to attend every one. But I wanted to accompany Frederick to at least one evaluation, partly to give Bernadette a break and partly to act as his cheerleader and advocate.

I chose the psychologist appointment, mainly out of curiosity. What valuable insights could a psychologist get out of an essentially non-verbal 30-month-old boy? Plus, the psychologist in our case was also our "Team Leader", the one who would be the point person as we navigated the evaluations and eventual school placement, so I wanted to meet her and size her up.

Nancy the psychologist was prim, proper, and preppy. When I walked into her office with Frederick, I noticed the papers were neatly stacked, the bookshelf was tidy, the pens were in a cup. On her desk, she had a picture of a girl, presumably her daughter, dressed in full riding chaps and standing next to a horse. I suspected there was nothing out of place in her home, that the kid said "May I be excused" after dinner. Nancy was someone who liked things a certain way.

She certainly didn't like Frederick walking across her desk, which is what he did about five minutes into the evaluation. Not sure why he did it, or really how it happened—one moment I was answering some questions when Nancy stopped me in mid-sentence and pointed over my shoulder. I turned around to see Frederick hustling across her desk, presumably trying to get to the bookshelf on the other side of the office. It was a small room, and Nancy and I were in chairs, almost knee-to-knee as we faced each other, and Frederick was blockaded into one little segment of the room to my left. Behind me was her desk, so instead of pushing his way through Nancy and I, Frederick took the route that did not involve human interaction by sneaking behind me.

I yelled, "Frederick, get down" but he had his mind made up to get across, so when I stood up he jumped out of his crawl and tried to run, and before I could finally grab him he was hurtling across the desk, knocking down the pen holder, his feet slipping on papers and sending them flying, looking like a mini version of Godzilla marching through Tokyo.

I got him down, and Nancy decided to begin the actual evaluation process, but it was futile. Frederick was in his own world that day, and nothing she asked him got the appropriate response. Bernadette had a code word for this. When I would get home from work and ask how the day went, and she knew what I really meant was how did Frederick act, she occasionally said, "It was a real 'A' Day," meaning he acted very autistic.

This was a real 'A' evaluation, and Nancy abandoned it less than halfway through the scheduled time. "I think I have enough to go on," was all she said. At the exact same moment she uttered those words, Frederick dumped her trashcan onto the floor. We received the evaluation a few weeks later and I wasn't surprised to read this line: Some scores may not be a true indication of Frederick's skills, as most results were received via parent report secondary to Frederick's unwillingness to engage in testing activities.

As I carried Frederick in my arms on the way out of Nancy's office, I passed Ms. Mercer, the wonderfully buoyant and cheerful Developmental Readiness evaluator. Bernadette had taken Frederick for that evaluation a week earlier and raved about her kindness and understanding.

As I walked by, I said "hi" but then Frederick jumped out of my arms and landed in a heap. He got up, raced across the room and pointed to a large clock on the wall.

"Ffffreeee. Frrrreee."

I ran over to pick him up, "That's right, buddy. Three."

I smiled at Ms. Mercer; she smiled back and said, "They love their numbers."

I froze. Did she just say, "They love their numbers?"

I felt my face get flushed, and my breathing got rapid. "They?"

She had just reduced Frederick to his least attractive attributes. She pigeonholed him, and it got me fighting mad. But three things stopped me from responding. First, Frederick was wriggling out of my arms again so I prioritized getting him out of the building and into the car. Second, Mrs. Mercer was really nice and a good person and didn't mean it as a slur. Third, she was right.

One of the hallmarks of Autism is that kids usually gravitate toward routines and sameness, and an offshoot of that is a love of numbers and letters. Frederick was no different. He'd rather carry around the "C" from his alphabet game or the "7" from his foam puzzle than carry a toy hammer or a football. One therapist explained it this way: "Imagine if your sensory system was so off-kilter that bright lights and loud noise bordered on painful. And because of that, simple things in life were actually very hard for you. Now add to that the fact that you don't understand language the way most people do, so it's harder for you to learn things. So someone tries to teach you what a shirt is, but some have zippers, others have buttons, some are short sleeve others are long sleeve, but they're all a shirt. And then they teach you the word shoe, which can mean sneaker or dress shoe or laces or Velcro and sometimes even sandals or flip-flops. So there's not a lot of certitude in your world, not a lot of things that can anchor you. But an A is always an A. And the number 1 is always a 1. Those things are comforting."

But Mrs. Mercer was on my "Team," and it was a good team. After a few weeks we finished all the evaluations and received all the written reports. And the team didn't fight us on anything; they were completely on-board with our thinking that Grace needed a little jump-start with speech and Frederick needed all the help he could get, so that meant choosing a school outside of our local district to find a placement that met Frederick's needs. Haddon Heights was a small town, with a population of maybe 7,500 in less than two square miles. Yet, like most little towns in New Jersey, it had its own autonomous school district. This setup was one of the reasons the state has such onerous property taxes; there's hundreds of little townships and boroughs, each with their own school district. But in our case, it worked to our advantage. Haddon Heights was so small they didn't have a real "Autism support class."

So now we moved on to the phase of Transition where we shopped for schools; our first visit was about fifteen minutes from home at the Campbell School, which used Discrete Trial Methods as its curriculum. In brief, Discrete Trial means that all lessons are broken down into small "discrete" sections taught one-on-one. They work on the "ABC" principle—Antecedent, Behavior, Consequence. The Antecedent would be the request by the teacher for the kid to perform a task. The Behavior is that kid's response to that request. And the Consequence is either a reward if the task is performed properly or no reward if it's not.

I watched one set of drills: the teacher had several shapes—circle, square, triangle—all with different colors, and a data page that looked like graph paper, where she scribbled after each question.

Teacher: "Daniel, show me the red square."

No response. The teacher notes on the sheet that Daniel did not point to the red square.

Teacher: "Daniel, show me the red square."

Still no response. The teacher guided his hand to the square. He picked it up.

Teacher: "Yes, that's the red square."

All these cubicles, with all these severely affected children who were nonverbal or noncompliant or both, all doing tiny little tasks for tiny little rewards. It was really,

really hard to watch. If Autism was drunk driving, all they'd have to do was give people a tour of this classroom and no one would ever drink again.

Bernadette and I stayed ten minutes in the classroom, thanked our hosts, then left, shaken. As we walked to the car, I had to support her the way a husband shoulders a grieving wife down the aisle when a funeral mass ends.

Our next stop on the school tour was John Shea Elementary, about ten miles away from our house. It was a "regular" school in that town's district but they had just launched an Autism support class for pre-K in an unused classroom. The school was a beautiful old brick building on a tree-lined block, surrounded by houses. When we visited the sun was shining and the leaves were turning; it seemed like paradise, or at least a Norman Rockwell painting.

The classroom itself was the opposite of Campbell: a big, open room with a bright, multicolored area rug with geometric shapes that looked like the back of the Partridge Family's bus. There was a lot to like with this class, and this school. But there were also a few things I didn't like. Maybe more than a few.

For starters, I asked the teacher about her background. She smiled and began her answer by saying she had "many years of experience working with this population."

Cue the record-scratch sound effect.

She prattled on through her resume but I had stopped listening. I had never heard the word "population" used in this manner before, and it stunned me, even worse than "They love their numbers." At least Ms. Mercer was stating a fact; this teacher had taken Frederick and dehumanized him. He was no longer an individual, just a data point in a larger cohort.

Another problematic thing was their teaching method, which wasn't as severe as the Campbell Discrete Trials but seemed pretty repetitious and rote. At circle time, they spent fifteen minutes holding up a cartoon cloud on a stick and saying to each kid, "What's the weather like outside?" One kid kept getting stuck. The teacher said "Is it sunny or raining?" The kid kept saying rainy. "No, no it's sunny, look outside." I'm thinking, "Who gives a flying flip about the weather? I'll just put a raincoat on Frederick if it's raining. I want him to be able to interact with people when he gets older, not be a weather geek."

And one other thing bothered me. There were six kids in the classroom; five of them seemed to be doing relatively well, or at least pretty much even in terms of skill set. But one boy wasn't. He was a big kid, a little heavy, with a shock of straight black hair. He was obviously in the deep end of the Autism pool, with a lot of challenges and adverse behaviors. Any question to him went unanswered. The teacher and the assistants spent the vast majority of their time getting him to comply. He was on a different planet.

In a follow-up call to one of the class administrators, I mentioned the kid. The administrator was obviously reluctant to discuss him, but I kept pressing, kept bringing up my opinion that he was a fish out of water in that class, and the other kids were suffering because most of the teacher's time and energy were spent on him and not on the curriculum. Eventually, the administrator spilled the beans: they knew it, they were working on it, and he would soon be placed in a more appropriate classroom for his skill-level.

At the end of that conversation I was both relieved that those plans were in motion and sick to my stomach that I had even brought it up. I realized an ugly little truth, one that I wasn't proud of: I'm all for equal educational opportunities, and believed every kid had the right to the best schooling possible—unless it impacted my own kid.

Our final visit was to the only school on our tour that was a campus setting. With three buildings and several acres, St. Joseph Community Services catered to a wide range of disabilities. I had a built-in bias toward St. Joe's since they were the only school in southern New Jersey that used Stanley Greenspan's Floortime method. It felt like divine intervention that I had discovered the Floortime method and read the books and attended the conference and tried to implement it at home, and then when school-age arrived there was a Floortime school five miles from our house, and the next closest Floortime school was 90 miles north.

We went to the classroom and met the teacher, Miss Kay, who greeted us with a big smile. She was always "on," the type of person that would be good as a human character in a *Sesame Street* or *Wiggles*-type kid show.

I was hoping Bernadette was impressed with the place, but she had one major hang-up. At every other school we visited the teachers sent home a daily communication book, which told the parents how things went that day and what activities the class did. At St. Joseph, the communication book only came home twice a week. Kay and Bernadette had a polite little conversation about it, which eventually grew to a five-minute back-and-forth. Kay reached the "we can agree to disagree" stage, but Bernadette was adamant: if she couldn't be there for her babies every day she wanted to know the play-by-play of how their day went. Kay parried back and forth for a few more minutes until finally ending the conversation with some unassailable logic. "You know the thing about those communication books is that they have to be written by the teachers, and you're better off when your kid has a teacher maximizing the teaching time rather than taking the last 20 minutes of each day writing up what just happened."

Well played, Kay. Well played.

On the day we visited, I got to see Floortime in action, administered by professionals.

It was fascinating. The way this class was run was less academic and more stagecraft. Yes, the kids were learning, but every nugget of information and every piece of academic knowledge (or what passed for it in a pre-K class) was based on interaction and emotion. Later in the day, we met with the principal, who I'd been "courting" for several weeks.

A few months earlier, one of the early intervention therapists had told me that St. Joe's, since it was a relatively new program, was only looking for high-functioning kids. She said it was important for a newer school to prove they could take kids for one year then place them back in the kindergarten in their school district. Grace wasn't a worry; she was like thousands of kids her age who had delays they would quickly outgrow, the kind of kid who wouldn't have qualified for any services 20 years ago. They would love to have her breeze through their program then be ready for mainstream kindergarten. But Frederick could easily be looked at as a stat-killer.

So I wasn't taking any chances.

I initiated an all-time brown-nosing campaign that began in the summer with me taking the cutest picture of each kid I could (Frederick in a preppy sweater vest while seated on my mother-in-law's couch; Grace clutching a book on an outdoor bench amidst flowers) and then creating a one-page fact sheet on heavy resume paper. It had each of their names in large font on top of the picture, along with their birthdates, social security number and my contact information. It was the equivalent of a head shot for models or a casting one-sheet for actors. I mailed them to the principal along with a letter explaining that the twins would be eligible for a school such as St. Joseph and that we would be interested in speaking with her and touring the school at the appropriate time in the fall.

**If you want me to attend
your school, call my agent.**

I handed her another copy on the day we visited just in case she needed to refresh her memory. During our conversation, I also let it slip that I was a TV producer, so if they had any classroom video projects, or if they needed a DVD touting the program's efficacy, we could certainly brainstorm about how I could be of help in that area. I also told her I was sure my mother or mother-in-law would love to volunteer at the school if the twins ended up attending.

She said there were currently two slots open, and they were available to Frederick and Grace when they turned three. However, if another kid was qualified and turned three years old before Frederick and Grace, then that kid would get the slot. So it turned out that the college campus visit analogy wasn't far off—this stuff was competitive. I was consumed with getting them into the absolute best school, and with the recent rise in Autism diagnoses, the school slots weren't keeping up with the diagnosed kids. Had these slots been subject to supply and demand pricing, they might have cost more than one of those $50,000-a-year Manhattan preschools.

And this opened another ugly little truth about me. During our St. Joseph visit, it dawned on me that even though I was part of the Autism "community," I was also in competition with everyone in that community for the best possible care within the limited amount of resources and school placements available. I would have tackled the other parents or taken out a second mortgage to bribe someone in order to get the best services for Frederick.

It didn't seem right, or fair. It was just the way it was.

As the days dwindled, a decision was needed. The Child Study Team needed an answer. We were down to two options: St. Joe's or Shea. St. Joseph was Floortime, Shea taught using A.B.A. Would it be both kids at St. Joseph? Both at Shea? Frederick at one school, Grace at another? Or should Grace just go to a regular pre-school? Which was the right school? What would happen if they went to the "wrong" school?

It seemed like Bernadette was leaning toward Shea, and so were most of the Early Intervention therapists. In fact, one of our therapists accompanied us to a visit at St. Joseph's, and afterward I told her that I liked this school because "they weren't sitting around just trying to teach kids how to read a bus schedule."

She replied, "Sometimes kids need to learn that, because that might be as much as they can ever learn."

Not my kid, I thought.

By the end of the process I had lost the capacity for rational decision-making, plus I was a wreck—cranky, snapping at Bernadette, not eating or overeating depending on my mood. The little voice inside my head kept reminding me: Don't screw this up.

I started to ask myself, "What do you want from Frederick? What are the goals?"

The answer was simple: I wanted him to be able to relate to people, and to be able to participate in a regular classroom in the not-too-distant future.

Clearly, I was leaning toward St. Joe's. But then I got cold feet. I wondered, Is this a case of wanting to be a know-it-all? Do I want St. Joseph so I can prove to everyone I was right about Floortime?

I called my friend Sola, who was a close confidante. He had worked with me at the NFL and then left to get a master's in Clinical Social Work, so I often had "shrink sessions" with him. I remember pacing back and forth on our little front lawn on the day before Haddon Heights wanted our answer. I had Sola on the phone and I was trying to convince him (and myself) that St. Joe's was the right place. I used an analogy: "If you tear your knee up, what's the most important thing to have—a crutch, or rehab? A.B.A. learning is a crutch, but Floortime is like rehab. It tries to rehabilitate the kid back into a typical kid."

"Yeah," Sola said, "but sometimes you need a crutch in order to walk across the parking lot to get to rehab."

I hate when someone uses my metaphors against me.

When the decision day arrived, the Haddon Heights school district called, but we weren't ready. They said they'd give us another day. When they called back the next day, I said we still weren't ready. Finally, on the third night, we put the kids to bed and sat down on the couch.

"We have to do it. We need to do it right now," Bernadette said.

Prior to having three kids, that might have been an invitation to go upstairs.

"I'm ready to give up," I said. "I'm done."

I had thought long and hard that night about what to do and how to say it. I had finally decided that this ordeal would end—not with a bang, but a wimp-out.

"I'm ready," I said. "I think it's time I give in and say it: Shea's the right place."

I was hoping she'd use some level of decorum. Jumping up and yelling "Yes! In your face!" would have been over-the-top. Instead, she shook her head. "No, no. You've been right all along. My babies are going to school together. And they're going to St. Joseph's." And then she walked away.

And that's how it ended. After six months of research and school visits, lots of praying and ulcer-inducing rumination stretching three days past the deadline, I finally gave in, and then I got overruled.

But we were in total agreement on one thing: Frederick and Grace's 3rd birthday fell on a Monday, but we would give them the day off, and begin school on Tuesday.

# 11 THE SURGERY THAT MIGHT NEVER END

On November 30, 2004, Frederick and Grace were three years and one day old. On that morning, Bernadette and I were getting dressed as if we were going to a funeral; we didn't talk to each other, didn't make eye contact. We weren't fully crying, but both of us were sniffling and taking deep breaths to calm our nerves.

When she was finished with herself and moved on to dress Frederick and Grace, Bernadette kept repeating, in a whisper, "You're going to school today. School is fun. School is fun."

I know she didn't believe it, so I doubt Frederick believed it, even if he understood it, which was unlikely.

Since kids with Autism are much more rigid and set in their ways than typical kids, they need to be managed with picture schedules and lots of "prep work" before embarking on anything new. Children on the spectrum have been known to get hysterical if they're riding in the car to Grandma's house and a roadblock forces the parents to take a slightly different route. Just a little change in routine, or a toy in the wrong place, or a jacket hung on the wrong hook can ruin the whole day for a kid.

So taking our essentially language-less son to a completely new environment with teachers he had barely met and then leaving him for six hours was probably not something he would have wanted. Neither did we.

But like it or not, the big day was finally here. Early Intervention was over and the next phase was starting. It was just another day for Anna, who was in first grade at the time, so after we walked her to the corner bus stop and waved goodbye Bernadette, the twins, and I took the seven-minute drive in our minivan to St. Joseph School.

It was a quiet ride. I drove, Bernadette stared straight ahead, and Frederick and Grace just sat there. When we arrived, I turned the engine off and unsnapped my seat belt. Without warning, Bernadette threw herself onto my chest. "This is wrong, it's wrong. It's not right. This isn't fair." Her body convulsed as she sobbed.

Comforting people has never been my strong suit. I probably shouldn't look for a job as one of those people who meet the relatives of airline crash victims. Anytime a plane goes down you always read in the newspaper that "relatives were escorted into a room where grief counselors were made available." I should never be made available. To anyone. Ever. Especially my wife.

As Bernadette sobbed on my chest, her body thrown across the cup holders of our van, I kissed her head and then rubbed her shoulder. After about five seconds of comforting, Emotionally Supportive Right-Brain Digger stepped aside and Capt. Left-Brain took control. "It's ok, Honey, it's going to be good for them. It's like chemo—it might make you throw up and lose your hair but it's ultimately for the best."

Normally, Bernadette would call me an idiot for comparing her children's first day at school to a physically-draining, vomit-inducing treatment for a lethal illness, but she just didn't have it in her. The day was too big.

We entered the building and walked down a long hallway past equipment that was used for the most physically-challenged children—wheelchairs with halos to keep the head upright, body boards, walkers. Bernadette was sobbing harder. I whispered under my breath, "Honey, try to stay positive. Don't let the twins see it. They'll feel the tension."

Her head snapped toward mine. "Shut up, they know this is horrible," she muttered. "They know they should be home with their mommy."

We knocked on the classroom door. Kay, the teacher, looked up and gave a reassuring smile.

"Look everyone, it's Grace and Frederick. Say 'Hi' to Grace and Frederick." I saw four kids scattered around the room. One said hi, another meekly waved. The other two ignored us. (You can always count on two things in a Pre-K Autism class: there won't be many kids, and the welcome is always underwhelming.)

I knelt down next to Frederick. "Look buddy, it's your new classroom. You go to school here. It's fun."

His eyes were as wide as saucers, and they didn't blink. His body was rigid. He was not on board with this.

Kay smiled and said, "It's best for you guys to leave as quickly as possible. It just helps in the transition."

Bernadette gave a kiss to both kids; forehead kisses that stuck for an extra second, the kind of kiss you give to your child before they get wheeled away for a long, delicate surgery. And then an assistant teacher came over and hustled us out.

Just outside the classroom was a large window, the one-way kind they have in Law & Order so the Lieutenant can watch the detectives grill a perp. Parents could look in but the kids could not see out.

The first few minutes were excruciating. Grace was understandably nervous, like any kid at her first day of school. She held hands with an assistant teacher, walking tentatively, but soon she relaxed and got into the flow. Frederick, meanwhile, took the opposite approach. When an assistant reached for his hand he threw himself down and banged the back of his head on the floor. Repeatedly. And then screamed. Loud. Really loud.

Frederick eventually calmed down and was encouraged (dragged) by his 1-on-1 aide, but anytime the subject changed—anytime they were done one activity then moved on to another—Frederick would assume the position: on the floor, banging the back of his head.

We were waiting for it to get better, but it didn't, so after an hour we left.

Bernadette went home, I went to work, but not before we had a good long cry in the parking lot together. It really did feel like we had just watched our son get wheeled into surgery and we were crying in the waiting room. But in this case, no one was coming out to tell us if the surgery was successful. It would be a few years before we'd know the outcome.

By law, special needs students get door-to-door transportation starting at age three but Bernadette would not allow a stranger to take her kids to school. Occasionally I tried to talk her into using the bus but she would always say, "What if something goes wrong, or God forbid the driver is molesting him. Frederick can't tell us."

Good point, I guess.

Over the next few months I drove Frederick and Grace to school as often as I could because I knew Bernadette felt like her heart was being ripped out every time she dropped them off. And sometimes when I drove, I day-dreamed about what it would be like to have a completely neurotypical family. I imagined we would go out to dinner once a week and all the restaurant patrons would notice my handsome, well-groomed brood and nod approvingly as they sat down and placed their napkins on their laps. My three spry, quick-witted children would have delightful banter, and my only son might crack a funny one-liner because he's a smart-ass like me, and I'd tousle his blonde hair and say "Hey buddy, watch yourself" as I smiled.

And then I'd pull up at the school, snap out of it, and walk them in.

I was trying my best to convince myself that this was a special calling, that I was meant to be Frederick's father, that I had to wake up every day and put the cape on. But I sure as hell wasn't Superman; I was just a guy who sobbed uncontrollably every time he dropped his kids off at school.

For the first few weeks I was worried that we didn't make the right choice. I wondered if Floortime was the proper fit for Frederick, and I wondered if Grace would be too advanced to get any benefits from such a specialized classroom. When it comes to deciding what's right for your special needs kid, you experience a very special kind of buyer's remorse, about a gazillion times worse than fretting between the Camry and the Accord.

But it turned out to be one of the best decisions we ever made; it was a phenomenal class for Frederick and a great education for Bernadette and I, because we took huge strides in understanding him and what he was going through.

Kay and the teachers in the classroom had a mission: each child had to be stripped down to the joists and rebuilt into a child capable of someday performing in a regular school setting. In order to do that, they had to put them in position to succeed each and every day. Every morning began in the Sensory Room, a spacious area that had soft blue lighting and an assortment of swings, cushions and ball pits. The kids had a blast in there, but there was an overarching purpose behind it: Kay called it "getting organized."

To "get organized," each kid had his or her own "Sensory Diet." Some kids began the day overstimulated and rambunctious so the Sensory Room was their place to calm down and organize themselves before the class work started. Some kids were always under-stimulated and needed some moderately strenuous activity, like climbing ladders and crashing into cushions, in order to get ready for the academic day.

The typical daily schedule read like this:

Sensory Room
Morning Circle Time
Self-Help Skills (grooming, etc.)
Table-Top Manipulatives
Lunch
Sensory Room
Afternoon Story Time
Obstacle Course
Dismissal

I would look at the schedule sometimes and wonder about some things. For instance, I understood circle time, and self-help was obvious, but what was "Manipulatives?" I was considered "manipulative" as a youngster, and it wasn't a compliment. So what were they teaching Frederick—how to talk another kid into trading a brownie for an apple at lunchtime?

As it turned out, it was another example of the strip-him-and-down-and-build-him-back-up work that needed to be done.

Autism had robbed Frederick of some of the most basic building blocks of development that a neurotypical kid goes through. For example, Frederick's sensory system was overly sensitive (like most kids on the spectrum) and as a baby, he didn't like to lie on his belly because too much of his body was in contact with the ground. As a result, his trunk and neck muscles were weak, and those are the muscles you use to sit up straight, which gives you a solid base in order to hold a pencil and write. So in the Sensory Room, Frederick sometimes rode a 'scooter board'—a square board with four wheels—in order to replicate (in a fun way) a baby lying on his tummy, which strengthened his underdeveloped core. And the Manipulatives sessions also mimicked the intricate movements necessary for writing; stringing beads helped his fingers learn to use a pincer grip. Puzzles helped him learn to move his eyes, pick up a piece, and move it where it belonged, because that was a precursor to sitting in class, looking at the board, then looking down at your desk and taking notes.

Manipulatives also helped in "crossing the midline," another concept I'd never heard of, and never understood, until Frederick started school.

Pediatricians often gauge a baby's development by asking the parents, "Is he right handed or left handed? Does he have a dominant hand?" They could care less if your kid is right or left handed; what they care about is whether the child can "cross the midline."

The midline is an imaginary line that runs down the middle of the body, separating it into halves. To cross the midline, your left hand has to do something on the right side of that imaginary line, or vice versa, and to accomplish that both sides of the brain need to be communicating. You cross the midline when you itch your elbow or cross your legs or put on your shoes and socks; it's even necessary for reading, since your eyes need to pass the midline as they scan from left to right.

When a kid establishes a dominant hand and a "helping" hand, it's a sign of a properly developing brain, one that flawlessly communicates across the hemispheres. But for kids who are lagging in that area, doing table top activities in which they're forced to cross the midline can kick-start their development.

And if the midline deficit wasn't enough, people on the Autism spectrum often have poor motor planning and poor muscle tone.

There's a guy at NFL Films named Gene who has worked in the mailroom for decades. He has Autism, and I always noticed how he shuffled more than walked. And one winter day I was looking out my office window and saw a guy shuffling across the parking lot. I immediately thought it was Gene until I realized that Gene never drove to work; he was dropped off at the front door every day. It took me a few seconds to realize what was going on. The lot was still icy from the previous day's storm and the guy who looked like Gene as he walked was actually a former college quarterback and a pretty spectacular athlete.

Wow, I thought. Gene walks down the hallway the same way typical people walk across an icy parking lot. His sensory system is so strangely wired that he needs to walk tentatively all the time, as if every surface is unfamiliar or slippery.

Frederick was also a kid with an unsure gait and low muscle tone. From the day two years earlier when I noticed he was unable to navigate a three-inch concrete slab in our backyard, it was clear he had some motor planning problems. So almost every day the teachers at St. Joe's made an obstacle course and forced the kids to break down each individual part, plan what they had to do, and then execute the whole thing. The obstacle course played a big part in Frederick's ability to more confidently navigate his world.

But it was never his favorite. One notebook entry read, "Frederick has been giving us a tough time at obstacle course in the morning. I think he just decided he doesn't want to do it! You know Frederick – he thinks it is always his way!"

No matter how hard he protested, they always made him finish. But he didn't go down without a fight.

Midway through the school year, his 1-on-1 aide told us they were having trouble finding the picture for the obstacle course. In their class—as in most Autism support classes—the teacher would have a picture-schedule board for the class to see every day, and on that board would be rudimentary photos or drawings of each activity. His aide told us that over the course of a few months they kept losing the obstacle course image and had to continually download, print and laminate a new one. Eventually, a teacher discovered a dozen or so obstacle course pictures behind a bookshelf. As it turned out, on days when there was an obstacle course, Frederick would wait until no one was looking, grab the obstacle-course photo off the schedule board and dump it behind the bookcase, hoping the teachers would skip it if it wasn't on the schedule.

I take a lot of pride in that story, and it highlights the strange alchemy that exists within Frederick. He was (and remains) mostly non-verbal and years behind in development, yet he's also really clever.

Frederick was, and is, capable of yanking your chain. He has a smile that's closer to a smirk when he's messing with you, and he defies the Theory of Mind conundrum because you can tell that he knows he's getting a reaction. A notebook entry from the spring said, "Frederick was in rare form. He had a silly day. Really acting like the class clown."

Soon, the notebook was coming home with wonderfully exciting little nuggets. "Frederick has been bringing the Jack-in-the-Box over to us to play a surprise game." And "Frederick was chasing Trevor in the sensory room yesterday to play tickle. It was really cute."

Another time, Kay wrote, "Frederick is making many sounds and using many words. He is trying to play with Tess." When I came home from work that day, Bernadette greeted me at the door with the notebook. I read it and looked at her, wide-eyed.

"Oh my god, oh my god," I said.

Bernadette smiled back. "I know, I know," she said.

I was short of breath, maybe even having palpitations. "But what does it mean? What does it mean? How is he trying to play?"

We wrote back in the notebook, asking for clarification. The next day, Kay wrote "He seems to position himself near Tess. He will touch her and then run and look back at her." We read it together and jumped and screamed, hugging each other.

Near the end of his first year at St. Josephs he had come so far that one entry from the Speech Teacher read, "Wanted to let you know Frederick is doing so well. In circle time he is regularly smiling, greeting and waving all at the same time. He is so happy now with his interactions."

It was a wonderful time, probably the best time since his diagnosis. The class was small, only six kids, and he made some tremendous strides in the 20 months he attended St. Joseph. And you got the feeling that every teacher and assistant and back-office person would take a bullet for him.

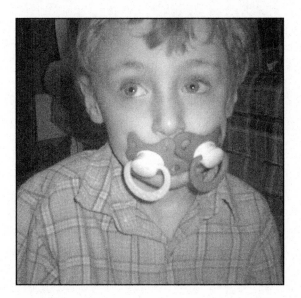

**Unfortunately, they didn't make him twice as calm.**

But the best part of that year was feeling like there was still hope.

I would sometimes bug out of work at lunch and take the 30-minute ride down Interstate 295 just to watch him for a few minutes behind the one-way window. It was amazing to see Frederick play, laugh, sing, scream and melt-down, sometimes all in a single 30-second span. I remember thinking how small he looked. How vulnerable he was. I remember thinking I would always remember these stolen few minutes when I would watch my little boy, like God peering down from the clouds. I watched with pride—but occasionally with a sense of dread—because Frederick wasn't just going to school. He was there to be 'jump-started.' To have the trajectory of his life altered. So in that way, I wasn't a dad watching school, I was a dad watching surgery from one of those glass operating room amphitheaters.

I had two open-heart surgeries when I was little. The second one, at the Mayo Clinic, lasted 14 hours and my Dad always said, "That 14 hours was the longest two weeks of my life." As I stood peering through that window I often wondered when Frederick would be wheeled out of surgery. After this year? After several years of intense schooling? Or would he never be wheeled out, never made whole?

# 12 I WISH HE HAD SOMETHING WORSE

I've seen every Seinfeld episode, so I feel qualified to make the following statement: there has never been a child who had Autism in Monk's Cafe.

Granted, it was a controlled set for a television show, but if "Seinfeld" purported to be about real life the way it's really lived, and if so much of the show was shot with Jerry, Elaine, George and Kramer sitting in a diner and chatting, don't you think they could have had one kid pitch a fit in the background during the course of 180 episodes?

I bring this up because when Bernadette's birthday came around that year, she wanted to go out to dinner and celebrate. So we went out to dinner. We're still waiting on the 'celebrate' part.

Frederick's development was obviously slower than a typical kid's, but it wasn't until the school year at St. Joseph was ending that we realized all of the ramifications. Prior to that, when Frederick was two or three, he didn't seem to have any strong interests. Sure, he liked some TV shows more than others and had some preferred food and drinks, but there was no "must-have" toys or video game because he wasn't that 'into' anything. He wasn't really invested in the world. But around age four, the beast was unleashed—he started getting 'into' things. Really, really into things.

On Bernadette's birthday we packed the kids into the minivan and drove a few miles down the Black Horse Pike to a diner with a vintage 1950's feel. When we arrived, everyone hopped out except Frederick, because this was the beginning of his hoarding habit and he never left the house without looking like Steve Martin in The Jerk ("…all I need is the ashtray, this paddle game, and this remote control, that's all I need…")

He eventually stepped out of the car with a tote bag full of books and placed it on the parking lot asphalt, then went back into the van to grab his other bag, which contained at least 15 Sesame Street figures. He put that bag down in the parking lot and retrieved his final object, a talking Sesame Street electronic thing.

I wasn't terribly optimistic that this excursion was a good idea, but I thought we'd at least get in the front door successfully. We didn't. As I held the door open, Bernadette, Anna and Grace entered but Frederick dropped to the ground—suddenly, there was nothing more captivating than the seven letters that greeted him on the "Welcome" mat. Frederick was on his belly, tracing the grimy, shoe-stained letters while his books and figures and talking toy blocked the entrance.

It was 5:15 p.m., just a few minutes into what Bernadette and I call the Magic Hour, that window between the Early Bird crowd and the normal people, the one hour where a restaurant is least crowded. An elderly couple was trying to shuffle past us to get out. They made it through Bernadette and the girls but then ran smack into Frederick's Welcome Mat roadblock. The couple looked at Frederick and smiled, looked at me and smiled, then looked back at Frederick, then back at me, no longer smiling. They were in their mid-80's and most definitely on the clock.

I had to get Frederick up; Bernadette knew it too, so she swooped in for the toys and books. I got behind him and applied a bear-hug hold and lifted. He started kicking and flailing and then thrashed the back of his head into my nose (luckily I'm not a bleeder.) As we moved into the diner and up to the hostess stand Frederick was still writhing in my arms. I put him down to see if he would stay put. He did, by laying on the ground.

To Frederick, floors are like Tiananmen Square or the National Mall in Washington—the perfect place to stage any and all protests. Although he couldn't verbalize his thoughts, my guess is that he was saying:

"Look Dad. I know you're hung up on this whole 'normal family' thing and you're always like, 'We're not giving into this; we will enjoy things that normal families enjoy!' But I hate to break it to you, dude: we're not a normal family. First of all, you never told me where we were going, or if you did tell me I didn't understand you, and now you drag me into this strange place with this fluorescent lighting that gives me a headache, and it seems like everyone's looking at me and I'm not a big fan of eye contact, so since you didn't let me vote well, guess what? I'm now voting with my ass—my ass is staying on this grimy linoleum until you get it into your thick skull that I would rather hug a cactus than go out to eat. And since I can't talk, this is how I'm going to express my opinion. Have fun trying to scrape me off the floor."

Everyone was looking at us. I knelt down and tried to reason with him.

"C'mon buddy, let's walk back to the seat and see Elmo. We'll look at Elmo book back there. It's ok; Elmo wants to see you back there with Mommy and Grace and Anna."

His only response was to scream louder. I gathered his books and toys then picked him up. He wouldn't walk, and he kept his body rigid for maximum lifting difficulty, so the only option was to carry him over my shoulder.

As I walked between the tables I caught the eye of a heavy-set man who looked like he could have been a stand-in for John Goodman when he was on the Roseanne show. This guy stared at me, shifted his eyes to Frederick who was slung over my shoulder, then fixed his eyes back on me. He never said a word. His stare was simple and declarative, with nothing lost in translation.

"Boy," he was saying, "If that was my son, I'd whip his ass. What in THE hell is wrong with you people today? The back of my hand on his bottom would solve all your problems."

With Frederick still slung over my shoulder I caught up with the hostess and the girls. We were in the back of the Diner; only a handful of tables were occupied.

The hostess put menus down on a table for six, right next to a senior-citizen couple who were sipping coffee. But regular tables don't work for Frederick; a booth is our only hope to contain him.

"How about a bout a booth, ma'am?" I asked.

"Oh sure." The hostess gathered the menus and moved a few feet to her left.

"Actually," I said, interrupting before she could place the menus down again. "How about that booth?"

I pointed to the far end of the 30-foot-long room. There was a booth way back there, isolated, as far as possible from other patrons.

"There's no place-settings there," the hostess protested.

I started walking toward it, with Frederick pounding my back and kicking my stomach. "That's ok. We eat with our hands."

"It only seats four,' she protested again.

"We'll mix and match"

With my free hand I pulled a 4-person table up against another table. The back wall of the room had bench seating, so we could fit the entire family on the bench, stretching left to right across two tables, and leave the chairs opposite us unoccupied. That allowed us to deploy in the optimum seating arrangement for our family: Frederick goes in the middle, the girls on either side of him, then Bernadette at one end and me at the other to form adult bookends. That way, Frederick has the maximum number of people to climb over in order to get away, which hopefully discourages any breakout attempts.

Anna immediately piped up. "I wanna sit next to Grace."

"Sorry, honey," I explained, "you know it's assigned seating."

In the fine tradition of South Jersey diners, the waitress brought us our waters in brownish-yellow glasses with big smears that made it look like they'd been licked by a cow. She introduced herself, although I didn't hear a word of it since Frederick was already standing, hopping up and down, rhythmically babbling.

"Can I start you with drinks?"

Eating at a restaurant with Frederick is like having a ticking time bomb next to you. There's no way to know when he'll go off, but you have to work under the assumption that you don't have much time. Although it was Bernadette's birthday, and I had hoped she could have an enjoyable experience, I needed to move fast in order to salvage the evening.

"No," I said, pulling Frederick off the table, which he had just tried to walk across. "We're ready to order."

Bernadette, who had yet to take the menu from the waitresses' hand, looked at me dumbfounded.

"It's a diner—do you really have to look at a menu?" I said. Her scowl was worth a thousand daggers. "Ok, you can go last," I told her.

After everyone ordered, there was a surprising lull. The first two or three minutes were pleasant, almost enjoyable, except for the knife-like tension in my back and shoulder blades. But it was nice. Bernadette was helping Grace color with crayons on the kiddie menu. Anna was asking why she couldn't get a large root beer instead of the small we ordered her. We were almost a normal family. It was wonderful.

And brief.

The inevitable descent began innocently enough: Frederick knocked over Grace's juice. Nothing wrong with that. Happens all the time. But as we were cleaning it, Frederick sensed that our guard was down, and he made his move. I noticed, almost too late, that he was sneaking behind Bernadette as she leaned forward to soak up the spill.

"Bern!" I yelled. "Jailbreak."

She caught him at the last second and tried to put him back in the middle of the booth. He wailed and smashed his hands up and down on Bernadette's head as she deposited him back on the bench.

I noticed Anna was turning another shade of red as she scanned the diner, looking at the handful of people who were now staring at the commotion at the far end of the room.

Frederick had been one step away from getting out, and had briefly sampled the sweet taste of freedom. It was intoxicating. He wanted more.

I tried to appease him with books and a sippy cup, but he would have none of it. Every time he stood up, I wrapped my right arm around his waist, pushed my left forearm into the back of his knees, and guided him back down. But like a Jack in the

Box, he always popped back up.

Anna tugged at my shirt. "Can you make him sit down?"

"I'm trying sweetie, I really am."

Bernadette leaned forward and shook her head.

"Just once, just once I'd like to...." Her voice trailed off. She didn't have to finish the thought.

I gave him his Sesame talking toy but he threw it, then arched his back and wailed. I tried to put the toy back in his hand, but he raised both arms, arched his back, and began sliding under the table.

"C'mon buddy, come back." I reached for him but he pulled away.

"Bern, grab him." She leaped up and hustled around the table as Frederick was emerging. She grabbed him, but as she went to pick him up, he made his body into dead weight, with his arms straight up, and he slid through her hands. He lay on the floor, purposefully kicked off both shoes, and wailed as he thrashed about.

Game, set, match.

I stood up and shrugged my shoulders. "We'll go. You guys take your time. Enjoy dinner."

Bernadette had a one-word response. "Funny."

I pointed out the window, toward a handicapped ramp on the side of the building. "I'll pull around there. Take your time. We'll be fine."

As we turned into the front section of the diner, I carried Frederick on my right side with his legs sticking out on the left and took a wide turn, hoping the John Goodman guy was still at his table so Frederick could maybe scream in his ear on the way out. But he was gone. At the front door a really, really old man with a cane was coming up the steps. I waited so I could hold the door, despite Frederick burying his nails in my neck.

The old man finally made it up. He winked at me. "Don't get old."

As he passed through the door I mumbled under my breath. "Don't get Autism."

With Frederick back in the van and buckled up, I drove around to the other side of the diner, near the exit of the non-smoking section. We sat in the car with the engine idling and both of us were trying to take the edge off—Frederick was listening to Veggie Tales music on an iPod and I reclined the driver's seat a little and turned on sports talk radio.

Occasionally I would look at the girls through the window, trying to imagine their conversation. Happy Birthday, Bernadette.

Later that night, as I tucked Anna into bed, I gave her a kiss and said, as I always do after days like this, "Thanks for all your help today. You're a great big sister."

"You know Dad," she said, no hint of tears or remorse. "Sometimes I wish Frederick had something worse. Maybe like…Down Syndrome."

I was taken aback. She knew about Down Syndrome because my cousin has a daughter with Down's, but Anna was only seven years old at the time and I had no idea where she was going with this.

"Why's that, honey?" I asked.

"Well, if Frederick had Down Syndrome then people could see something was wrong with him. But because you can't see Autism, everyone just thinks he's a bad kid. But he's not. He's a good kid. He just can't help it."

She was right. No one at the restaurant knew what the real problem was. They just thought they saw a bad kid eating dinner with his overindulgent parents. But that wasn't the sad part—I was more upset that a fantastic big sister had to wrestle with stuff that was way above her pay grade. And the saddest part of all was that a great mom had to celebrate her birthday dinner with only half her family, while the other half waited in the car.

**Frederick and his big sister.**

# 13 THIS IS NOT A GOOD PLACE

Some say doing the same thing over and over again and expecting different results is the definition of insanity. It's also the definition of a Special Needs parent.

We felt like we had to keep trying new experiences with Frederick, even if the results were almost pre-ordained. Bernadette took him to his first movie, starring the Veggie Tales. He loved the TV show so she figured he would do ok at the theater. She was wrong. The woman in front of them complained that Frederick was kicking her chair, and he spent as much time on the sticky floor as he did in his seat. They left after 20 minutes.

We also took him to his first concert to see *The Wiggles*, the ultra-successful kids show from Australia that had taken over the children's market on American TV. Their touring company was nice enough to sell special-needs seating so we were in the third row, center aisle. There were giant vertical monitors on either side of the stage which showed videos before the concert and then projected the Wiggles during the performance. When they came out to start the show, Frederick went bonkers. He was screaming their names. He was jumping up and down. It was awesome. And then I noticed something peculiar—Greg, Murray, Jeff and Anthony Wiggle were no more than ten feet in front of us, basking in the applause center stage, and Frederick was still watching the monitors.

I screamed above the noise. "Frederick, Frederick, look! There they are!"

I put both hands on the sides of his head to turn his vision to the stage but he kept snapping his eyes back toward the screens. The Wiggles walked straight in front of Frederick but he preferred to watch them on video, because that's how he did it at home. In the span of the 90-minute concert he probably watched five minutes of live, in-the-flesh action. The rest of the time he stared at the video boards.

In high school I had to read *On Death and Dying* by Elizabeth Kubler-Ross and, maybe because of my open-heart surgeries, it had always stuck with me. Recalling the book, I was beginning to wonder if there were stages that I was going through in dealing with Frederick's condition. If so, I was definitely entering the "anger" phase. I started noticing things I had never noticed before, and they were starting to piss me off.

For instance, in the summer after Frederick's first year at St. Joseph's, Hurricane Katrina hit. The news coverage over the next several weeks had stories on donations of clothes, food, books, and anything else you can think of. Conspicuous for its absence was any mention of charitable efforts for children with disabilities. If you estimate that 1 million people were displaced during Katrina and even if you use a generous ratio by saying 1 in 150 children had a diagnosis, that means thousands of kids with Autism were uprooted from their homes and schools across the region. Put yourself in their shoes: the day before the storm they were in their usual routine then suddenly they were out of their home and being bussed to a shelter then driving to a new town then eventually settling who-knows-where and now the kid is so out of whack maybe he's starting to do things he's never done—like hitting himself or biting himself—because he's not in his regular classroom.

When I started seeing the pet rescue stories from Katrina, I officially lost it.

No pun intended, but you couldn't swing a dead cat without hitting a Katrina Pet public service announcement. But where were the PSA's for the kids with Autism and their families? Seriously—you were better off being a beagle or a tabby than being an autistic kid in New Orleans in the summer of 2005. When I typed "Katrina Pets" on an internet search engine I got 13,700,000 hits. Typing in "Katrina Autism" got 949,000 hits. That's a 14 to 1 ratio.

It also bothered me that for all the talk of an Autism epidemic, for all that I read about school districts being overwhelmed with special needs students, I was the only one in my circle of friends with a special needs kid. Out of the six guys from high school that I'm still tight with, out of the 25 or so guys from college that were my core group, and out of the friends from my first job at the NBA and my closest friends from my current job, I'm the only one in the group with a compromised kid.

It wasn't Frederick's fault. I wasn't angry with him. But it did bother me that he chewed the front of his shirt all the time and left a saliva stain on it the size of a saucer plate. It bothered me that he couldn't just go straight to bed—he had to collect a dozen toys or papers or figures, and it was never the same dozen things, so I couldn't help expedite the process. It bothered me that I worked for the NFL and he couldn't go to the Super Bowl with me.

And it was starting to bother me that he was so good looking. Frederick was on his way to being tall, handsome, and thin—three things that had eluded me during my lifetime. He looked like one of those kids on the beach in a Ralph Lauren Polo ad, their sandy blonde hair tousled by the wind. On some days I dreamed that he'd be the first autistic model, but it was unlikely considering he couldn't sit still for more than a nanosecond.

**Holding Sesame guys helps him take a good picture.**

Autism was beginning to really impact our home life; in little things, like going out, and big things, like moving. We would talk about wanting a bigger house, and maybe even moving back to my hometown in Pennsylvania. Then we'd think about a new school district and a new process and it would scare the hell out of us.

I was getting sick of making color-coded excel sheets to keep track of his doctor visits. I was angry that I no longer did any reading for enjoyment's sake; instead of non-fiction history and biography books, I kept buying the latest special needs "fix-it" manuals which, by the way, never worked. One day I took Anna to see the Disney movie *Cars* and wondered if I was the only one in the theater who realized that C.A.R.S. is also the acronym for "Childhood Autism Rating Scale" used by pediatricians.

During this anger phase, I also realized I hated the word "autistic."

When Frederick first showed signs of being developmentally delayed, Bernadette and I couldn't even muster the courage to say the word. We called it "the 'A' word."

Somehow, we figured if we didn't say it then he didn't have it. Unfortunately, the therapists and doctors didn't share our hang-up so they started using the word quite freely when it came to Frederick. Eventually, we had to use it as well.

But I still hold my nose when I say it. It's a nasty word—all jagged edges and mouth contortions. Say it out loud: aw-TIS-tik. It starts off terribly because the first syllable, "aw," is a pity party. "Awwww, your child has a lifelong disability that has mystified the scientific community," or "Awwww, your child repeats cartoons verbatim and has no friends."

The next syllable, "TIS," isn't horrible. Lots of nice words contain "tis." "'Tis the season to be jolly," etc. "Tis" is fine, but hopefully "tis" was wearing a seatbelt because it slams right into "tic" like it's a concrete wall. What word ends with "tic"? Septic? You mean the tank that stores human waste in a backyard?

There are so many other diseases I'd trade names with. Multiple Sclerosis? It has an abbreviation: M.S. That's cool, like "F.D.R." or "J-Lo." I'd switch names with Crohn's Disease any day. It sounds like "crony," and it's named after someone, so it's not your fault. It's just someone else's disease (Mr. Crohn? Dr. Crohn?) you happened to get.

Huntington's Disease is another cool one. It's so elegant. "Huntington" could be the name of a high-end hotel chain or an expensive private school or the best model in an upscale development ("There were a lot of great floor plans but we chose the Huntington model with cherry cabinets and Corian countertops.") I didn't even know what Huntington's Disease was, so I had to look it up on the Mayo Clinic website. They define it as a "progressive, degenerative disease that causes certain nerve cells in your brain to waste away."

Ok, the name is better; the symptoms—not so much.

Maybe the worst thing about the word "autistic" is the fact that it's a label. It's like a cattle brand. You can't get rid of it. It becomes your identity. Nobody says, "That kid has Autism." What they usually say is "That kid's autistic."

If you have cancer, do people say you're "canceristic?" No one says a kid is "Cystic Fibrotic." But they do say, "That kid's autistic." It's like their height, hair color, and personality are washed away and the person becomes their disability.

After a few years on this adventure, I'd come across a few more words and phrases I couldn't stand. My least favorite was "good place."

Occasionally, I would have a conversation with someone about how Frederick was doing, and I'd give them the Cliffs Note version of what we were going through and end it by saying "but, you know, we're hanging in there." Invariably, the person would then say, "Well, it sounds like you're in a good place."

Good place? I had a son who kissed the computer good night but walked past me on the way to bed; that was not a "good place." We had to change his diaper within minutes of a poop or he would dig it out then wipe it on the wall; that was not a good place. When you dread the weekends and look forward to Monday it is, in fact, a very bad place.

And oh by the way—when people would ask me if my son was autistic, I'd say, "No, he's not autistic. He's Frederick."

# 14 HIS WATER ISN'T WARM
## AND HIS CAR ISN'T FAST

When it came to Frederick's long-term future, Bernadette and I shared a Don't Ask, Don't Tell philosophy. It had been nearly two years since D-Day (Diagnosis Day), and for those two years since 02-03-04 we tried to take things one day at a time. We were concentrating on working hard, doing what we could, and not interested in the view from 30,000 feet. We were still optimistic; in fact, we had some estate planning done at that time and as the lawyer took the necessary information to write our wills he mentioned something called a Special Needs Trust, which shelters money if a child's disability was so severe that they couldn't live an independent adult life. I assured him that Frederick didn't fit that criterion. "Knock wood," I said. "We're lucky."

But maybe we needed a bit of a reality check. So we made another appointment with our favorite guy, Dr. Mark Joplin, the same doctor we saw to get a second opinion after Dr. Landau gave her gloomy prognosis on D-Day.

Two weeks before the appointment, I mailed Dr. Joplin a letter that had some questions I didn't want to pose in front of Bernadette. I listed Frederick's current strengths and weaknesses so Joplin could get a sneak preview, but the last two paragraphs of the note stated what we were really coming to see him for:

"The main reason we're bringing him to you is to get a glimpse into the future. I realize no doctor can say with certainty what will happen to a special needs child in the future, but we're wondering if our heads are in the sand.

"We still talk about Frederick getting married or having a career, and maybe that's not a healthy or reasonable outlook. No matter what you or any doctor says, we'll never stop fighting for him and working with him. But we would like to have a dispassionate and detached discussion of what is likely to transpire."

Don't Ask, Don't Tell was officially repealed. We were asking, and we were about to be told.

Dr. Joplin was in private practice now, a HMO casualty who broke off from

C.H.O.P., but we were going to follow him wherever he went. In the waiting room of Dr. Joplin's new digs were dozens of pamphlets, the kinds I had now seen way too many times: Autism conferences, advocate services, horse riding therapy camps, etc. I noticed that the pamphlet bins were full. They were always full, wherever I went. Did that mean the staff was diligent in re-filling them, or did no one ever take any? Probably the latter. If they had more truthful titles, maybe more people would read them.

Screwed: How to Get On With Your Life

Futures are Overrated: How to Handle an Autism Diagnosis

Welcome to the Club You Didn't Want to Join:
Parenting a Child With Autism

Dr. Joplin walked around his desk, greeted us, then waved Bernadette and me into chairs along the wall as he sat down at a tiny little table with two chairs.

Within the first minute of his session with Frederick, I got this feeling in my stomach that I only get at work. When I'm producing a segment or a show for NFL Films, I pick the shots, edit it, write it, etc. And I try to be as critical as possible as it evolves from a rough cut into a finished show. Before it's completely done, I have to show it to the bosses, but even that isn't a daunting task at NFL Films because my immediate bosses are my age and my best friends in the building, and when the big boss, Steve Sabol, used to watch it, he wasn't overly critical. So I'm never nervous or scared during this stage. But there's something about watching it with another person that makes all the bad edits and weak interview bites stand out in a way that you didn't see when it was only you working on it.

And that's the feeling I had very early in Frederick's evaluation. It was like I was seeing him for the first time, and I couldn't believe my eyes.

Frederick was asked to draw a line, and he either didn't want to or didn't understand the question. He then was asked to make a three-block stack but, despite Dr. Joplin telling him to stop at three, Frederick kept going to six or seven until his tower fell down and he laughed. Joplin gave him a ball and said "Throw it to me" but Frederick ran away with it. He asked Frederick to read him a book, which didn't happen, then told Bernadette and I to read him a book. He stayed on my lap ten seconds before fleeing.

This went on for about 30 minutes. There were no moments of triumph. There was never an instance where I thought, "He nailed it." Then it was time for Frederick to go back out to the waiting room.

After he pulled his chair toward ours Dr. Joplin began, as always, with a metaphor, the same one he used on our first visit with him. "IQ is like water temperature, and atypicality is like ice. The higher the IQ, the warmer the water, and the atypicality will melt away over time. But if the IQ is lower, the atypicality doesn't melt away. Frederick has a fairly high degree of atypicality, but my intuition says that the water won't be warm enough to melt it away."

Ok, I thought, he's telling us Frederick is different. Got it. Not a shocker.

"And because his IQ is lower, his peers will begin pulling away from him. Imagine Frederick and a typical four-year-old are both in cars. Frederick is going 20 miles per hour, but the other child is going 40 mph. The gap will widen each year. Frederick will always improve, yet he will always fall farther behind."

Ok, so now Frederick's in a car. Did he drive the car onto the ice? I was getting confused.

"Obviously, it was difficult to do a full, formal evaluation today, but even with maximum allowance for his attention span he presents with an overall IQ level that is not age-appropriate, and combined with his atypicality he may have some skills but not enough common sense to get by in the world."

Whoa whoa whoa whoa. Now he was talkin' smack about my son. I had to interject.

"Hang on doctor," I said. "I'm not following you. I think Bernadette would agree with me here—there are some obvious problems with Frederick. We know he's not going to be Student Body President or anything. He may not even get married. But I'm not sure what you're saying." I tried for a second to collect my thoughts, but I didn't have any. "So I guess my question is…what are you saying?"

Dr. Joplin sat back and sighed. "If you're asking me my best guess what will happen to Frederick as an adult, I see him in a group home because skills like money-management and hot-food preparation may elude him, and he would need adult supervision. I'd be pleasantly surprised if he learned how to manage money or drive a car. Intuitively, I feel there's a degree of mental retardation. He will be part of the community, he will be gratified, but he won't be flying solo. He may be able to acquire some skills but he won't have enough common sense to get by in the world."

Part of me died right then and there.

I'm still alive, still have a life, it's just different than the one prior to that. Dr. Landau said it was bad, but Dr. Joplin was saying it was over.

I sat with my mouth open, unable to stop him, as he continued. "I recommend you take him for full genetic testing, because I sense a hint of dysmorphia with the nose and ears. There could be a genetic component. The degree of mental retardation is not profound, but it's to an extent that I think a good goal for Frederick would be for him to get to the stage as an adult where if he got lost he could ask a stranger for help."

I attended a good college and have a nice career. And although I didn't have any fully articulated dreams and aspirations for Frederick yet, I'm sure they would have been higher than hoping he could ask a stranger for help if he was lost. As an adult.

Bernadette and I sat there for ten seconds, silent. Then we turned and looked at each other right at the same time, and burst into tears. And even though we were sitting next to each other, the arm-rests of our chairs touching, our heads no more than eight inches apart, neither of us leaned over to hug or comfort each other in any way. I wish I knew why. I guess we had nothing left.

Dr. Joplin leaned in toward us. "Have you ever heard of Dayenu?"

I figured it was a non-profit organization that helps families in need or some special school where the kids run free and the sidewalks are made of gumdrops. Either way, I wasn't interested. But he continued.

"Dayenu means 'It would have been enough.' It's sung at Passover and it says, 'If God had just brought us out of Egypt, it would have been enough. If he had just given us the Torah, it would have been enough.' So I would offer that to you as you move forward in life. You have enough. You do."

We hustled into the minivan and, for the second time in two years, had a long, lonely drive back from a place where we had braced for bad news and had received much worse. After that first visit with Dr. Landau, I spent the ride home strategizing next steps and developing a plan to beat Autism. On this ride home, I didn't.

Two weeks later, another report—also printed in Courier font like the first one from C.H.O.P. —arrived by mail.

```
Re:   Frederick O'Brien
DOE: 01/19/06
CA:   4 years two months
    This was the first visit at this office for this 4
year old child with previously diagnosed Autism, who
comes for follow-up having previously been evaluated by
this examiner at Children's Hospital.
    Current Development of Status
    Fine Motor/Adaptive: Frederick can use a spoon.
He can remove simple articles of clothing such as his
pants, shoes, and socks. He cannot unbutton or button
up (33-36 months skills). He does not spread with a
knife, or initiate zippers or snaps (48 month skills).
He is continent for urine in the daytime, but otherwise
```

not toilet trained. He is engaging in mild fecal withholding, possibly because he is apprehensive about flushing his stool away.

Gross Motor: He can walk, run, and with some encouragement he is able to pedal a tricycle (36 months skill), but this does not really hold his interest.

Speech, Language, and Hearing: Frederick's speech includes greater than 200 single words, plus the recent emergence of two-word phrases ("Cup, please" for example).

Personal/Social: Frederick likes letters, numbers, looking at books, and playing on the computer. He has a large vocabulary of single words that he uses primarily for labeling of objects rather than for communicative purposes. He has certain preferred DVDs and CDs, which he memorizes. After a CD is loaded into the player he will advance it track by track to listen to a few seconds on each track. The CDs "must" be in the car, and returned to their proper place on the visor, or he will become upset. He has difficulty with transitions, although this is getting better according to the parents today. Frederick does not understand concepts such as "Wait," becoming very upset if his desires are not gratified immediately. He does not have significant motor stereotypies (flapping, spinning, etc.). The parents are concerned because of the short attention span and increased activity level. He has significant food selectivity, craves deep pressure, "shuts himself off" when the environment becomes overstimulating (for example, over Christmas, when there were lots of family and friends over to the house). He has an increased pain threshold.

Neurodevelopmental assessment

Mental Status: Eye contact was intermittent and brief. Attention span was short and activity level was increased, both for his age and his developmental level. Frederick was neither cooperative nor uncooperative.

Rather, for the most part, he seemed to be unaware of this examiner's intentions or wishes (i.e., that Frederick was being expected to imitate actions modeled by the examiner). He had frequent "stimming" behavior, such as repetitiously banging objects.

Cognitive Assessment: Frederick was briefly engageable with the one-inch cubes, and we did succeed in getting him to imitate alternating from a three-block stack to a horizontal string of three cubes. He scribbled spontaneously, and on one occasion appeared to imitate his mother, alternating from a scribble to a stroke. He completed the Cattell 3-hole formboard in the primary position without difficulty (24 months), and with some trial and error in the reversed position (27 – 30 months). Frederick's speech consisted of infrequent single words and rare two word phrases, with less than 50% intelligibility. With some difficulty, Mrs. O'Brien was able to engage Frederick in a picture-pointing and picture-naming task. Frederick had a score of 38 on the Childhood Autism Rating Scale. (The CARS is a 15-item inventory of atypical features. Each item is scored from normal(one point) to severely atypical (four points). The lowest, or best possible score on the CARS is 15. Children with mild atypicality consistent with a diagnosis of Pervasive Developmental Disorder (PDD) commonly have elevations on the CARS in the 25 to 29 range. The cutoff for Autism is 30. The highest, worst possible score on the CARS is 60.)

Discussion

Today's evaluation documents the persistence of moderate to severe atypicality, consistent with a diagnosis of fully expressed Autism. Autism can be accompanied by any degree of general intelligence from superior, to profound mental retardation. Frederick's adaptive skills, as well as his abilities with manipulable's today in the office, suggested he is functioning, overall, somewhere around the 24 month to 30 month level, for a developmental quotient of approximately 50%. Likewise, Frederick's overall cognitive skills were at approximately half of age expectation when evaluated through the school district 9/04. Thus, today's findings represent a continuation of previous observations, and suggest to us that Frederick's level of cognitive development will remain significantly slower than that of other children for the indefinite future. As Frederick gets older, he will continue to learn new skills. At the same time, however, his overall level of ability will continue to fall further behind that of other children. From an operational standpoint, this is the functional definition of Mental Retardation, which we believe accompanies Frederick's Autism. We cannot give a precise IQ, although we suspect that Frederick's mental retardation is in the Mild to Moderate range.

Follow-up:

We would like to see Frederick back in the office in six months

The parents may wish to come back in 2 months, without the children, to meet with our social worker, to review any questions they might have at that time.

We were sorry to have to broach the diagnosis of mental retardation. However, this information will be useful to the family in terms of long-term planning.

We look forward to seeing Frederick again in the spring, and encourage the parents to remain in touch with us during the interim.

# 15 MORE QUESTIONS, NO ANSWERS

The Black Dog. Rock Bottom. In a hole. In a funk. Whatever euphemism existed for being depressed-as-hell, it suited me at this point. There had been many dark days since 02-03-04, but even in the darkest day there was always hope. Now it seemed gone.

Those first few weeks after Dr. Joplin told us Frederick was driving 20 miles per hour were probably the hardest of our marriage. But more than Joplin's dire prognosis, I think the burden of constantly being in an unnatural mode of child-rearing had finally caught up with us. I'm not even sure you could consider us married during that period; Bernadette and I were more like two adults who shared parenting responsibilities.

I needed an outlet. Maybe a hobby. I considered starting a blog about my experiences with Frederick. When I went to look for a website name I tried AutismSucks.com but it was taken. So was IHateAutism.com. So were AutismStinks, AngryAboutAutism, and virtually every domain name regarding anything from a casual to a vehement dislike of Autism.

Talking about it didn't help much. My older brother Kevin was a good listener, and I occasionally poured my heart out to him; he did his best, but ended up being more of a sounding board. I also turned to my best friend Dave except that he was a "fixer;" any problem or complaint that I voiced to him was quickly followed by a pithy solution. One time I was on the phone with him saying how I couldn't believe Frederick may not have a real career or live independently and Dave cut me off and said a friend of his parents had an adult child with Autism. That kid, Dave told me, was living in an apartment and had someone help with his money management, so I should realize that these things "always work out."

"Work out?" I screamed. "Do you really think it's 'working out' for those parents? Pretend that was your own kid! I would not define that as 'working out!'"

I had to figure out a way to get a smile back on my face while raising a child with Autism and two other kids. I was looking for answers to Frederick, and I didn't even know what the questions were. What I really needed was someone in between a listener and a fixer—in other words, a pro.

Dr. Kohley was a psychologist who practiced near where I worked. He had a way of putting my jumbled thoughts and emotions into a succinct, coherent package. Within the first few weeks of seeing him he said, "You and Bernadette can now identify with what was lost. It's been over a year since the diagnosis and you see the trajectory he should have been on. And what is lost is foreshadowing the future."

One of the biggest problems I had was my non-stop obsession with Frederick. No matter how much I did, in my mind, it wasn't enough. At one point in one of our sessions, Kohley said to me, "It sounds like you'd be pretty happy if you could get to a point where you do everything you can for Frederick within reason, while also having a balance to your life, and feeling ok and healthy about it."

Exactly. But easier said than done.

On another day, I was in a pissy mood, railing about this and that, and Kohley said, "Well, anger is a natural part of the grieving process."

I immediately sat up, my spine suddenly a rod of steel. "Hang on, hang on, Frederick's not dead. He just has Autism."

Kohley nodded his head while also shaking it side to side, as only a trained psychologist can do. He agreed, but not totally. "Be that as it may, grieving is part of the process."

"Hang on, hang on a second. There's no body. He's not in a grave. I'm not grieving about my son who's alive and well. (Pause) Alive and doing pretty well." Then my eyes got misty and I wagged my finger at him. "I am not grieving. That's not fair to him. I will not do that."

Kohley smiled a small smile. He wasn't gloating, just explaining. "The first stage of grief is reality setting in, and pervading. At this stage there is no alternative to the pain; nothing makes you feel better. Slowly, very slowly, you gain the capacity to see meaning and joy in life once again. You find out a way to live with the pain and also create joy. But right now, you deserve to grieve and you deserve to cry. You had hopes for Frederick's horizons to match or exceed your life, and now it won't happen."

And that did it. I broke down into a bawling mess.

One of my best friends from college is a guy named Demps, and he's a Cardiologist. Because of my heart issues we've spent a lot of time talking about my condition and my various doctors. One time I told him that my Electrophysiologist wanted to perform an electrical procedure on my heart, and Demps responded, "If you go to a pizza place they'll offer you pizza." His point was that a doctor is likely to focus on what he knows best, and does best. I was at a psychologist now, so Dr. Kohley brought up my childhood.

I had never talked with a professional about the health issues I had as a little kid. I remembered a lot of things from the surgeries: from the first surgery in Philadelphia I remember getting a Snoopy stuffed animal that friends, family, and the hospital staff signed like a cast on a broken arm, and I remember much more vividly a Nun coming by as I was alone on the gurney, in some type of staging area right before going under the knife, and she said "Don't worry, you're not going to die." For the second surgery in Minnesota I remember accidentally locking myself in the bathroom of the Northwest Orient flight and thinking we were being hijacked, which was a word I only vaguely understood. But Kohley and I also got into specifics about how, leading up to that second surgery when I was a kid, my mom never talked about it and my dad kept telling me it was no big deal. And then the neighbor across the street, Mrs. Quinn, called me the day before I left and started crying, repeating over and over, "You're a brave little soldier. You're a brave little soldier."

Dr. Kohley told me that a big impediment to my present situation was the fact that I was never able to grieve as a child about my surgery. I never emotionally explored my life-threatening heart problems and that's why I was having a hard time dealing with Frederick. I told Kohley that my mood had very little to do with my heart operations and everything to do with my only son getting a diagnosis of Autism and mental retardation.

He disagreed. "Kids don't have a sense of their own mortality until much later in life. Yours came early. You should have been able to grieve your loss of innocence. You never got to grieve back then so you're having a hard time grieving now. Grieving can't change things but it is cathartic. The 'ouch' when you pull off that particular band-aid is both helpful and necessary. You feel that it's not fair, that life should not hurt you or your spouse like this. But that's why you need to grieve, because grief has hope, depression doesn't."

There were times when I drove away from his office feeling like it was a waste of time, and there were other days when I drove out of there feeling so physically and emotionally drained that I was afraid I'd fall asleep at the wheel. But, hey, maybe if I was only going 20 miles per hour like Frederick I might not get hurt.

Although I was devoting a little time to therapy, my main concern was still Frederick, and I had gone from big-picture thinking all the way down to the cellular level.

In his report from our visit, Dr. Joplin recommended we pursue genetic testing. That recommendation was on the second-to-last page, one page before this classic line: "We were sorry to have to broach the diagnosis of mental retardation. However, this information will be useful to the family in terms of long-term planning." I guess we were supposed to go into our Microsoft Outlook Calendar and scroll down to the year 2050 and make a note: put self in nursing home; figure out what to do with Frederick.

In the previous two years, when Bernadette and I would pursue therapies or new diets or speech teachers, we did it with the zeal of a true believer. Now, it seemed like a chore. We had crossed some invisible line that separated "fixing" Frederick from managing Frederick. I hated those thoughts and I hated those words, but that's what it felt like.

We were robots at that point, so we followed Dr. Joplin's orders and made an appointment with a C.H.O.P. geneticist, Dr. Helen Mackay, and naturally, we couldn't get in to see her for over a month. And that meant I had time to search the internet.

As a rule, guys who majored in English and work in sports should not Google chromosomal defects in the hopes of pinpointing what's wrong with their child. For starters, I had forgotten how many chromosomes a human had (23 pairs). I couldn't even remember which were female (X-X) and which were male (X-Y). After I got the basics down I looked up every malady I could find: Russell-Silver, Prader-Willi, Smith-Magennis, Pelizaeus-Merzbacher, Yin-Yang, Shirts-Skins, and Hall-Oates.

I was so overloaded with information that, by the time we went to the offices of Dr. Mackay, I wasn't sure what they were looking for. When we first arrived we were met by an assistant who asked all the standard questions, and we gave the same answers we'd given to so many previous doctors: Yes, it was a full gestation. No, he was not in the intensive care for any length of time. Yes, he took to feeding right away. No, he didn't lose any language skills, just never acquired them.

In walked Dr. Mackay, who after getting through the requisite introductions lobbed this bombshell as her first question: "Do you happen to know if you are related?"

"He's my son," I answered.

"No, I meant with your wife," Dr. Mackay said.

"She's my wife," I said.

"Yes, but does the possibility exist that you are related?" she asked.

"We're related by marriage."

The doctor shook her head. "I mean blood relatives."

I was dumbfounded. "I think that would have come up by now."

Mackay shrugged. "Yes and no. Is it possible that a few generations back that you might have been related? What is your ancestry?"

"Fifty-fifty, Irish and German," I said.

Bernadette ticked off at least five nationalities, including Irish, German, and Hungarian.

The rest of the questions were more mundane and then, for the first time in our adventure with Autism, Bernadette and I were participants in a physical exam. Dr. Mackay looked at my hands and then Bernadette's, really studying them intently, like there was fine-print hidden in the crevices. Then she asked us to remove our shoes and socks and appraised our feet. She inspected the soles and then peeled apart each toe. Without a word, she moved on to Frederick.

She started with his hands and feet, and did the same careful inspections. And then she pulled out a little tape measure made of cloth and began to measure the length between facial features: ear to ear, nose to ear, length of nose, eye to eye. It was strange to watch—so strange, in fact, that Frederick was taken aback and didn't complain or try to get away. Dr. Mackay had this Jedi-thing going where she was so quick and smooth that it seemed like she was measuring mannequins, and that feeling must have transferred over to Frederick. He just sat there as Dr. Mackay said the numbers aloud as her assistant wrote them down. She was fast and efficient, and in the time it would take me to measure the width of a refrigerator in our kitchen to see if it could go in a different spot, she banged out ten measurements and then announced, "We're going to take our findings and compute them. We'll be back soon. Just wait here."

She left, and we waited.

Fear of the unknown is powerful. Since I didn't fully understand why we were there, nor the full inventory of genetic maladies, I didn't know what to expect when Dr. Mackay came back. She wasn't going to simply say 'yes' or 'no' upon arrival, she'd have to painstakingly explain what she was diagnosing him with.

She was probably gone only ten minutes, though it seemed like a half hour. When she returned, Dr. Mackay said the three words no parent ever wants to hear. "Have a seat," she said.

Have a seat.

It was that same feeling all over again. The feeling I had when Dr. Landau said, "The engine driving all of this is Autism." The same feeling I had when Dr. Joplin said "A good goal as an adult would be to have him be able to ask for directions if he's lost." It's a hollow, slightly warm feeling in the stomach that slowly seeps upward. It takes about five seconds from when you first feel it until it reaches your head, and you're left with a hot, flushed face and a distant ringing in your ears.

Frankly, I was sick of the feeling.

But then I had a rush of adrenaline and excitement: it occurred to me that I was standing up when she entered the room! So this might not be, "Have a seat, I have terrible news" it might be "Have a seat, this could take a while." But then I realized if the explanation was going to take a while then it can't be good news. Dr. Mackay had been back in the room five seconds and I had gone from despair to elation to despair again.

"After examination, we don't see any genetic markers, but that doesn't mean there is not an underlying condition that we're not seeing. So what we would like you to do is get a full genetic screening, more than was done last year and not just the ones Dr. Joplin suggested but a fuller spectrum analysis."

That was it.

Bernadette and I looked at each other.

"Hang on," I said, trying to get my bearings. "Wait…what? How do you do a genetic screening?"

"Just blood work." Dr. Mackay shook hands and left. The assistant handed us a lab form for blood work and pointed us to reception.

So we trudged down to the lab.

When it was Frederick's turn I sat in the blood-draw chair and put him on my lap, then explained to the nurse that Frederick had Autism and didn't like blood tests. I was experienced enough that I kept my head to the side as the nurse shoved the needle in his arm; that way, when he tensed and threw his own head back it would hit me in the chest, not the teeth. And as I sat there holding him snug to my chest like a policeman pinning a 300lb meth-head, I imagined what it was like to be Frederick—a little kid in a strange place with strange people tying a rubber hose to his arm then sticking him with a sharp object, and being unable to ask or understand why.

But, hey, we had to do it.

Or did we?

It was a seemingly unending process, and there was never any chance for joy because whether the doctor's report was good or bad, there was always another one, the next one.

Every time we ran the ball, someone moved the goal line. And that wasn't the only thing that was moving.

We were.

That spring, genetic testing results weren't the only thing that had us on edge—we had accumulated enough time talking about moving that we went ahead and put our house on the market, even though we had yet to decide where we'd end up. Bernadette of course wanted to stay in the area, near her parents. I wanted to move 40 miles north to my hometown in Pennsylvania.

To say that Bernadette is "family-oriented" is like saying Tim Tebow is "Jesus-oriented." We bought our first house in her hometown of Haddon Heights, New Jersey. That was in 1995, around the same time her parents were moving out of her childhood home. We got to know the couple that bought that house and, wouldn't you know, a few years later they ended up moving so we sold our first home and bought the house she grew up in, and lived happily there until I started agitating about moving.

She loved that house but I had never completely warmed to it; it was always "her" house, not "our" house. The basement room where I had a desk and treadmill was never "my office" or "the workout room," it was always "Freddy's room," the room where her only brother had slept.

So when I floated the idea of moving back to my hometown of Yardley, Pennsylvania, just 45 minutes away from Haddon Heights, her initial reaction was something like "over my dead body." She was concerned about being too far away from her parents and her sisters and her friends. I countered that by pointing out that we weren't moving to California, we were moving across the river, a few congressional districts away. It was still the same TV market, the same radio stations. We could leave one town at halftime of an NFL game and get to the other town before the third quarter ended. We could bring a Carvel ice cream cake to a family party and it would still be edible by the time we got there.

But we were not a normal family, and that had to be factored into the equation. Bernadette never imagined her only son would be unable to eat the Carvel cake because of egg and peanut allergies and oh, by the way, he needed to be in a restraining seat at the kitchen table. Every night, Frederick sat in a food-encrusted navy-blue booster chair that attached to the chair. It had a big strap, secured with Velcro that kept him in his seat. Most nights, he pulled and whined and cried, trying to get out, and after

**Yes, he's playing with the computer while on a trampoline.**

a few minutes we just unstrapped him and let him wander in order to salvage what was left of dinner with 2/3 of our children. Giving in to him violated the rules sets down by every doctor, therapist, and how-to manual ever, but we were either lazy or bad parents or just wanted ten minutes of peace and quiet—or all of the above.

Frederick was closing in on five years old, and he was getting more and more unconventional. We always knew he was obsessive about carrying certain toys and having his "things" with him but now he was doing "things," and none of them were constructive or age-appropriate.

For a while his "thing" was to take a pile of items—usually a basket full of toys—and dump them all onto the ground. Then he'd jump in the air, land in the pile, and yell "oops." We had no theory on this one; we just knew it was annoying. But it was also endearing, or at least pretty damn funny. It was hard to get mad because after I'd say "clean it up" he would look out of the corner of his eye, dangle a toy in his hand, and drop it, like the last anvil dropping from the sky in a Road Runner cartoon. He knew I was watching, he knew he was doing something he shouldn't, but the devilish grin and the upturned eyebrow could melt me.

Frederick dominated the house, dominated our marriage, and dominated our conversations about moving. Should we move away from the school district we know, and that knows him? Should we buy a second property that we could rent until Frederick was old enough to live there? (That idea quickly faded when we realized we could barely afford the first property.)

And we had to consider the educational services he'd get in either state, and they were philosophically different.

In New Jersey, kids with Autism who could not be mainstreamed into a regular classroom would attend school at a regional center. Frederick was looking like he'd fit that bill so he would likely be bussed to a large education center that would be responsible for teaching him through 12th grade. In Pennsylvania, the kids are usually taught at a self-contained classroom within a local school.

There are pluses and minuses to both. In New Jersey you know the whole school or center is geared toward Autism—they've seen it all, they know it all. Every nurse, every janitor, they all know what the kids are about and why they're there. But the downside is your child doesn't get a chance to be around typical kids. In Pennsylvania, the downside is that you're at the mercy of the school district as to what school your kid will be in. It doesn't have to be the school closest to you; it could be one on the other side of the district, which in the case of the Yardley area meant up to a 25-minute car ride away. But the good thing about that setup is your child can have lunch and maybe gym or art with typical kids his own age.

We were worried about Frederick's development, yet I had regressed to a six-year-old's level when discussing our impending move. I would say things like, "We've lived in Jersey for ten years...You get more house for your money in PA...The taxes are lower....It's my turn to live where I want."

As pathetic as it may seem, I think part of the reason I wanted to move so bad is because I wanted to get my way. I wanted to win. But it had nothing to do with Bernadette—it was the culmination of years of never getting my way when it came to dealing with Autism. That goddamn thing always won.

Was it selfish? Probably. But I kept pursuing it even though it was likely to derail another dream of mine. The thought of adopting a baby had first percolated before the twins arrived. In the past few months, despite the insanity that was our daily lives, we talked about maybe—maybe—considering it again. We had taken tiny, incremental steps with an agency that placed children from Korea. We talked about adopting a boy, attended a seminar on adoption, and even bought a tiny little N.D. t-shirt at the Notre Dame bookstore when Bernadette and I went out for a football weekend. We even had all the initial paperwork at home, just waiting for someone to start filling in the blanks. I actually think Bernadette was ready and willing to adopt, but moving could potentially scuttle the idea. If we ended up in Pennsylvania, even though weren't moving far from our home in South Jersey, crossing state lines meant we'd have to find a new agency. And something told me that the process wouldn't start again anytime soon if we moved to the Keystone State.

About a month after meeting with Mackay and getting the blood drawn, Bernadette and I dropped the kids at her parents and drove to look at a house near Medford, New Jersey, a sort of compromise town that would be near her parents and still somewhat near my parents, but something new. It was just a shot in the dark, something to break the stalemate between staying (Haddon Heights NJ) and going (Yardley PA.)

My cell rang. I looked at the number.

"I think it's the genetics people." I said.

Bernadette was driving, and she started freaking out. "Oh crap, oh crap, oh crap. Should I pull over?"

I waved her off. "Hello."

"Mr. O'Brien?"

"Yes."

"This is Children's Hospital." It was the assistant from our visit with Dr. Mackay.

I could hear Bernadette in the background talking to herself. "If it's bad we stay in Jersey. If it's good we move to Pennsylvania."

"We have your son's blood work in and it's negative."

"It's negative!" I shouted, thrusting the phone in the air.

Bernadette shouted back, "Negative good or negative bad?"

"I don't know." I got back on the phone. "Negative good or negative bad?"

"The tests are negative. He has no chromosomal abnormalities."

"So that's it?" I asked. "We're done? No more tests?"

"This only covers what science currently knows about genes. That doesn't mean he has no abnormalities, it just means of all the ones we can test for, he has no abnormalities in those."

These people would crap on a birthday cake.

"Thanks for calling," I said, and hung up.

I felt like I could breathe again for the first time in months. Somehow it all seemed over. In a flash, an absolute millisecond, I projected forward and saw Frederick getting therapy and responding well and being a little bit different than most kids, but not by much. And that was good enough for me. Bernadette turned toward me, staring, and kept staring, the way actors do in movies when they're not actually driving, except that she was actually driving.

"Well.....?" Bernadette asked.

I sat back and exhaled. "He's fine. There's nothing wrong with him."

As generalities go, that was a stretch. There were still a lot of things wrong, but we could scratch off genetic abnormalities.

"Oh my god, oh my god, oh my god." Bernadette started crying; so did I.

She drove for about a minute, and neither of us talked. It occurred to me that this was the first piece of truly unambiguous good news we had heard on Frederick in over two years. That's a long time, 24 straight months of every black cloud bringing rain.

Bernadette finally swallowed and said, "So Dr. Joplin was wrong? He doesn't have retardation?"

Back to reality.

I didn't want to get into it. The accurate answer to her question was this: the tests ruled out all known genetic abnormalities, but did not rule out genetic malformations that do not have a test yet. Furthermore, even if all genetic abnormalities, known and unknown, could be ruled out, that does not on its face mean that mental retardation is still not an accurate piece of the diagnosis.

I opted for the short answer.

"Yup."

There was more to it than that one phone call, but we ended up moving to Pennsylvania.

Months later, as we were packing up our house in Haddon Heights, there were the typical stresses of moving, and a lot of worry and uncertainty, but there was one thing I knew for sure: I wouldn't miss our house on Bryn Mawr Avenue. This was her town, not mine. It was (literally) her house, not mine. But surprisingly, on moving day, Bernadette and I walked through the house one last time, and I cried like a baby as I stood in the doorway of the "therapy room." It used to be called the toy room, and years before that it was her parent's first floor bedroom, but for the past year it had been the therapy room. It was the room where we hung the shelves up high so Frederick had to request the toy he wanted, the room we painted in bright pastel colors with a sand-based paint so they would be tactile to improve his sensory inputs. It was the room where we were going to work for an hour a night and "hit it hard" and do Floortime and somehow undo Frederick's Autism.

It didn't happen.

That room was more than a room—it was the metaphor for our efforts and frustrations and the first step toward a healthy surrender. We were moving on from the house and we were moving on with our lives.

# 16 WHERE'S THE PLAYBOOK?

"Back to School Night." Millions of parents in America have done it; you arrive at the classroom, sit in the same desk where your kid sits, and the teacher waxes about how "extraordinary" it is to have your child in their class.

In the fall of 2006, a few months after we moved, Bernadette and I attended Back to School Night at Lakota Elementary, Frederick's new school. The walls were decorated with photos of the kids in the classroom, and the parents were pointing out their child and giving a state of the union. One Caucasian woman said, "She's mine" and pointed to an Asian girl. "Oh," Bernadette and I responded in unison. It was a three-syllable "oh" with a dip in the middle, the one that conveys 'I get it' and 'that's cool' with a single two-letter word.

"Yeah," the mom continued. "We adopted from China because they said they have the healthiest babies." She looked away, wistfully, for about five seconds. "Yeah, that's what they said."

And we uncovered an ongoing mystery, one that even Inspector Clouseau could have deduced after hearing the information. One dad said to us, "My son's doing great, yeah, they've really done wonders for him here. I mean, he does still tend to bite when acting out his aggressions but, overall, he's doing great."

No need to subpoena the class for dental records—that's the kid who bit Frederick last week.

At a neurotypical Back to School night, you hear from one teacher and maybe one aide if the class is large. But when your five-year-old is in the "Autism Support Class" there's so many people talking it's like the opening debates of the 2016 Republican Primary.

We heard from Frederick's main teacher. We heard from the speech teacher. We heard from the classroom aide. The Applied Behavior Analysis (ABA) specialist was also on hand. Did I mention the physical therapist? All of this was fine and dandy until a woman in her early 50's stood up, looking like she'd walked out of a "Better

Homes & Organic Gardens" magazine ad and introduced herself as the Occupational Therapist.

"My name is (removed to protect the insensitive) and I've had many years of experience working with this type of population…"

Once again—cue the record scratch.

This type of population. If you're scoring at home, that's twice in three years now for the "P" word.

So the prim and proper Occupational Therapist who probably passes herself off to friends and family as a bastion of open-mindedness has now stripped my child of his wonderful quirks and his delightful personality and thrown him into an abyss where the nameless autistic children are writhing together in all their uncommunicative and self-stimulatory glory.

Maybe I was being harsh. Maybe I was overreacting. It's probably a legitimate piece of diction. Then again, I tend to think of "this type of population" as my son.

Or maybe I was a little sensitive that day because I was beginning to realize that sending Frederick to this school had been a grave mistake.

To recap:

We took our Special Needs child out of our familiar school district in New Jersey and moved to a place in Pennsylvania where we knew none of the teachers or school administrators—check.

I doubled my commute to work—check.

I uprooted my wife from her childhood home and town—check.

Maybe things would have been ok if we had a smoother start in our new house, but Closing Day was a debacle of epic proportions. You know how the drill is supposed to work—show up at your new house for the "walkthrough" to make sure everything is in working order, flush some toilets and flick some light switches, then head over to the real estate office and sign the papers.

But when we pulled up to our new home, all of the current homeowner's belongings were on the front lawn, there was a moving van with the gate open but nothing in it, and a cop car with its lights flashing. Apparently, the homeowner either vastly underestimated the amount of stuff and the movers were rebelling or the movers pulled the classic "get everything out of the house then tell the homeowner it's gonna cost more" gambit. Somehow, Bernadette didn't faint, and after speaking with the police we walked into the house. When Bernadette opened the washing machine and saw clothes in it, that's when she burst into tears and fled.

Twenty-four hours later, we finally had settlement. The misadventures of our house hunting were hard on Bernadette; maybe if we had found the perfect school for

Frederick, it would have helped her psyche.

But we didn't.

When we moved from New Jersey to Pennsylvania we did a few meetings with the Special Ed department in our new school district that were as cursory as speed dating, and their recommendation was that Frederick attend a specialized classroom in an underused public middle school called Lakota Elementary. Most any school would have paled in comparison to our experiences at St. Joseph's, and my first impression of his new school did not disappoint.

I'm no scholar of Native American languages, but I suspect the word "Lakota" translates to "uninspiring venue" or "foreboding place of learning." It was once a big, bustling elementary school but was now only used for Special Ed. There were a few Autism support classrooms and also an "alternative" classroom for teens; the criteria for admission to that class was apparently Goth makeup, trenchcoats, and those wallets with the long silver chain. There were days when Bernadette would call me on the phone, hysterical, because she dropped Frederick off and a roving band of teenagers were walking outside the school, looking like they stepped out of a violent video game.

Bernadette hated it from day one; it didn't take Frederick much longer.

After about a week, Frederick would start crying when he was a half-mile from school—it wasn't full-bawling, hissy-fit type tears; it was actually sadder. Just big drops that moved slowly, maybe an inch a minute, down his face.

If a playbook existed, I could have used it right then, but there were no "Special Needs Parenting for Dummies" books.

But I needed help, and not just for Frederick's school placement. It was now painfully apparent that having a special needs brother was taking a toll on Anna. She was nine years old, and it was getting harder to be Frederick's big sister. Anna now came to me with questions and problems and feelings that I never thought I would have to discuss with one of my children.

The first few years of Anna's life were great. In fact, they were probably more peaceful than if Frederick was a typical boy. Since he wasn't interactive, he largely stayed out of Anna's way. I didn't have to referee too many fights, just listen to the occasional complaint of, "Dad, Frederick has my Barbie in his mouth again."

When Frederick first got the diagnosis we didn't have any big sit-down with Anna because she was just six years old. But she was always precocious so, about a year later when she started asking questions about why he didn't go to school with her, we had The Talk. Not the birds-and-the-bees Talk, which wasn't scheduled for a few more years. This was a different capital-T Talk—the one where you explain why people stare at your little brother.

I prepped for this Talk. Wrote an outline, scratched some stuff off, added a few others, and then typed it up.

When we were ready, Bernadette and I walked down the basement where Anna was in the middle of a Powerpuff Girls marathon on Cartoon Network. "Hey sweetie," I said as I turned off the TV. "Mom and I want to talk to you for a minute." Bernadette sat next to her and I knelt in front of the couch so I could place my bullet-point cheat sheet on the floor and glance at it. The full list is below:

He is a little difft, has a name—Autism
Means difft way of relating to the world
Lots of people have it
Harder time talking and interacting
We feel how you feel—happy, sad, angry
Special school for a while, slower to talk
Floortime, way you play—helps him
Future—little harder, but confident
Every day will get easier
Your feelings—talk to us
He's very lucky to have you as a big sister
Your're lucky; will learn so much from him

It went over like a lead balloon. I'm not sure how much of it she assimilated because she asked, almost every thirty seconds, when she could go back to watching the Powerpuff Girls.

But now, a few years later, she was maturing and things were changing. It wasn't a sudden, light-switch type conversion. She didn't wake up one day and say "Holy crap! I have a special needs brother!" Over the years, I wrote down some of Anna's quotes, as she slowly began to understand what Autism meant and how it impacted Frederick and our family.

Age 7: "I'm glad Frederick has Autism, because if he didn't have Autism he wouldn't be the way he is. And I love him the way he is."

Age 8, when asked who we should bring to the Bingo Social at church: "Let's bring everyone! No wait, let's not bring Frederick. He might run around...and do goofy things...and talk funny...and point to the numbers on everyone's bingo cards...and steal their chips."

Age 9, when asked how she felt about Frederick's Autism: "It makes me sad for him. And I'm sad for myself because I'll never get a second chance at the life I wanted.

I'll never have a normal brother. Somedays I wish he wasn't like this. Other days I wouldn't change a thing."

Tough stuff.

Should we only discuss things when she wants to, or do we force the issue? Should we throw her into the deep end of the pool by aggressively looking for and attending "special sibs" meetings? Should we take her to a shrink?

I really needed a playbook the day she started crying for what seemed like no reason. Her friend Caroline wanted Anna to come over and play but Anna didn't want to. Not knowing the situation, I pushed her. "It's a nice day. Just go over for an hour." Then she burst into tears.

I sat her down on the stairs and her tears started slowly, at first. She tried squinting and shaking her head to make them stop, but they just came out harder.

"Why don't you want to see Caroline?"

Anna just shook her head.

"C'mon honey. You can tell me. You'll feel better."

After a few minutes of sitting and stroking her arm, she spills the beans.

"Caroline said that word."

In most families, the words you have to worry about are the seven George Carlin words. If you live in a family of a certain ethnicity, it might be racial slurs. In our house it's the "R-word," as in overhearing a kid saying, "I'm not watching that show. It's retarded." Or "I went to my sister's school play. It was so retarded."

"So she used the R word?" I asked.

She nodded, sobbing.

"Tell me how it happened."

Now she started getting fired up.

"Oh like she only used it once? Are you kidding me—she's used it like three times. I don't want to see her. I haven't gone to her house in two weeks and she keeps calling but I'm not answering. I want to rip her face off. The next time she says it I'm going to punch her."

Since no playbook existed, I began to make up my own, channeling my inner Dr. Kohley. "Let's slow down honey. Slow down. First of all, it's very hurtful when you hear the word 'retarded,' right? It's painful. You can feel it like a knife, right?"

She nodded.

"I totally understand that. Totally. That hurts because you think of Frederick and you know how wonderful he is."

More nodding. More tears. Her hand curled up in a fist, her fingers white. I hugged her.

"It's ok. You can cry. It's sad. It is sad."

She sobbed so hard it shook my shoulders.

"It hurts and it's supposed to hurt. But now let's look at what happened. Do you think when Caroline said the word retarded that she was making fun of Frederick?"

She shook her head 'no.'

"I agree with you. She wasn't making fun of Frederick and she wasn't even thinking of Frederick. She might not even know that the word retarded is a technical term about someone's intelligence level."

She perked up. "Yeah well that makes her a stupid idiot because she doesn't even know the words she's using. How stupid is that?"

"Pretty stupid," I admitted. "But you're at least realizing something. When she says that word, she's not doing it on purpose. It's just ignorance."

"Right, she's a stupid ignoramus."

I hugged her again. "I know it hurts honey. Did you know I used to use the word 'retarded' like that? Not proud of it, but I did. Until Frederick came along and he got his diagnosis. Then I stopped. And guess what—Dave said the R-word once in an email"

She was shocked. Dave's my best friend and Anna's known him since birth.

"Yeah, he emailed that the Eagles were retarded for cutting a certain player, and it hurt me. Real bad. So I emailed him back and told him how I felt. And he instantly got back to me and said 'My bad, my bad, totally understand. Sorry. Won't happen again.'"

She sat upright. "No way!"

"Yes, way. So if my best friend can use it, you can see that people don't always mean it the way you're taking it. It doesn't make it right, it just makes it a lot less wrong."

She nodded. I moved in for another hug. I held her tight for this part, because it wasn't what she wanted to hear.

"And you know I'll always support you and always love you and do everything I can for you, right?" Her chin tapped on my shoulder as she nodded. "But the bad news is I can't help you completely out of this one. We can talk about it as much as you want. But at some point it's up to you what you do next. And I think you have three options: first, you can ignore Caroline and try to let it roll of your back, like water off of a duck. Just say to yourself, 'I know she doesn't mean it so I'm not going to let it bother me.' Second, you can ignore it and let it eat you up inside. You can avoid Caroline and just get angry and feel like you're on fire every time she says it, but do nothing."

"Fine with me," Anna said, her face now contorted again with rage. "I'm gonna punch her anyway. Yeah, that's option three. Just punch her."

"Well I have another option so we'll call punching Caroline option four. Option three would be to talk to Caroline. The next time she says it you can ask her if she knows what it means. Tell her it offends you. And you can even explain why and talk about Frederick."

The tears began again. I hugged her again. "Unfortunately, sweetie, the best option is usually the hardest. That's not an easy conversation to have. We can rehearse it if you want, when you're ready."

She just cried some more and buried her head in my arms.

**Our Christmas cards rarely included photos.**

I had been telling myself for years now that having Frederick as a brother would be the best thing that ever happened to Anna. But now I wasn't so sure.

It was painful. Anna had so much to offer a typical brother. Hell, if I had an older sister like her growing up I never would have worn sweatpants to parties in college. I might have held a door for a lady prior to the age of 30. Frederick had the ultimate weapon in dating—an older sister—and he would never be able to use it.

As the weeks went by, our laundry list of grievances with the school grew. As the mother of a nonverbal kid, Bernadette relied on communication from the teachers to know how Frederick's day went. But there wasn't much communication from Lakota. One particular day Bernadette went through his backpack and discovered a note from the school nurse—Frederick had been bitten in school, but "the wound looked fine." That was the extent of it. No call or note from the teacher. Just a scribbled message from the nurse, as if she was a M*A*S*H doctor performing triage: "Head wound: right into surgery. Femoral artery: put a tourniquet on it. Five-year-old bitten by another five-year-old: he's fine, just write a note and get him out of here."

Because of her unease with the school, Bernadette would often "check up" on Frederick surreptitiously. Other jurisdictions call it "stalking." On one October day she was "checking up" at recess and parked well away from the playground. When the class came out to the fenced-in playground, Frederick did what he always did: wandered aimlessly. No interaction with the other kids. They were kryptonite.

She noticed a teacher arguing with a kid who was standing on the top of a sliding board. The boy was in a different class than Frederick and looked maybe a year younger. Bernadette rolled down the window and could make out the teacher saying, "Don't jump. We don't jump. Come down the steps."

Special needs kids aren't that different from typical peers in one respect: they enjoy disobeying. So the kid jumped. The teacher collected him and sat him down, wagged a finger in his face, and said "We don't jump. We don't do that. Now you sit until recess is over."

In Frederick's class, they use pictures to tell the kids when it's time to go potty. It's a little picture of a toilet. So the odds of that kid understanding a pissed-off adult who rapid-fire tells him "Wedon'tjumpwedont'tdothatnowyousituntilrecessisover" is pretty slim.

Bernadette stayed put and looked at the clock. Nine minutes. The teacher left the nonverbal kid there for nine freaking minutes. The boy cried the whole time. And so did Bernadette. She cried for a lot of reasons, but mainly because we had left a school that made students feel like part of the family and now we were strangers, parents of a population, resigned to spying on our kid at recess.

It was the slow trickle of a lot of little things that made us decide we needed to pull Frederick out of the school. But since we were in Special Ed it wasn't that easy. With a typical kid you can move them from a public to a private school, or vice versa. But we were at the mercy of the district.

We called an Individualized Education Plan (I.E.P.) meeting—a necessity for any change, big or small. It's very procedure-oriented with lots of forms and several representatives from the school district side. We called the meeting specifically to say we wanted Frederick to move to a new school.

When the meeting began, it felt like we were on trial. We were across the table from the teacher and school district representative and, ironically, the woman who considered Frederick a "population."

Our argument was that Frederick needed to be around typical peers. The only school that could serve Frederick's needs—and have typical children included—was Butterfly Academy, the school Grace attended. It was a school for typical kids but had a small number of slots for kids with special needs.

The school district disagreed. They said "typical peer" involvement wouldn't really help Frederick at this stage. In fact, they made that argument in about 30 seconds and then said "sign here." They told us we were wrong and then they wanted us to sign a document that said we agree with their recommendation to keep him at Lakota.

At that point, Bernadette said "Do you want to know the real reason we want to pull him? He's sad. He cries every day. He used to be happy. Now he's not."

Oh no.

Naturally, Miss Population spoke up first. "Sometimes, kids don't like what's best for them." Her arrogance was obscene. And it stiffened our resolve.

We eventually got our way and, at the semester, we got him out. Things started to change after that—Bernadette was happier, and Frederick was happier. He no longer cried going to school. Instead, he leaped out of the van with his sister every morning and waved goodbye to Bernadette without turning around. He was at a school situated on a picturesque five-acre farm, having fun with 60 other kids, about a quarter of whom had special needs and an IEP and the proper support.

So the Lakota saga was over in one semester. It wasn't the end of all our problems; when you're a special needs parent the problems don't end, even with your own death. But perhaps switching schools was, to use Churchill's phrase, the "end of the beginning." We don't have a lot of happy memories from Lakota, but we did learn one important lesson there: always listen to your child, even if he can't talk.

# 17 IT FALLS APART SO EASY

Another year flew by. Slowly, painfully, it felt like we were emerging out of a long tunnel. Grace was finishing a successful year of kindergarten and was ready to take the leap to join Anna at our local parochial school, and Frederick was finishing a banner year at Village Park Elementary, a busy public school in our district that had a few classrooms of various special needs kids. The teachers adored him in a way that you knew they weren't faking it, and they loved his impish sense of humor in the classroom. Even when they had to re-direct him when he was doing something wrong, their mock-stern "Ahem—Mr. O'Brien!" was done with a smile. Our only complaint about the school was the "Autism Walk" flyer they sent home one day in Frederick's backpack. I understand they can't make a few hundred of the same flyers and then five custom ones for the parents of the kids in his class, but did they really need to send us something that began with "Autism is a condition that has a tremendous impact on families…." Really? An impact? Hadn't noticed.

His behavior in school had improved, but his academic progress had not. In fact, it hardly seemed like he was learning anything. His homework assignments were rudimentary and, although he was technically on the verge of first grade, he had not progressed past number and letter recognition.

Since we had been seeing Dr. Joplin regularly, he had prescribed medication that seemingly gave us the "best possible Frederick." Risperidone was relatively new for kids on the Autism spectrum, but for us it had been nothing short of a miracle drug. When we started that medicine after our last Dr. Joplin visit, our lives were completely transformed: he went from completely unmanageable to almost pleasant.

Yet, his teachers always noted his inability to concentrate. And one of my big concerns was academics, in the sense that I wanted him to eventually move beyond tracing his hand and making a Turkey to give to Bernadette on Thanksgiving. So near the end of the school year we consulted with Dr. Joplin and he agreed that it might be worthwhile to try a stimulant in the hopes of helping Frederick's attention span. From what I was told about stimulants, we'd quickly find out if they were working. If they didn't work, we figured we'd get right back on Risperidone and have a great summer.

What I didn't know about switching medications is there's a process involved. The physician's assistant told us "We're going to have to ramp down and then ramp up. So take his Risperidone from 1 pill in the morning, 2 pills in the afternoon and 2 pills at night to 1 pill three times a day. Then the next week we'll go 1 pill in the morning 1 at night. Then he has to be completely off for the third week to get all the medication out of his system."

This would not be as quick as I hoped. And I shuddered to think about what week three would be like without medication. But I rationalized that it was for a good reason—we thought Frederick on Risperidone was the best possible Frederick, but maybe there was an even better Frederick lurking.

Well, there was another Frederick lurking, but not the one we were interested in seeing.

By the second day of his cold-turkey week, Frederick had gone from Bill Bixby to the Incredible Hulk. In an instant, he had regressed three years and we were back in the same dark hole we'd been in when we were coming to grips with Autism and simply trying to get through the day. We would tuck him in at 8:00 p.m. and he'd bounce on the bed until 9:30. His feces withholding got worse and he was constantly touching his underwear to the point where we would find flakes of poop on the TV screen. His fingernails looked like an auto mechanic's fingernails, but it wasn't grease under there. And his "agitation," the pleasant euphemism the doctor used, had gone into overdrive.

His patience was measured in nanoseconds. If he wanted to go outside but only had his socks on, we'd say "Let's put your shoes on" and he would start kicking, thrashing, and crying. It would take at least 30 seconds for him to downshift into merely angry, at which point you could maybe slide one shoe on. But then he'd pop up to go outside and you'd say "Frederick, other shoe," and the whole sordid mess would repeat itself, but this time for twice as long.

When it was time for bed, we used to say "Get your guys" and he'd grab maybe 20 Sesame characters and a book. Now, without his usual meds, he made two trips up and down the stairs, both times loaded down like a pack mule. And after a few days of getting tired of two trips he got smart and emptied out a toy basket in the living room and started using it as luggage. So now when we said "Ok, time for bed" he started filling up the basket with a staggering inventory of items that usually included Cookie, Oscar, Elmo, Grover, the guys from Wonder Pets, Greg Wiggle, Anthony Wiggle, all the tools from Handy Manny, some small plastic animals, little pieces of paper he cut out of books, plus at least five actual books and any photographs of family members he could find, framed or unframed. After two days of this I tried to stop it. I told Frederick he had to pick just a few guys. Twenty minutes later, with him still screaming on the floor, I gave up on that idea.

But the real hard part was when he forgot someone. Remember, he's Frederick, and he doesn't do random things. It's all thought-out, all calculated. When he filled up the toy basket for bed he knew exactly who he wanted and why. So when we'd put him to bed with a basket filled with 50 items, it was hard to imagine him caring that he left a man behind. But he would have made a great Marine. If one little piece of paper or one minor Sesame character who got less screen time than Prairie Dawn or one three-inch plastic figurine wasn't in there, he'd throw a fit. And in another regression to three years earlier, he made very little effort to communicate what was missing. He would tantrum in bed because he was convinced I knew what he was missing (Theory of Mind), but I was refusing to get it. No matter how often I said "Which guy? Who's not here?" it wouldn't help. Just slaps to my face and kicks to the family jewels as I got his pajamas on.

So this is what we were dealing with during his cold turkey week. When it was finally over, I was on the phone to the doctors at exactly 9 am Monday, ready to get moving on new meds and reclaim our lives.

Not so fast. I was told that we needed an EKG before starting the stimulant.

The quickest we could get an EKG appointment was a week later. Then a cardiologist had to read the EKG and fax the results to Dr. Joplin. One day passed. Then another. Then three more. We called Joplin's office. Still not there. On day five, we called the EKG doctor, and found out their office was faxing it to the wrong number.

In the meantime, we tried to live our lives, but that wasn't working out so well either.

One hot summer day when I was at work, a neighbor up the street invited Bernadette and the kids over to swim. Later, as she recounted the story to me, she said, "My head told me to say 'no.' But I'm sick of living like this. I'm sick of giving up before I start. So I said we'd be up, but could only stay for an hour."

They ended up staying about 57 minutes short of an hour.

When they got there, half the neighborhood was already in the pool. Anna jumped right in, Grace started playing with the host's kids, and Bernadette put Frederick on a big raft and walked him around the shallow end. He loved it. The raft was big enough that he could sit up or turn around, and he must have felt like he was on an island in the middle of the pool. Bernadette then turned to talk to the moms who were sitting in the deck chairs, chatting about summer plans and the ridiculous heat wave, when one of the ladies pointed and asked: "Is Frederick all right?"

Bernadette turned to see him on all fours, with a pained look on his face, and brown stuff trickling out of his bathing suit.

"Ohmygod, ohmygod" was Bernadette's feeble response as Frederick Baby Ruth-ed our neighbor's pool.

All the kids screamed and jumped out as Bernadette picked up Frederick, who was still muttering, "Ish coming now, ish coming now." She lifted him from the water and carried him down the sidewalk back to our house, while Frederick crapped on her with every bouncing step.

Bernadette quickly got him bathed, but the damage had been done. The host called a few minutes later to tell Bernadette it was all right. She said "With our three boys, this has happened on more than one occasion. One day we were swimming and my mother-in-law asked me, 'Cheryl, why is there corn in the pool?'"

To her credit, Bernadette got him dressed and walked back up to the neighbor's house and sat with the moms for an hour as Frederick ran around the yard. But none of the neighborhood kids were there; they were across the street at another house, playing in a sprinkler.

**The summer of meltdowns.**

By the 4th of July, we were working on nearly four weeks without medication. It was taking a toll on us, but it was also beginning to show on Frederick. Risperidone had helped his appetite, and made him a little more adventurous with his diet. But without the medication he reverted to being a picky eater, then lost his appetite altogether. He lost four pounds—nearly 10% of his bodyweight—and looked like a stick figure.

The following week, Dr. Joplin's office called. The EKG report was finally ready.

"This is great," I said when they called. "Things have been really tough without meds."

"I can imagine," the woman at the office replied.

"Well, I'm just glad he can start the new medication," I said. "Can you call the pharmacy today?"

"No, actually, it's a controlled substance, they only accept paper prescriptions. I'll have to mail it to you."

My first impulse was to slam my head into our kitchen countertop. Then I thought it might be better to use the receiver and pound my skull like a hammer until I went unconscious. Ultimately, I was too worn out for either.

"That'd be great," I said, then wished her well and hung up.

We got the prescription filled just in time for Frederick's first day of summer school. In Bucks County, Pennsylvania, if your child qualifies for "ESY" (Extended School Year) you get roughly four weeks of summer school, beginning in July and running through early August. But it's not with your regular teacher in the same classroom from the regular academic year. It's all new—new building, new teachers, new bus driver. And Bernadette made the tough decision that she'd allow Frederick to be bussed both ways, so she wouldn't have to pile the girls in the minivan and transport him every day.

So let me reset the scene: a child, diagnosed with moderate to severe Autism, who craves sameness and routine, is now off the "miracle drug" Risperidone and will be put on a new bus with a new driver and taken on a new route to a new school with all new teachers.

Shockingly, it didn't go well.

On the first day, getting Frederick into the school bus was harder emotionally than physically. It was one of those moments that every parent goes through, whether they have neurotypical kids or special needs kids. When do I give in? When do I stand strong? When a kid cries as the mom leaves for a first sleepover, what do you do? Ultimately, you have to decide what's right for the child. And sometimes the medicine tastes bad, but it will cure what ails them. In this instance all three of us—Frederick, Bernadette, and I—tasted the medicine, and it was bitter. But it was for the best. If we gave in and let him stay home on day one, then day two would be worse. If we drove him in our car, the next day would be even harder. The best medicine for Frederick would be to get him in that bus, get him into a classroom, and re-introduce the structure into his life that had been missing since school ended in June.

I got in my car and followed the bus. I stayed a few car lengths behind, figuring it would be insulting if the driver knew I was shadowing her.

The trip took ten minutes. When I pulled up there was a long line of buses that outnumbered the amount of planes on a runway after a weather delay. Kids were getting unloaded everywhere. How would they manage to take care of Frederick?

I was a little too enthusiastic with my surveillance because I suddenly realized I had pulled into the buses-only lane. After a frantic, high-speed reverse, I pulled into the general parking lot and drove forward until I had a good view of where each bus unloaded their precious cargo. I was maybe 50 yards away, but I kept my head down so Frederick wouldn't see me. My eyes were just above dashboard level as I watched one bus after another smoothly pull up, get greeted by a new set of teachers, then quickly unload.

As I waited, I wondered where security was? Shouldn't their walkie-talkies be crackling right about now—"Unidentified male Caucasian, parking lot, staring at kids, please apprehend."

Finally, Frederick's bus pulled up to the drop-off area and two teachers walked over to greet it. They got the first kid out and walked him to another teacher who escorted him into the school, then went back to the bus for the next kid. They repeated the same sequence each time until there was only one child left—Frederick.

A teacher got in, and then 30 seconds passed. Another teacher then got in. Finally, after nearly a minute had elapsed, Frederick was led out by two teachers, one on each arm. As I watched his forced march the only thing I could think of was the Kentucky Derby in reverse. Each year, at least one horse doesn't want to enter the gate so a few track people get summoned to do the dirty work—they put a guy on each side of the horse's butt, clasp hands across its tail and use their arms to shove the horse into the gate. I was watching the opposite. The bell had rung, the horses had left the gate, but Frederick refused to go.

After a few steps, he yanked his hands away. The teachers stopped without reacting. Frederick looked around, not recognizing where he was, getting led into a strange school by two people he'd never met. I wanted to run over, pick him up and run him back to the car, telling him "No school, no school, Daddy and Frederick go play."

But this was for the best. I hoped.

After a long, slow walk to the school, Frederick disappeared. As I drove away, the same thought kept popping into my head. And even though I was alone, and not a real big fan of talking to myself (or bad grammar), I kept muttering that thought out loud—"Breaks your heart, don't it? Breaks your heart, don't it?"

For the ten-minute ride home, every time I got overwhelmed, that phrase fell out of my mouth and hung in the air. "Breaks your heart, don't it?" It was a detached observation, as if I was telling it to another person as we observed something tragic that had no personal connection to us, like reading an obituary about a child dying. "Breaks your heart, don't it?" you might say, then move on with your day.

The experiment with stimulant medication ended with a whimper, not a bang. He was on it for five days, with no change. None. It would have helped almost instantly if it was going to work, but it didn't, so we quickly gave up. Naturally, we couldn't start right back on the Risperidone. First we had to endure a few days of cold turkey (again), then very slowly reintroduce the medicine, ramping up over several weeks.

Summer school was a disaster. Each day, the teachers sent home a sheet about what activities the kids did, and on that sheet were two pre-printed faces: a happy one and a sad one. They circled the appropriate face each day to tell the parents what kind of mood the child was in, or what kind of day they had overall. Frederick never got a smiley face. Every single day, for four weeks of summer school, he came home with a sad face—on his paper, and on his actual face.

The teachers were doing their best I guess, but they were dealt a bad hand because of our useless medication experiment. One day, the sheet read "Frederick did not participate; we allowed him to wander the classroom."

By the time we ramped up to the full dose of Risperidone, things were back to 'normal.' He was still a handful, but he was ten times better than he had been all summer and most important, he was eating. But that was August 7, which meant our "summer" lasted less than three weeks.

# 18 FAMILY VACATION OR ENJOYABLE VACATION?

With the twins now at an age where they could (Grace) or should (Frederick) begin to enjoy some big-kid adventures, our thoughts turned to the possibility of a family vacation.

My childhood had ingrained in me three basic principles: the first was that family vacations should be tense. Second, they should lack enjoyment. And third, they had to include the whole family.

Over the years, my sister and brothers and I were subjected to dozens of vacations, ranging from stressful to awful. Honestly, I'm surprised there isn't a form of PTSD called PFVD (Post Family Vacation Disorder.)

My family outings were like those 1970's chain gang movies where the prisoners are shackled together by the ankles; if one convict tries to run away, he brings down the whole group. Their freedom is compromised by the mere existence of every other person. And that's what it was like on the Ocean City Boardwalk or at a cabin in the Poconos. We were forced to move as a group, and if one person was slightly out of sync it ruined it for everybody. It was a zero-sum game. My siblings and I were scavengers, each of us trying to score a little sliver of time to enjoy exactly what we wanted to do without it being ruined by a brother or sister.

I'm sure Bernadette's family vacations were slightly more palatable than mine, but she was also from the school of No Child Left Behind. Her parents, like mine, had their children travel in a pack. Another common thread between Bernadette and I was that we were both Disney Dorks. To us, Walt Disney World was sacred ground, like Lourdes or Graceland. When we got engaged and were discussing wedding plans, we talked about honeymoon locations. "I know where I want to go," she said. "I know where I want to go too, but I'm embarrassed to say it," was my response. We wrote our preferred destination on pieces of paper, exchanged them, and then read each other's at the same time. Both papers said Disney.

During our honeymoon, we talked about bringing our kids back to Disney World someday and showing them all the dorky things we did there. So now it was time.

I did some research on Disney's accommodations for kids with disabilities. I'd heard that kids with Autism can go to the front of the line, but that was only a small part of the equation. I had to visualize every moment of the week and put myself there with Frederick to see if all obstacles were surmountable. Some practical points included: can we legally acquire enough elephant tranquilizer to get Frederick to behave on the flight down? Could he wait the 10-20 minutes for the bus from the Disney hotel to the Theme Parks? Would he behave on the bus? Would we spend most of our time trying to calm him down within the parks? And—God forbid—what if he actually had to poop during the week? He never had a "road win" to his credit; every time he had gone #2 it was in the confines of our own home.

I came to the inevitable conclusion that if we were going to do this, we had to leave Frederick behind. I thought about the Disney Super Bowl spot we used to do at NFL Films each year. If I had won the MVP my commercial would say:

Digger O'Brien, you just won the Super Bowl. What are you going to do next?

"I'm going to Disney World—but leaving my son with Autism at home!" Cue the fireworks.

But it was the right call. If we had brought Frederick, every day would have been two separate vacations—one for him and the parent with him, and another for the girls and the other parent. Bernadette fought the idea. "I am not going on a family vacation without my whole family." But she eventually came around and understood it was the right call. We booked it, then told the girls. Afterwards, Bernadette cried, and Grace said "What's wrong with Mommy?"

"She's just so happy," I said, lying through my teeth. "And excited."

I thought at the time, and still think, that this was a big step for Bernadette and I as parents. It was accepting the way things were and doing what was best for our daughters and for Frederick instead of trying to pretend we were a "normal" family.

The weeks leading up to the vacation were a nightmare for Bernadette. Every waking thought involved Frederick: How would we tell him? Would he understand? What if he thinks we're never coming back? She decided to make a booklet that my parents or her parents could read to him every morning that would serve as a day-by-day, step-by-step tour guide through his Week of Abandonment. We left on a Thursday, so page 1 of the booklet said "Thursday" and had a photo of his school, our house, and one of her parents. The next page was Friday, and it had the same thing. Saturday and Sunday had photos of her parents and their house, since they were taking him to South Jersey. Monday and Tuesday had photos of our house, school, and my parents because it would be their turn to relieve her parents. Wednesday had a photo of school and a photo of us since, barring delays, we'd be home by 8:00 pm.

The morning we left, we drove him to school. Before walking him up, we stood outside the car with him so Bernadette could debrief.

"Frederick, Mommy and Daddy and Anna and Grace are going bye-bye for a few days," she said.

Frederick hopped in the air. "Few days," he repeated.

"But we'll be back soon so you don't have to worry."

In a sing-song voice likely borrowed from a *Blue's Clues* episode, he lilted, "Don't worry, ish okay."

Bern's eyes were gushing tears as she hugged him. "Yes, it will be okay. It will be okay."

You would think it's easier when your child doesn't get it, but somehow it's not, and I don't know why. The guilt hit me hard, so I began making a mental list of why we should take him. It's not Frederick's fault he has Autism; his inability to wait in line for 10 seconds is not his fault; his penchant for falling on the ground and laying there for a minute is not his fault; his desire to hit strangers every time a child cries is not his fault. None of it was his fault, but it felt like we were punishing him for it.

Those were the thoughts running through my head as our flight left Philly for Orlando.

I selected middle and aisle seats, rather than a pair of middle and window seats, and naturally, the window seat next to me was unoccupied, just in case I had forgotten we left my son behind.

The girls didn't mention Frederick. Anna was reading, and Grace was bugging a salesman in the window seat next to her.

"Where you going?" she asked

"I'm traveling to Orlando for work," the guy answered.

"Are you married? Where's your wife?"

"She wasn't able to come with me."

"How old are you?"

He just laughed.

"Where are you going?" she asked again.

"I said Orlando."

"I thought this plane was going to Florida?"

After we landed and checked in, we changed into bathing suits and made a bee-line to the centerpiece of Disney's Port Orleans Hotel—a giant swimming pool with a humungous water slide that looks like a dragon. The vacation had begun.

Professionally, I took a break that week—didn't bring anything to watch for work, didn't bring scripts to rewrite, didn't bring books to research. Unfortunately, I couldn't shelve my hobby, which was scoping out special needs kids. When we got to the pool, Anna jumped in, Bernadette jumped in, Grace jumped in with her little vest on, and I was about to jump in when I noticed him: a kid, maybe 17, tall and gangly, almost imperceptibly talking to himself. I looked closer: the nose seemed misshapen, the bottom teeth and jaw seemed too far forward. And then the not-so-subtle markers appeared: he walked up the steps on the spine of the dragon, ignoring the long line of kids waiting; they stared, mouths open, at this big kid who butted in line. He walked to the top, entered the Dragon's mouth, and slid down with his hands up. Diagnosis: Fragile X Syndrome.

I had become a secret agent in the field of special needs. In *The Bourne Identity*, Matt Damon's character sits in a diner and explains to his lady-friend how his radar's always on. All he ever does is memorize the license plates in a parking lot or size up who's in a room and what his escape route is. He can't stop. It's his obsession.

That was me. If I had a pair of expensive sunglasses, a loose-cannon partner, and a police chief who popped Tums like breath mints, I could have starred in a prime-time TV show.

Another kid caught my eye, maybe 10 years old, very overweight. Bright yellow shorts, almost blinding. He never looked up, only down. Had subtle little stims where he would roll his hands around his wrist, the way people do when their wrist is stiff or sore, and he did it constantly. He stayed by himself in the shallow end and hopped. That's all. Didn't play with anyone, didn't swim, just hopped. Then he got out and an older woman, at least 70, put a towel around him. Where were the parents? Dead, divorced, or back in the room taking a well-deserved break?

The third kid I saw was a beautiful little boy with Down Syndrome. He was really skinny, really huggy and really kissy, the stereotype of the sweet and innocent Down's kid. He had the little floaty-things on his arm and he was swimming with his sister, his mom, his dad, and his grandparents. For a moment I watched him jump around and splash and make his sister genuinely laugh. And then I glanced at his parents, who were my age but better looking and in better shape, and I thought "I hope I look as happy as they look."

But I knew I rarely did.

I didn't know them, and could only observe them from afar, but they seemed to be locked in, content, happy, in the moment. In a word: accepting. I had the urge to talk to the family. I wasn't sure how I would start the conversation, but I kept edging near them every time Anna and Grace were around them, hoping to bump them or lock eyes. I wanted to tap the kid's sister and say "Hey, you see that redhead over there, the one your age? That's my Anna and she has a special needs brother just like you. And you're both awesome big sisters. You guys get to use the EZ-Pass lane on the way to heaven."

And I wanted to talk to the guy, dad to dad. The conversation would go something like this

"We have a son, her twin." I'd point at Grace. "He had to stay home back in Philly. Too much for him."

"Down's?" he'd say, catching my drift.

I'd shake my head. "No, Autism."

That would be it. Just to let him know we're not a clueless, lucky family with only typical kids. Before walking back I'd glance over my shoulder.

"Hey. You're doing a helluva job, man. This stuff ain't easy."

I feel like I have an affinity with these guys, the dads who have the special needs kids. I feel like I could come up and converse with them the same way I've ambled over to old guys wearing sweatshirts of my alma mater, Notre Dame.

Maybe I should start a tradition. At big vacation resorts like Disney we could start a Special Dads Club, complete with an interlocking "S" and "D" logo like the interlocking "ND" of Notre Dame. We'd all meet at a bar wearing the ribbons of our cause. I'd walk over to a guy, read his ribbon like it was a nametag and say, "Wow, Cerebral Palsy. That's no picnic."

It's silly, but in some ways, not. When I see a kid with Down Syndrome, or a kid in a wheelchair, or a kid with any kind of special needs, their Dads and I have as much or more in common as the guys who walked the same college campus I did. The special needs dads are an alumni group, or maybe we're current students at the same Life University, the same School of Hard Knocks, the place where we learn to laugh and cry and cope.

Luckily, the Magic Kingdom is still Magic even when you're missing a child, so it was a memorable and worthwhile week. But as we walked with the girls and went on rides, I looked at every other family and wondered: are they missing one too? Did they leave a kid behind? Or worse, bury one? It's sick, but that's how I think. And most times, I figure other people don't have some sad backstory and are actually as blissfully happy as they look. Or, if they are cranky and miserable, I try to tell them telepathically that they don't deserve healthy kids because they don't appreciate them. No one has ever telepathically answered back.

During the week, Bernadette and I kept a running score, tallying all the things Frederick would have liked and all the things he could not have handled. He would have loved "It's a Small World." He would have loved all the stores and all the stuffed Mickeys and Goofys. And he would have really loved that Dragon Slide at the pool.

But he would not have liked the 90 degree heat, or the relentless afternoon sun. He would not have liked the crowded fast food joints, where he'd have to wait until the girls got their food before sitting down for his eggless waffles and soy yogurt. And of course, we would have had to refrigerate them back in the hotel room and bring them every day.

Those are things he wouldn't have liked. But there were also things he just could not have handled. He couldn't have waited 10-15 minutes for a bus every day or sat still as it took the 20-minute ride to the parks. He was not cognitively or physically able to stand in line for long, and would have occasionally lain down in the middle of Main Street USA and screamed. He was a full-time job for two people, which means that Anna and Grace would have gotten the shaft.

**The girls at Disney, without their brother.**

Several times during the trip, Bernadette or I would spontaneously look at the other and say "He couldn't handle this." Maybe we were assuaging our guilt. But most likely, we were accurate.

But we also had moments where we knew if we could beam him into this exact spot, skipping the plane ride and the bus ride over and the line into the park and the blistering sun and the noise and the colors and the lights, that he would have loved what we were doing. Bernadette had more of those moments than me.

But Bernadette doesn't have her own special needs radar, and mine was on constantly. I noticed every kid in a wheelchair, every mom using sign language. Selfishly, I saw a lot of struggles with these children that made me feel pretty good about Frederick and our whole family situation. But I also noticed sadness in the parent's faces, and I saw what was missing, the what-could-have-been feelings registering briefly, like a candle flicker, in parents' eyes. Most notably, I saw it on a bus from Epcot back to our hotel.

Every seat was taken, and a dozen people were standing (and, by the way, how do they get away with no seatbelts on these buses?) And I noticed a woman and her son, and the boy had some type of disability. I immediately looked around to see if anyone else noticed. When you see a kid with severe cerebral palsy, sitting in a wheelchair with his head lolling around, moving to a separate rhythm than the rest of his body, you can look around and see that everyone has noticed. You watch people's eyes, they flit back and forth. Some of the brave ones even try to make eye contact with the parents, conveying some sense of "I noticed, and I feel for you." But on this bus, no one else, including Bernadette, seemed to notice this kid.

He looked to be in his mid-twenties with wispy, dirty-blond hair and a soft, fine beard you see on high school kids when they try to grow one before they're ready. He wasn't short, but everything about him was dainty—thin nose, delicate fingers. He was sitting next to his Mom, and never stood up or spoke, which is why no one but me understood what was going on. But I could just tell he had some kind of intellectual disability because I watched him look around, and it was the way a child looks around, the way a little kid's eyes register newness when he's on a bus in Disney World. Anyone else in their mid-20's would have been indifferently observing; this kid was watching.

And he wore the full Disney Tourist Uniform: Mickey hat, Disney T-shirt with several characters and the Cinderella Castle behind them, and a Disney fanny pack. No typical 20-something guy would be caught dead in that outfit. His t-shirt wasn't an ironical Mickey t-shirt favored by hipsters, it was the kind Grandmoms wear as they scooter around the mall.

And if I needed further proof, I got it from his mom. She was in her 50's, attractive, handsome might even be an appropriate word. She seemed intelligent and comfortable and manicured. But her eyes flitted from one family to the next, always looking down at their child and then up at the parents. She was doing what I was doing—taking her own mental roll call of the "normal" families, playing the bitter game of what might have been.

Then she closed her eyes. Not to sleep, but to stop her brain. And without saying anything, she put her hand on her son's, patted it, then left her hand there. It wasn't overly lovey, it was just a "I'm glad we're here" type of gesture. But the kid pulled his hand away. Because even though he was in his mid-20's, he was only a little kid developmentally, and little kids of a certain age don't want their mommies to hold their hand. So his mom suffered one more reminder.

We had the Big Reminder all week. But in the end, it was a good vacation. And worth it. But it wasn't complete.

On the final day we went shopping at Disney's Pleasure Island, had a nice lunch, another dip in the pool, then off to the airport. Because of a delay out of Orlando, and waiting on bags in Philly, Frederick was asleep by the time we got home. We snuck in on him and kissed him, and then Bernadette looked at me and said "In his book, the picture said we'd be home today. He thinks we're liars.'"

But he was happy the next morning, jumping up and down on his bed when he saw me, and hugged Grace and Anna until they screamed for mercy. And he loved his Goofy stuffed animal and the Mickey Mouse poster for his room.

So Frederick was fine. But Bernadette and I were not fine.

We knew he was unable to grasp the concept of a missed family vacation, yet all we could talk about was how to make it up to him.

# 19 ANYTHING YOUR HEART DESIRES

I was confident that leaving Frederick home and going to Disney World with the girls had been the right thing to do, but it didn't make the decision any easier to live with. So that first week after we got back we made a list of "Things To Do With Frederick In Order To Make Up For Screwing Him Out Of A Disney Vacation." It ended up being a short list because we scratched out everything we came up with.

~~Sesame Street Island in Jamaica~~ (If we couldn't fly him to Orlando how can he handle a flight to the Caribbean?)

~~Big Bear Lodge Water Park~~ (Frederick regularly drinks his bath water, and those pools are petri dishes.)

~~Take him to Bouncing Off the Walls~~ (It's an ordinary Kiddie Gym five minutes from our house, so to make it fair based on what he missed in Disney we'd have to take him every night for six months)

We couldn't think of anything extravagant or memorable, so we settled on our go-to excursion—Sesame Place.

**Frederick's mood when we get there early.**

Sesame Place was a *Sesame Street* theme park tucked away a few miles from our new home in Pennsylvania. It had plenty of rides and shows in addition to the water park aspect, but it was relatively small and not too overwhelming. I had taken Frederick to Sesame a few times that year, always with a game plan. I had found over the years that taking Frederick out of the house without thinking through the effects of the crowds and the noise at our eventual destination was a recipe for disaster. Even taking him to church involved as much planning as the Normandy Invasion (Where do we sit—front or back? Do we bring snacks? One juice box or two? And don't bring the toys he talks to. Or the books he pretends he can read out loud.)

A typical trip to Sesame Place was quick and clean. We'd get there right as the park opened, put in about an hour, and then go home. In and out. But on this day, the day I was going to make up for leaving him behind on the Disney trip, Bernadette stayed home and my mom decided she wanted to go with us. By the time she was ready it was after lunch.

When we got there the park was jammed. We should have turned around and gone home, because there's one thing I've learned with Frederick: don't force it.

But I owed it to him. So I forced it.

We got in the back of a line at the entrance gate, a line that appeared to be a minimum ten-minute wait. I held his hand tight. He looked around, and it took about five seconds for him to understand what was happening. *I have to wait in this line?* he was thinking. *I never wait in a line at Sesame.* Then he lost it and started screaming. "Go see Elmo! Go see Cookie!" He pulled my hand, trying to drag me to the front.

"We have to wait. Frederick, you have to wait."

He lay on the ground, arching his back, kicking. His face was instantly soaked with tears. I looked around: of the two hundred or so people in the four lines, roughly half were staring at Frederick.

For the second time since arriving, I contemplated taking him home. And I had an opportunity here for a teaching moment. I could have picked him up and said "No crying, Frederick, if you don't stop we go home." He would not have stopped, and we could have left. I'd be getting out of a bad situation, and Frederick would (hopefully) understand that his behaviors could jeopardize a preferred activity.

Instead, I put him over my shoulder and carried him the way a firefighter carries an unconscious victim, except that this unconscious victim was punching my back and kicking my chest.

I walked to the far left side of the gate, where there was a guard manning a turnstile, but no line of people. I knew from previous trips that this was the re-entry line, used only for people returning to the park who had been there earlier in the day.

The security guard stood up out of his chair. "Sir, can I see your stamp?" I checked to make sure he wasn't armed.

"My son has special needs and he can't wait in line," I explained. "We get the orange band every time."

The guard waved his hand "I'm sorry, you're going to have to wait in line."

I was a little pissed off Frederick couldn't wait in line, I was more pissed off he couldn't go to Disney World, and I was unbelievably pissed off about Autism and this semi-retired security guard.

"Do you have eyes? Can you see what the hell is going on here?" I said.

The guard stepped back, stunned. I shoved our season passes under the barcode scanner, pulled them out just as quick, not sure if they had registered but quite sure I wasn't checking. I put Frederick down, knowing he'd run into the park. He did.

I shrugged my shoulders at the guard. "Oh well. Gotta catch him," I said, gesturing toward Frederick as he raced into a gift shop.

I caught up to Frederick as he was poking and kissing Abby Cadabby dolls. My mom arrived a few seconds later. "You could have been nicer," she said.

But "nice" wasn't why we were here. It was guilt, pure and simple.

Next up was Guest Relations to find Frederick's name in the computer so he could get an orange band that allowed him to cut in front of all the neurotypical kids and their parents, who stare daggers through me as we do it. I forced a smile at the young lady behind the counter. "Hi, I'm here to get my orange band for my son, who, as you can see, either has Autism or is in need of an exorcism."

"Last name?"

"Let's try O-apostrophe-B-R-I-E-N."

She typed it in. "I can't seem to find it."

"Of course not," I said. "Let's try without the apostrophe."

As the young lady was entering the info, a kid and his dad got in line behind me. The boy was a tall, lanky teenager. I nodded hello and turned back to the counter.

"I've been here before. We usually get the orange thing no problem."

She shrugged her shoulders. "I'm sorry sir, I have to look you up and enter a condition." And then out of nowhere....

"OH MY GOSH LOOK ITS BIG BIRD. BIG BIRD'S ON THE FLOOR. LOOK DAD IT'S BIG BIRD. HELLO BIG BIRD!" I slowly turned around at the smiling teenager whose voice level was not so much shouting or screaming but the same voice you use to be heard in a noisy room.

The kid's eyes caught mine.

"LOOK THERE'S BIG BIRD. YOU'RE STANDING ON BIG BIRD!"

I looked down; the welcome mat had a Big Bird image embossed in the carpet strands.

The Dad put his hand on the kid's shoulders.

"It's ok Billy. We'll see Big Bird later."

"YES, SEE HIM LATER, AND WE'LL HAVE LOTS OF FUN!"

Normally, this is where my comparison tool kicks in. I spot a special needs kid and go down the list of strengths Frederick has over the kid. *Well, at least Frederick can walk. Well, at least Frederick's not self-injurious.* And this pointless little exercise usually ends with me saying a silent prayer of thank you that my road ahead will not be as tough as the other parent's. But in this instance, I weighed Billy's Autism causing him to be childish and unable to regulate his voice level and inflection, versus Frederick being unable to wait in line for more than three seconds, and for one of the very few times in this ridiculous mind game I play, I thought to myself, "If that's Frederick in ten years, sign me up."

I finally got the orange band; the winning combination was O(space)Brien, after unsuccessful attempts with O-Brien, O_Brien, and Obrien.

We went back into the gift shop and Frederick immediately went to his favorite spot where there are television monitors running loops of the *Sesame Street* DVD's. After 15 minutes of awkward silence between my mom and me as Frederick repeated the videos from memory, I gently suggested to him it was time to enjoy some of the rides.

He hit the floor, screaming so loud I thought someone would perform a citizen's arrest and charge me with child abuse, and then he began rolling around on the ground. Every time I whispered "Hey Buddy, let's go see the Elmo show" or "Time to see Cookie and give him a hug" he unleashed another paroxysm of wailing.

The obvious decision was to buy whatever he wanted, but he didn't want to buy anything. All he wanted to do was stay in the gift shop and watch videos, and maybe occasionally meander from one stuffed character to the other, poking them ritualistically.

So maybe Frederick, my mom and I should have spent the day in there, or stayed as long as we could until someone asked us to move along.

I knew it was all my fault. He's usually great at Sesame Place because we show up before it opens and leave before it gets crowded, and maybe I should have gone home the minute we saw the crowd. But goddamnit, I was going to make up for the Disney Debacle. And if Clark Griswold could drag his kids across the country to see WallyWorld, I could drag Frederick out of this gift shop to hug the real Big Bird.

So I took him by the hand and dragged him out of the gift shop. When we got through the door, Frederick collapsed on the pavement, still wailing. He needed to come to terms with the idea of not staring at a ten-inch Super Grover for the rest of the day, so I decided to give him a minute to properly mourn.

The only people in the immediate vicinity were a couple who were in the middle of an argument, most likely concerning how dismaying it was that their neurotypical three-year-old was acting like a three-year-old. I would have lectured them about how lucky they were, but at this point Frederick was on the ground, screaming.

The husband wore a tank top, probably stood 6'2" and weighed over 300 lbs. Frederick was on his back, kicking his feet and rubbing his eyes. The guy glanced in my direction, then darted his eyes down to Frederick. A brief look of disgust washed over his face. He caught my eye again then looked back at his wife, and speaking at a volume and tone meant for my ears, he answered his wife's chirping with "Hang on, I can't hear you. It's a little loud around here." He glanced back at me with a look that told me if his kid was the same age he would never pull a stunt like Frederick was pulling.

I'm not a tall man, so maybe it's a Napoleon complex. Or maybe just anger. Whatever the cause, I'd become much more confrontational since Frederick's diagnosis shattered my world. So it was 'go time.'

I closed the ten feet of space between us in a millisecond. EnormoGuy was reaching into his stroller for something and I stood almost on top of him.

"I dare you. I dare you to say something."

His head spun around and his eyes widened, probably more shocked than scared at the rage in my voice. He took a second to process the scene, then dove back into the bottom of the stroller, looking for whatever it was he had already found, hoping I'd go away.

And then my mom walked by, pulling Frederick, "Ok say 'Cmon Daddy, time to go on the rides.'" I slowly backed away, hoping the dude would look at me. He didn't.

I had officially lost my mind.

Frederick can be the most enjoyable, effervescent little boy you've ever met. But there are days when Autism makes him less tolerant and less tolerable. I thought I'd seen him at his worst but this day at Sesame was his low point and, by extension, mine. He was a wild child, his natural human instincts overrun by an animalistic fury. He was biting, kicking, throwing himself down and slamming his head on the asphalt; this was the side of Autism I'd read about in books and always thanked my lucky stars I didn't have to deal with. But I did that day. We were at the park for 45 minutes, probably 44 too long, and by any definition it was torture. For me, for my mom, and for Frederick.

But I was not going to be denied. As we were walking toward the exits, I saw one last opportunity to salvage an enjoyable, memorable moment.

The daily character parade was about to begin, so the three of us sat down on a brick landscaping wall. All around us, parents were settling in with their children. Everywhere I looked there was a typical family enjoying a beautiful day. Some kids sat on their mom's laps while others danced and held their dad's hand. For some unexplained reason, Frederick was calm at this moment. I turned to my Mom and shrugged, "Let's see if he can chill for a minute. I'd hate to leave without him seeing any of the guys."

After two nice minutes where Frederick was relaxed and enjoying himself, the loudspeaker blared an announcement, and he slammed his hands over his ears. I tried to bear hug him, hoping the deep pressure would calm him, but to no avail—he was cooked. He thrashed out of my bear hug then fell out onto the parade route, kicking his feet, rubbing his eyes, and shaking his head back and forth.

"We're done" I said, and threw Frederick over my shoulders. I adjusted him so he was sitting on my neck, his legs dangling down my chest. I held his ankles so he wouldn't fall but as we walked out he tore at my face with long fingernails that he would never let us cut, each swipe opening up a hot, stinging line on my face. I let go of his feet and grabbed his wrists, but within a few steps I was barely keeping him in balance, so instead of risking him falling I let go of his wrists and grabbed his ankles again. I was partially blinded for the last few hundred yards of the walk; Frederick managed to scratch both of my eyeballs so all I could see in front of me was a watery blur of figures, but the Sesame patrons who walked close enough so I could make out their facial features all wore horrified looks on their faces.

As we headed toward the exit, it felt like I was walking through a wall of thorny vines as Frederick's fists and fingers kept hitting and cutting at ferocious speeds. But I kept moving. It was the only way to get out of there.

As we neared the gates, I felt a hand on my arm and heard my mom's voice, which was quivering, as if she was trying to keep from crying.

"You know, this isn't easy. Frederick's a lucky guy."

I could also hear the parade starting behind us as we walked through the entrance gate, and I thought back to the parade in Disney World, sitting there in the hot sun with Bernadette and Anna and Grace, but no Frederick. That whole week in Orlando I had mostly stayed in the moment and tried to enjoy a vacation that was missing one person. But I did cry once—during the parade down Main Street.

There in the heart of Disney World, I was baking in the sun and already bored with the slow-moving cavalcade of characters. They all ran together for me—Tinkerbell,

Cinderella, Beauty and the Beast—I couldn't tell one from another, and I was mentally looking ahead for what happened after the parade. Should we get a bite to eat? Should we take the kids to the bathroom? Or go back to the hotel? If so, bus or ferry boat?

And then the Pinocchio float came into view.

If I had been given a quiz on *Pinocchio* prior to this parade, I would have failed it. I vaguely remembered Pinocchio as a doll that came to life, and that was pretty much it; sort of a wooden version of Frosty the Snowman. But the Disney folks know how to boil a narrative down to its essential elements, and as the Pinocchio float approached, the loudspeaker told the gist of the story in about 20 seconds.

Apparently, this Geppetto guy wanted a son so he made the wooden puppeta a substitute. But in order for Pinocchio to become human he had to prove himself, because it's a Disney movie and it needs a heroic arc. And when the float passed us, the loudspeaker blared the words, in Pinocchio's voice, that stabbed me like a knife: "I dreamed of becoming a real boy."

And I cried. I cried so hard in that hot Disney sun I had to stand up and walk away so my daughters wouldn't see me. I cried because my only son Frederick was 1,000 miles away in Pennsylvania, sitting in an Autism support class with four other boys. Maybe they dreamed of being real boys, too.

I don't know if Frederick dreams of being a "real boy." I don't know what he knows and doesn't know about his disease. I'm not sure if he realizes he's in a similar body but is completely different than other kids.

In the movie, Jiminy Cricket sings that "anything your heart desires will come to you." My heart desires a lot of things I'm never going to have. One of my simplest desires is the ability to take Frederick to places we'd enjoy together. But I couldn't take him to Disney for a family vacation. I couldn't take him to any of the Super Bowls I attended. I couldn't take him to a Notre Dame game and show him the dorm where I lived.

My heart was in my dream, but apparently the request was too extreme: I couldn't even take Frederick to a little theme park five minutes from my house.

# 20 REGRETS ONLY

I was already in bed the night Hank Aaron broke baseball's all-time home run record. My Dad came up to tell me, and then he let me go downstairs to watch the replays and all the pageantry on the field.

The images of Aaron rounding the bases and getting mobbed at home plate are still vivid in my mind, but I honestly don't know if those memories are from that night or from seeing the replay a hundred times in the forty years since. Really, it doesn't matter. The most important thing from that night isn't the home run, it's that my Dad came and got me.

Sports had always been my passion and my hobby and, now, my profession, but I couldn't fully share them with my son.

I produced the open to Super Bowl XXXIX for NFL Films' "Game of the Week", which meant I was responsible for the first 4-5 minutes of the show that led up to kickoff. It was my job to tell the story of the teams and set up the characters and storyline. I was looking through the pregame footage from all the cameramen we had at the game and I came across a shot of Patriots Linebacker Tedy Bruschi cavorting with his young sons on the field, hours before the game, well before all the players and pregame entertainers turned the gridiron into a circus. They were racing, playing, and frolicking like ponies. At one point, Tedy got down on the grass and his kids ran over and jumped on him. We had the shots from a few different angles, including some trademark NFL Films slow-motion clips. The look of pure joy on Bruschi's face was priceless.

I hated those shots.

In fact, I knew it was a no-brainer to use a few of them in the open, but I wasn't planning to. It hurt too much. But then my boss, Steve Sabol, stopped by for a few minutes to ask how the show was going, and as he was leaving my office he said "How 'bout that shot of Bruschi's kids, huh?" So I had to use it.

My attempts to play sports with Frederick were equally depressing. I thought he might like golf since repeating the same swing over and over again is the key to success, and there are no teammates to interact with while playing. So one day we pulled up to the driving range at our local public course, where there were maybe a dozen people practicing. We had our fresh bucket of yellow balls with the double-black stripes nestled in the grass. I took out the tiny little driver I had bought for Anna years ago and said, "Ready?" and Frederick fired back "Ready?" And so we were ready.

I stood behind him and put the club in his hand. I tried to get his grip right, with my hands over his. I told him to bend his knees and when he didn't, I reached down to push the back of his knees and he started laughing because it tickled. I said "Here we go."

"Here we go," he answered.

"Swing!" I said.

"Shhhwing!" he repeated.

"Now hit ball."

"Hit ball."

We swung together and when club met ball it was all sweet spot. The sound was a brilliant, intoxicating "crack." Our follow through could have been bronzed and put on a trophy. And since Frederick doesn't play catch and has never kicked a soccer ball more than twice in a row, it was the first truly athletic moment I had ever experienced with my son. It seemed like it happened in slow motion. I watched the majestic path of the ball as it bounced six or seven times and then finally nestled about 40 yards in front of us.

And then Frederick took off running.

In retrospect, I should have seen it coming. Every time we had played in the backyard, and every time he had watched his sisters play with the neighborhood kids, the ball was ours and we re-used it. Simple as that. It was not disposable. If we threw a football and no one caught it, someone would jog over and pick it up. If someone hit a wiffle ball, it would be thrown back to the batter. When someone kicked a soccer ball, another person kicked it back.

So if I really had special dad superpowers I would have anticipated this. But I didn't. And before I could react, my son was running onto a live driving range to retrieve his ball while a dozen people of varying skill level were practicing.

When I caught up to him I grabbed his wrist and started pulling him back. He quickly dropped to the ground. I had to decide whether to reason with him and avoid a scene or drag him back. It wasn't much of an option. I didn't care if the Child Welfare police were going to come after me, I had to get him out of the line of fire.

"Git ball! Git ball" he screamed as I dragged him through the clumpy grass. By the time we got back to our clubs he was a dirty, sobbing mess. He arched his back and rolled over, kicking his feet up.

"Git ball! Git ball."

I waited about two minutes and tried to talk him through it, rubbing his back. "It's ok buddy, its ok. The ball went bye-bye. The ball went bye-bye."

When he finally got up, I knew that would be the theme to get him through it.

"Frederick," I said, with a big smile on my face. "Do you want to play bye-bye ball"

His eyebrows arched; this sounded tempting. "Bye-bye ball?"

"Yes, bye-bye ball," I nodded. "Watch!"

I crouched low with his tiny club in hand. "You swing, hit the ball." I cracked it a good hundred yards. "And then you wave and say 'Bye-bye ball'"

I jumped around, waving bye-bye.

He came right over and we hit another 20 golf balls, hopping, waving, and occasionally blowing kisses to each ball that scorched the ground on a multi-hop journey to its final resting place.

When we were done with the bucket we wandered over to the putting green. In order not to confuse him, I brought only one ball. We used the little driver and I set the first ball down three inches from the hole. We tapped it in together and he yelled "In the hole!"

And then I saw him.

Little Tiger. The Cub. Tiglet. Over the years I've given him many nicknames. His real name will forever be a mystery.

But there he was, at the other end of this expansive, multi-hole putting green. He was probably six years old and was pimped out: navy blue Nike hat, neatly pressed navy blue Nike golf shirt, beige chinos, and saddle shoe golf spikes. And his putting stroke was better than mine.

Maybe I would have dismissed him if he was minding his own business, but he wasn't. He was minding our business.

I guess if your child is in a wheelchair you might become fascinated with the physics of walking; you might stand there in awe watching another child move freely about and marvel at the intricacies of gait. Since my son is deficient in relating to others, I notice more than most parents about how the social dance is played.

Little Tiger was glancing at us, but he wasn't looking to play with Frederick. This dance was subtle. It was, in fact, close to a mating dance. Tiglet would take his stance, strike his putt, then look at us as his ball rolled to the hole, as if he was a 23 year-old in a bar playing pool, sneaking glances at a girl across the room. He wanted to be noticed.

Frederick wasn't interested. He was busy yelling "In the hole!" every time he knocked in a six-inch putt. But I got sucked in. As I was helping Frederick line-up each putt, I became the object of the affection, the girl in the bar, because I was using Frederick as a shield and stealing glances at Little Tiger. I was noticing how good he was. I was noticing that he was dressed to emulate his golf hero. Every time the kid took a putt and looked over, I was sad and angry and vengeful. I wanted my son to play 18 holes with me. I wanted to be the Dad who taught my son how to putt like that. And then I wanted to go home. So we did.

Any thought of kids enjoying sports with their Dads gave me a hot, hollow feeling in the stomach. It got so bad that back when we lived in South Jersey I actually rooted against the Philadelphia Phillies in the playoffs because it was too painful to watch the little boys next door wear their Phillies t-shirts and talk about how "Ryan Howard's gonna hit a bomb tonight." Mercifully, the Phils were swept in the first round.

For a parent, Autism has two sides. On the one hand, a child with Autism is so ridiculously close to being "normal"—no physical deformities, no wheelchair involved—that in some ways you'd think it would be easier as a parent to deal with. But the flip side is that you look back and wonder if there was just one little thing that tipped the balance, if there was ever a point where one moment or one decision that had gone the other way might have saved your child from this difficult life.

It's easy to beat yourself up over it, and the list of weapons to use is extensive. For starters, should Bernadette and I have at least debated the idea of trying to get pregnant through artificial means? I'm sure if Frederick had turned out completely neurotypical I wouldn't be thinking about how the twins were conceived at all. I would have moved on to more important things—like the type of car I drove or getting an in-ground pool with underwater speakers, etc. But I wondered if the IVF might have contributed to his condition.

Don't get me wrong—I don't think this is "God getting us back" for violating Church principles. And it was probably ridiculous since Grace was unaffected. But I sometimes had this sinking feeling that we upset the natural order of things. I sometimes wondered if Bernadette's body wasn't getting pregnant because it knew Autism was going to happen so it was performing its own version of natural selection by avoiding a pregnancy. I even mentioned this theory to our pediatrician and asked him point blank, "Could a woman's body know that it's destined to have a child with Autism and therefore do its best not to get pregnant?" He just shook his head. "No way. No way. Remember how close kids with Autism are to normal. They have the right number of chromosomes, nothing out of the ordinary except a difference in the brain that we can't even detect or see. They are so, so close."

So close. Yet so far. Please attend my pity party. RSVP- Regrets Only. Maybe if I invited parents with special needs kids, 'Regrets Only' would be taken literally.

I also regret all the infertility shots, even the ones before the twins were born. When she was pregnant, Bernadette had to get a RhoGAM shot, and I'm still not sure what it was for. According to WedMD, "Rh disease occurs when an Rh-negative mother and her husband conceive an Rh-positive child." So now I had Rh-egrets on top of my regrets—did that shot cause Frederick's Autism?

What about immunizations? Did all the shots in the hospital and the ones he got at the pediatrician tip him into the Autism spectrum? My sister Colleen, who the kids call "Crazy Aunt Chaz," used to email me all kinds of warning about vaccines and how I should request Thimerosal-free vaccines and never get more than one shot per visit. I shrugged them off as the mad rantings of my tree-hugging sister, whom I love dearly. I even gave her a know-it-all lecture where I explained to her that the odds of my child getting a disease that we don't vaccinate for is much greater than the odds of getting Autism.

Oops.

In the last twenty years there's been a lot of talk about the link between Autism and vaccines. Everyone was worried about Thimerosal, the preservative that was part of the MMR (Measles-Mumps-Rubella) vaccine. The MMR is given to kids at about the same time that developmental delays can really begin to be noticed, so maybe it was a coincidence. But the conspiracy theorists claimed that pharmaceutical companies dumped the measles, mumps and rubella doses into one shot to make it more cost-effective, and the adding of a preservative with mercury, a known neurotoxin, has led to the dramatic rise in Autism diagnoses. Since this theory reached its boiling point in the mid 2000's, several studies have concluded that there is no link between Thimerosal and Autism.

I always thought that the Thimerosal crowd was in the ballpark, just not in the right seat. I once read a study that suggested kids with Autism suffer from brain inflammations, and they went so far as to autopsy the brains of deceased children who had Autism and corroborated the idea that kids on the spectrum essentially have "swollen brains," which led me to believe that the guilty party might be the amount of vaccines that infants and toddlers receive. Didn't matter if there was Thimerosal or not, certain kids couldn't handle that much of a vaccine load in that short of a time span. Since vaccines are meant to fool the body into mobilizing the immune system in the face of a threat, and since inflammation is the body's response, it's a decent after-the-fact argument that kids with Autism are genetically predisposed to an overreaction to vaccines. There's a saying that's popular with the Autism crowd: "Genetics loads the gun, and vaccines pull the trigger."

But what the hell do I know? My last Biology class was freshman year of high school. I'm not a doctor or a statistician. I didn't even stay at a Holiday Inn Express last night. I guess we need the Freakonomics guys to figure this out. But the following seems hard to argue with:

1) You can't have an outbreak of a genetic disease. Disorders like sickle cell, cystic fibrosis and Down Syndrome remain fixed at a certain percentage of live births.

2) Autism has exploded in the past 25 years.

3) Therefore, there must be something more than genetics involved with Autism.

The only way to disagree with the premise above is to believe that there has not been an epidemic of Autism in the last few decades. For what it's worth, the website of the National Institute for Mental Health (NIMH) stated that a report by the Centers for Disease Control (CDC) "confirms other recent epidemiologic studies documenting that more children are being diagnosed with an ASD than ever before." Some said the increase in numbers came from doctors being more knowledgeable and diagnosing more cases. Personally, I think it is an epidemic. This is based on my own unscientific (English major) study, the methodology being as follows:

Ask anyone between the age of 55 and 75 if any of their friends have a kid with Autism. (And I mean full-blown Autism—severely affected kids, children really struggling to get along in the world.) Almost all of them say no. Ask anyone between the age of 30 and 50 if any of their friends have a kid with full-blown Autism. Almost all of them say yes.

The defense rests. But there was no rest from the regrets.

On any given day, a half-dozen or more regrets flashed into my mind. Bernadette was pregnant a full 40 weeks with the twins—maybe Frederick got overcooked. Did he run out of nutrients, or oxygen? Also, about two weeks before they were born, Bernadette felt a tiny trickle of water on her leg and we went to the hospital, thinking her water broke. But they said there was no amniotic fluid coming out. False alarm. They sent us home. But what if we had insisted right then and there that 38 weeks was plenty? What if we had said "Get these kids out—now!" Would that have done the trick?

And what if Bernadette's first delivery was a C-section? It came close to that. Bernadette had a long labor with Anna, and the doctor who delivered her admitted that she was a few seconds away from giving up on the natural birth and going to the C-section. If our first baby had been a C-section, the twins probably would have been as well. If we had a C-section with the twins, would Frederick have had the breathing issues and low Apgar scores that he did?

Frederick's difficult birth was another discussion with the pediatrician. Again, he didn't see a link. "I've seen kids have great Apgar scores and severe disabilities. I've seen kids with worse Apgar scores end up perfectly fine. The fact that he was only in NICU overnight, and breast-fed well the next day, tells me that it had nothing to do with anything."

But maybe he was just saying that to make me feel good. Maybe a doctor knows what's done is done, that you can't retrieve the time, and you can't go back and force air into Frederick's lungs sooner and restore the color to his body any faster. And maybe the doctor knew that any delivery is a crapshoot and Frederick was just the margin of error in births, the one per week or the one per month that doesn't get handled well, and it resulted in this.

I started having bad dreams. One night I dreamed we got into a car accident and Frederick had a fractured skull. The surgeon came out of the operating room and said he could do this dangerous procedure which could cure Frederick's Autism, but there was a 10% chance he wouldn't make it through surgery. I said we should do it, and Bernadette started slapping my face and screaming, "I am not gonna lose my baby!"

In another dream I'm living with Bernadette and the kids in the house I grew up in. Frederick is getting ready for the first day of first grade, and he's wearing the Catholic-school uniform I wore—navy pants, short-sleeve white shirt and clip-on tie. I kneel down to adjust his tie, then rub his hair. He looks at me and smiles (he never talks in my dreams.) I open the front door, the light streams in, and the walkway to the driveway is lined with friends and family and they're all applauding. There's a limo parked and my Dad is behind the wheel, beaming. As Frederick walks ahead of me with his backpack, I shake hands and hug everyone like a Presidential candidate working the rope line. And then suddenly, I fall to my knees, sobbing. I mumble over and over, "I'm sorry. I'm sorry. I tried. I tried." I stay there on the ground and no one helps me up.

At one of our follow-up appointments with Dr. Joplin, Bernadette asked him if Frederick would ever be able to say "I love you" to her and really mean it. And then she ran out of the room crying. I broke down sobbing as well, telling him, "You know, I videotape Frederick a lot because I want to freeze him in time. It's not fair that he has to get older. I'm ok with him mentally staying young but why can't his body stop? Why? I don't want him to be tall. I don't want to have to deal with armpit hair and boners and a cheesy moustache. It's not fair!"

This was the doctor who recited Dayenu, the great Jewish song that says "it would have been enough." But this wasn't enough. Not by a long shot. I needed more.

# 21 THE JOY DEFICIT

Bernadette and I were suffering from a joy deficit.

Yes, a "joy deficit." Sounds like an 80's Brit-pop band that could have opened on tour for Depeche Mode. But that seemed the appropriate term when evaluating the situation.

If I was looking at my life on paper at that time, there would have been a graph with two bars, like a debit and credit. The bar on the left represented the pain of Autism, and the bar on the right represented the joy in my life. It took me a while to realize it, but the pain bar never moved. I had no control over it. Autism had damaged our lives, and the pain was locked in. The other bar was joy, and that was the one I could control, and I needed to find ways to make the joy bar move up. At that point, we were losing the battle; Autism was winning.

In a football game, if you're losing and the clock's running out, you just throw deep and hope something good happens. So Bernadette and I thought about throwing a Hail Mary pass.

Back in 2000, when we were going through the infertility treatments—the shots, the doctor visits, the insurance nonsense—we decided to adopt if we were unsuccessful in conceiving a baby. After Frederick and Grace were born in 2001, we put the adoption idea on the back burner. And when Frederick was 19 months old and exhibited signs of delay, it went on the waaaayyy back burner. After Frederick's Autism diagnosis at 27 months, it just sat on the oven, forgotten and charred beyond recognition. After we moved it got tossed in the garbage can.

But I never let go of the urge, even when we were slogging through the painful months and years of trying to understand, then manage, then accept Autism. So now, in 2008, we were closing in on two years at our new house and rebounding from the low point of our Lakota School misadventure. Bernadette was now happy with Frederick's teacher and his school. There were a lot of nice neighbors on the block and she was making friends. So I slowly started talking about adoption again.

I knew Bernadette was considering it because anytime things were real bad with Frederick, if he was having a tantrum or trashing the toy room, she'd say "And you want to add another child to this?"

But we had to throw our Hail Mary pass soon, or the clock would run out.

We weren't necessarily racing the clock from a legal standpoint—most programs allowed the adoptive parents to be at least 45 years old at the time of referral, so we were fine from the letter of the law. But psychologically, age was a big barrier. Would we have the energy to change diapers or chase a toddler? Did I want to teach a kid to drive when I was nearing 60? Or pay college tuition at the same time I was thinking about retirement?

And there's more involved than simply the decision to adopt; you also have to determine whether you'll go domestic or international. From what we'd heard, domestic adoptions had less of a fixed timetable than international. In other words, we might get a child in two weeks or two months or two years, and that wasn't very appealing to us. Another unsettling aspect were the laws that give the birth mother a window of time to change her mind and take the baby back. It can be as little as 24 hours, but some states allow weeks to go by. I'm sure there are good reasons for it but I couldn't stomach the thought of adopting a child then having him taken from me, whether it was after one month or one hour.

Because it was all speculative at that point, and we were just dipping our toes into the water, it made some of the decision-making easier because there was no pressure. We quickly decided we'd go the international route if we ever did it. Then we had to pick a country. At that time, the most popular programs were China, Russia, Guatemala and Korea. We eliminated China because if we were going to adopt, we'd definitely want to adopt a boy.

If we chose Russia, the child would likely fit in well, and might even look like he was one of our biological children. But I'm not sure that ever really mattered to either Bernadette or me. What made us cross Russia off the list was the travel; Russia required two separate trips, and both trips needed to be two weeks or more.

That left Guatemala and Korea. We liked Guatemala because my little brother Mike had just completed an adoption from there. It would have been nice to add another Guatemalan baby to our extended family, but there had been rumors that they would change their international adoption laws, which would mean either slowdown or, worse, total shutdown. In Guatemala, the adoption process included an in-country lawyer who was the conduit between your agency and the orphanage or foster family. That lawyer obviously had a fee, and some were apparently giving a little cut of that money to pregnant moms. So that resulted in accusations that women were getting pregnant just to give up the baby and get paid by the lawyers, which is well within the realm of believability since, according to a World Bank Report, 50% of Guatemalans lived on less than $2 per day. They had threatened to change things for years and finally did; Guatemala eventually closed to international adoptions as they worked on their new process.

For years, Korea was the model International adoption country. Most referrals were quick, the babies got excellent care, and the process was devoid of corruption. But then the country got to thinking: "Hey, if we're a top-10 GDP nation, why are we exporting all these kids?" For years, orphaned children in Korea were considered outcasts because the ideals of family and lineage were so important there. This made it difficult for Koreans to adopt other Koreans. But, like every other taboo based on fear and ignorance, it was dying a slow death. Korea began a sort of "national conversation" on keeping their precious children in the country. Eventually, a new rule went into effect: Korean babies were not eligible for international adoption until they were at least five months of age. It was a noble effort, but a consequence for prospective parents in the U.S. was the wait time increased from roughly 6 month to 18 months. We didn't have the stomach for that kind of wait, and that opened the door for the new kid on the adoption block: Ethiopia.

When we first considered adopting back in 2000, I don't think Ethiopia even had a program. But it grew, year by year, and soon became the fifth most popular country for overseas adoptions by U.S. parents. And it fit our criteria on all counts: it was pretty fast and efficient, you could choose the gender of the child, there seemed to be little to no corruption issues, and the travel in-country was about a week.

The wild card to consider was race. When I asked George, my former roommate from my bachelor days at NBA Entertainment and an African-American, about what I would say to a black son if he ever came home from school and said "Dad, why is my skin different than everyone else's?" he said "Same thing we do. You don't think I hear that? It happens to us too. We just tell her, 'Your skin is beautiful and so is your friend's skin, they're just different colors.'"

I had already convinced myself I wanted to do it; I just wasn't sure if we should do it. And Frederick was the poster child for both sides of the argument. He was the reason we should do it, and he was the reason not to do it. A little brother would be great for Frederick; a little brother would take up precious time and energy that should be devoted to Frederick.

**At school concerts, his sensory issues seem like a critique of the music.**

In some ways, Frederick was a typical boy. He loved to laugh at farts. He never put the toilet seat up before he peed. But as the days and months went by, the grim truth was setting in: Dr. Landau at C.H.O.P. nailed it back on 02-03-04. Frederick was not "high-functioning," or a kid who would someday blend in with his "typical peers." For the first few years of his life he was just "different." But now he was undeniably autistic. Au-Freakin-tistic.

Frederick was technically in elementary school but his self-help skills were still at toddler level. He had increased his vocabulary, but still could not put on his socks, button a coat, spread jelly with a knife, or print his name. At least once a week he got off the bus with a plastic grocery-store bag tied to his backpack; inside the plastic bag were his soiled underwear and sometimes even the pants he wore into school (we kept the classroom supplied with plenty of spare clothes.)

Once a year, we took Frederick to a County psychologist so the state of Pennsylvania could determine if he still qualified for Autism-related services, and it usually took about 30 seconds for the evaluator to realize Frederick needed all the help he could get. That year, the psychologist's report read:

"Once inside the office, Frederick was overly active and restless. He paced around the office and was fairly impulsive in trying to touch things inappropriately. For example, there was a fire extinguisher on the wall that he tried to touch; however, his mother quickly redirected him. He finally sat down on the floor and played with some toys for a short period of time. Frederick did not show much interest in the evaluation or the examiner and he did not actively participate.

"Frederick presents with other behavioral issues, mainly in the home and community. His parents have a difficult time taking him out into the community due to his hyperactivity and impulsivity. He lacks safety awareness and he will take off if not watched. Additionally, he is prone to tantrums particularly when he is told no and it is difficult to redirect him. Overall, Frederick has made little progress toward his goals and he continues to present with a number of behavioral concerns."

I remember a therapist telling us to analyze his "destructive behaviors" and ask ourselves, "When he does destructive things, does he like it? Is he trying to communicate? Would he do it if we weren't looking?"

All valid questions, but the real question was "Should we be adding an adopted baby to a household where such questions were asked?" Or in a house where Anna could write this diary entry, which she showed me years later: "I hate Autism! I never knew that a six-letter word could cause so much trouble. It is so hard dealing with it. Dad says he might want to write a book on what it's like to have a child with Autism. I told him if I were to write a book it would be on anything but Autism. I am feeling so stressed!"

When I had quiet moments then, the times when all the kids were in bed and I was alone with my thoughts, it would hit me that I had a son with Autism. In some ways I think I was ok with it, but I also wanted to do something about it. To fight back. But I couldn't. The joy deficit remained.

# 22 THE NEW (AB)NORMAL

Bernadette was finally warming to the idea that this was the right move and the right place for our family. Grace was blossoming into a really fun, really inquisitive kid. Her curiosity was legendary within my extended family and they loved hearing stories about her latest unintentionally hilarious question, including the time we were discussing topics of a spiritual nature and Bernadette told Grace that "God made her." Grace replied, "Well, if God makes people how come God didn't make Frederick so good?" Big-sister Anna was a creative, independent middle-schooler. Where most kids her age were into boy bands or Harry Potter, she counted the days until Sunday when she could go on the internet and watch Saturday Night Live (she wasn't allowed to stay up until midnight, even on a Saturday). She had also declared that when she was old enough, she was moving to New York City.

Everyone seemed adjusted to where we were, and I was adjusting to where Frederick was. Things that used to come attached with guilt or "why us?" musings just started happening without drama or emotion. Like most kids who are severely affected by Autism, Frederick was a flight risk, so anytime I walked into my house it looked like the open to *Get Smart* when Maxwell Smart enters a series of doors which menacingly slam shut after him. In our house, every door that led outside had two locks, and most had additional security in the form of an eye hook, high enough so Frederick couldn't reach. I was so used to locking doors that I could walk into the laundry room from the garage and lock it without breaking stride, as smooth as a pickpocket. Every time I walked in the house, and every time I left, I locked the doors.

One time we went to a party for my buddy Rob's kids. After we walked in he laughed and said, "Don't you want anyone else to come?"

"What do you mean?" I asked.

"You locked the door."

I had to laugh myself. "Oh, sorry. Habit."

Like everything else with Frederick, I was trying to find the humor in it all. One story I recounted often was the time Frederick jumped up after a poop, looked down into the toilet, and said "The Letter of the Day is C!" Below him was a perfectly-curved "C" in the bowl.

Not that things were getting any easier in that department. When Frederick had to go #2, the process was much like the labor process—long, drawn-out, and painful to watch. And there wasn't much we could do about it. We gave him powdered laxatives in every drink. Plus, with his diet—mostly fruits, eggless waffles, and yogurt—he should have been living on the toilet. We tried everything. We had appointments with several pediatric Gastro docs including one who called himself "The Poop Whisperer." None of it worked.

Frederick also had some cringe-worthy moments in social settings. The previous year, his classroom only had five kids, one of whom was African-American. The boy's name was Cameron. One day I was at Dunkin Donuts with Frederick and as we were waiting at the counter an African-American gentleman walked in with his son, who was approximately Frederick's age. When Frederick noticed them in line he walked over and hugged the kid.

"Ahhh, Cam is here." Frederick buried his head in the kid's chest and squeezed.

I was mortified.

"Frederick!" I gasped.

"Ahh-ahh, ish so good to see Cam."

The kid he was hugging was so petrified he couldn't move. The dad's jaw was on the ground. I pulled Frederick away. "Buddy, that's not Cameron."

Thankfully, my coffee was ready. I slammed a few bills down on the counter, grabbed Frederick's hand and ran out as he was screaming goodbye to the kid.

Whether through laughter, or just the slow accumulation of days, it was getting easier. And we found out that it if you asked the right questions to the right people, things often worked out.

For years, Bernadette was worried that Frederick would not or could not make his First Communion at the same time as his twin sister Grace. But our parish had a wonderful program for special needs kids to receive their sacraments, so Frederick celebrated on the same day as Grace, and we had a big party in the backyard for both of them. At weekly mass (or the weeks when we thought he was in a proper behavioral mood to attend mass) either Bernadette or I would stand next to him at Communion to make sure he consumed it all. And it usually went well, except for the times he would walk back making loud, overwrought chewing sounds like Cookie Monster. Or the time the priest said "The body of Christ" and held up the wafer and Frederick said "hi-5!" and tried to hi-5 him.

**The original twins.**

I was slowly coming out of my hole, looking to get back in the game. I started reaching out to some old friends, started planning some Sunday football get-togethers, and even looked up my favorite teacher from high school who I hadn't spoken to in years. Mr. Cornelius taught Theology at Holy Ghost Prep and I always liked him because he was one of the smartest people I had ever met and also had more faith in God than anyone I had ever met. It was a unique combination.

The conversation eventually turned to family, and I updated him on the girls and our occasional thoughts about adopting. Then the discussion turned to Frederick. I told Mr. Cornelius how things were going well but there were still moments where I struggled, times when it seemed like every minute of my life was consumed by "What ifs?"

And then he said something that hit me like a bucket of cold water to the face: "All will be well."

I sat up straight. "What will be well?"

"All will be well," he answered. "God made it, God loves it, God keeps it. It's Julian of Norwich."

"Hang on a minute," I said. I borrowed a pen from the waiter and grabbed a napkin to write on. "Who?"

He explained that Julian of Norwich was a 14th century Nun living in a cloistered convent. She got sick and was near death, and it was at this point she had visions of Jesus and Mary visiting her. She eventually recovered, and wrote down her recollections, which became "The Showings of Julian of Norwich," likely the first published book in the English language ever written by a woman.

In the most famous of the visions, Julian claims that Jesus placed in her hand something small, the size of a hazelnut, and when she asked what it was Jesus said, "It is all that is made." There she was, holding the entire created universe from the beginning to the end of time, and in it she said she saw three properties. "The first is that God made it. The second that He loves it. And the third that God keeps it."

I drove home that night from the Macaroni Grill in Wilmington, Delaware with my pockets stuffed with napkins, after a dinner between old friends had turned into a theological seminar.

I immediately bought "The Showings of Julian of Norwich" in its modern English translation and I was hooked. I read it and re-read it and even bought a version written in the original Old English, although I was never able to plow through that one. I think the proper theological takeaway from the book was this: if God is the source of all existence then you can't look at things as good or bad, well done or poorly done. There's no in-between, no what-ifs, no Frederick without Autism. All will be well, and we will understand the how's and why's of things in Heaven when we shed the limited perspective of a human mind.

I kept coming back to the idea that, to God, there is no past or future. Everything has been created already, from the beginning of time to the end of time. And if that was the case, then there was no reason for me to spend time wishing or wondering about what Frederick would be like without Autism. But my mind doesn't work like that; I'd never be able to stop ruminating on what might have been. So I came up with a convenient construct: I began to think that were two options for Frederick: exactly as he is, or never existing. Those were the only two scenarios. Frederick "as-is," or Frederick "not-at-all." I'm not sure if that was the proper theological conclusion, but it's what made sense to me.

When I told Bernadette about the book, and how it changed the way I saw things, I said, with a great degree of conviction, "There were only two possibilities with Frederick: as he is, or not at all. We either have him in our family as he is, or he was never born. Those were the only two possibilities. I prefer the former." It became my slogan, a pithy bumper-sticker-sized thought that was easily digestible. I started repeating myself like an old man who forgets how often he's told the same story. "It's Frederick as he is, or Frederick not-at-all. I prefer the former."

My desire to have faith had always been greater than my actual faith. I was born and raised by parents who took us to Church every Sunday without fail, I went to a Catholic high school and college, but my brain usually got in the way of my heart when it came to the spiritual life. I was a chronic over-thinker, and that's not the best recipe for a strong faith. I had no problems believing the "Showings" book; after all, these were visions. She never claimed she bumped into Jesus at the grocery store. But I wasn't sure—certainly not 100% sure—that I believed my new mantra of "Frederick as he is, or Frederick not-at-all."

In his book *Brave Men*, the World War II correspondent Ernie Pyle talked about how the Allied army in Italy was relatively small compared to their Normandy invasion force. The fighting in Italy would have been easier with more troops, but the Generals decided they would use a limited force to tie up the Germans there and render them unable to pour soldiers into France after D-Day. In that sense, the Allies sacrificed many men in Italy to save many more in France. Pyle wrote, "If those things were true, then it was best as it was. I wasn't sure they were true, I only knew I had to look at it that way or else I couldn't bear to think of it at all."

# 23 FREDERICK'S CALL SIGN

I'm not sure if it was in a high school history class or a book I read, but for some reason I always remembered an anecdote about Richard Nixon flying home to California after he resigned. Apparently, Air Force One is only called Air Force One when the President is on board. When it's flying at all other times it has a normal airplane call sign. When Nixon got on board in Washington DC, it was Air Force One. But a few hours later, when the plane was over Missouri, Gerald Ford was sworn in as President and the call sign switched from Air Force One to SAM 27000.

I thought a lot about that story as Bernadette and I kept thinking and talking—but never committing to—adoption.

Bernadette and I had picked an adoption agency from the Midwest that had a great track record in facilitating adoptions from Ethiopia and fulfilled all the necessary steps to adopt a baby boy between the ages of 0 and 11 months old. Well, every step but one: we had yet to mail the application. Every time we came close to pulling the trigger I had one terrible thought I couldn't get out of my head—if I mailed the paperwork I'd be writing Frederick off. Or that somehow, he would be different after I mailed it, that our relationship would be altered. That his call sign would change from "Only Son" to "Not Good Enough; Needed a Do-Over."

For three solid months the adoption application sat on my desk at home. If we had a good day, one where Frederick was reasonably well-behaved and our lives did not seem like a 24-hour Improv sketch, we talked about mailing it. But that day would be followed by several days of Frederick dominating our time and requiring five times the attention we were giving to Grace and Anna, and the application stayed put.

The paperwork sat for over 100 days. FDR reached double figures in the amount of bills he passed in his first 100 days; in that same span of time Bernadette and I could not muster the courage to affix postage to a 10 x 13 envelope and put it in the mailbox.

FDR ended the Great Depression; in some ways, we were hoping to end ours.

Despite all the research and all the conversations, neither of us were ready to take the leap. It was going to be a team decision and she had her own reservations. My inability to decide came down to this: I don't allow any major life-decision to be quick and painless, even when I think my first instincts are correct. And when a decision is really, really big, I pray about it.

But not this time. For the decision on whether or not to adopt, probably the biggest one I'd ever make in my life, I didn't pray at all. I think I was so consumed with making the "right choice" that I wanted to give equal weight to the emotional "pros" and the practical "cons," so I thought prayer would give an unfair advantage to the "pro" side. Let's face it: what kind of God are you praying to if His answer is "no" to the question: "Should we enrich our lives by lifting a child out of poverty and giving this child a lifetime of security and love?" Seriously. How can you not adopt if you bring spirituality into the decision-making process?

I needed some guidance, preferably from someone here on earth, and for that I turned to my older brother.

Kevin was born an adult; from my earliest memories, he was a no-nonsense, cut-to-the chase guy. Even though we're only 15 months apart, he always seemed 15 years older than me. So I called him up, told him I would be in New York for meetings at the NFL headquarters in Manhattan, and asked if we could grab lunch.

We met at a small deli on 49th Street, waited in line at the counter, bought some wraps and iced teas and then took a two-seat table in the cramped, elbow-to-elbow seating area. It wasn't the relaxed setting I had hoped for, but here we were. It felt like I was having a sit-down with The Don. After one bite each, I jumped right in.

"I have a confession—I lied about working at the League today. I actually came up just to see you. I wanted to talk to you about something." Kevin took his second bite and chewed, expressionless. What was going through his mind? He was probably thinking I had cancer. Or lost my job.

"Bernadette and I are thinking about adopting a baby." His face still didn't change. He had no reaction. Just kept chewing, looking straight at me. Maybe this poker face was the reason he worked in the Wall Street investment community. "So I guess I just want to hear your thoughts." More chewing. Five seconds passed. He didn't say anything. It was unsettling, so I did what I always do when I'm uneasy—kept talking. "You know, see what you think, maybe talk about it. Or whatever…"

Kevin sized me up. This must be what it was like to sit across from him during a financial deal. "Here's what I think," he said, as he put down his wrap and wiped his mouth. "Everyone has only so much bandwidth. And you guys may be at your limit.

You have your hands full. You gotta ask yourself how much bandwidth you have left."

Bandwidth.

I was hoping for some encouragement, a helpful push off the cliff, maybe a hug and some tears, but all I got was a computer term.

I thought about my buddy Demps and his line that always resonated with me: "If you go to a pizza place, they're gonna offer you pizza." I guess if you go to a guy who works in finance you'll get the cold, hard, analytical facts. My brother looks at numbers for a living. If the numbers make sense, his firm does the deal. If they don't, they take a pass. And based on my data—I had a special needs kid, I had a history of heart problems, and I wasn't getting any younger—the numbers didn't add up.

**Typical family photo.**

I was starting to worry that Bernadette and I would keep talking about it, keep asking people, until one day we woke up in our 50's and said, "Guess we're not adopting, right?" Up until this point, there was never a moment where we both said "That's it, its official, let's do it, let's adopt a baby!" At each step in the process, with each notarized form or background check, we reassured ourselves by saying, "This doesn't mean we're doing it. It just means we'll be ready if we decide to do it." But as I said before, it was never a question of whether we wanted to do it. That answer was always "yes." We needed to come up with a satisfactory answer to the question, "Should we do it?"

"Why should we adopt?" was the hardest question I've ever had to answer in my life. We had three children, one with special needs who required lifelong care. My salary was the same as a lot of people's: more than I needed to survive but less than I wanted. We had a nice house but an old car. Our vacations consisted of one free week down the shore at my parent's house and a Mommy-and-Daddy-only getaway every five years using hotel points and airline miles. We had nothing to complain about, but nothing left over. On paper, adopting seemed like a bad idea. But in our hearts, it seemed like the right thing to do.

It's funny how breakthrough moments happen—when you least expect them, but exactly when you need them.

One night after dinner, Bernadette and I were kicking the question around. I don't remember which one of us mentioned it, but someone said something like, "Wow, if we adopt we won't be empty-nesters until we're like 65. Can you imagine?"

And then something that I had never thought of before slammed me like a punch to the face: in reality, we would never be empty-nesters.

It was now clear that Frederick would never live an independent life, which meant there would be two options on how he would spend his adult days. He might end up living in our home until he died or we died. Or he would live in a group home, presumably very near Bernadette and me, that was well-run by a trained staff who could cater to his needs.

But even if we chose the group home option (and knowing Bernadette I could not imagine the day when she would sign off on Frederick living under a different roof) that didn't necessarily mean we'd be "empty-nesters." To me, an empty-nester is someone who goes to bed at night knowing that his young-adult child is out there in the world but capable of navigating life and surviving—if not thriving—on their own. My boy could never do that. To be an empty-nester seemed as much about the mental relief as it was about where the children were physically living. Even if Frederick was in a group home, which technically made our house an empty nest, we would not be empty-nesters. Mentally, psychologically, it would not be the carefree retirement of a typical person whose kids are out of the house and making their way in the world.

Adding a child wouldn't be postponing the day when we would be alone and carefree in our home because we would never reach a point where all of our children were independent. I'm not sure why that concept mattered so much, but it was the last piece of a giant puzzle that I'd been mentally piecing together for years.

On June 6, 2008, we finally mailed the paperwork. In our house "D-Day" used to mean "Diagnosis Day," February 3, 2004. But now D-Day meant "Decision Day," and it happened on the anniversary of the real D-Day. We were officially placed on the waiting list.

# 24 THE WEIGHT OF THE WAIT

According to our agency, the process to adopt a child from Ethiopia would go like this: in about seven months we would get a call saying there had been a "match"—an available child who fit the criteria of age and gender that we had submitted. When we formally accepted the "match" then we'd have to wait a few months to "pass court" in Ethiopia (no trip required.) If we passed court, then it was a 12 to 16 week wait until we left to pick him up.

When Bernadette and I first discussed adopting from Ethiopia, the waiting period until referral was averaging three to five months. When we decided to adopt, it was four-to-six months. By the time our application finally moved from my desk to the mailbox it had moved to seven months.

In the previous year the agency had placed nearly 300 children from Ethiopia to American families. That's nearly one a day, more than five per week. In fact, it's higher than that if you remove the "rainy months," September and October, when the country essentially shuts down because torrential rains make nearly every road impassable and there are no referrals granted.

But those numbers had been consistent, so we settled in for the wait.

When you make a decision like this, and the full weight of it hits you, you start to think about things differently. Everything becomes a potential "Last (fill in the blank) before the new baby arrives." Some of them just happened, like celebrating the last Thanksgiving and the last Christmas before the New Arrival. And some were things we felt we should do before the baby arrived. One of them was a quiet vacation for Bernadette and me. So we cashed in the frequent flyer miles and headed to the island of St. John's for a relaxing five days, with her parents and my parents splitting the week of babysitting.

At least I relaxed. Bernadette was a nervous wreck.

Frederick had always had problems with bowel movements. Specifically, he held onto them as long as he could until his body was no longer capable of containing them, at which point he'd drag Bernadette to the bathroom and, with her sitting on a little stool in front of the toilet, face to-to-face with him, still fighting off the urge to go, he would engage in a 15-20 minute blowout that was painful and physically exhausting. For both of them.

I convinced Bernadette that the trip was a good thing because it would force Frederick to have to go #2 without his #1 supporter sitting in front of him. The few days before we left found Bernadette pleading with him to go poopy, and in the last 36 hours before our departure she gave him enough powdered Miralax to fill a sandbox. But when we got on the plane, Bernadette called home and stayed on the line until the flight attendants forced her to hang up. Frederick hadn't pooped. It was going to be a long week for her.

While we were away, Frederick didn't poop, but the front lawn did.

When Frederick couldn't go for a few days the solid matter built up in his colon, and invariably some looser stuff would push its way past the blockage and make his underwear a little messy. Our parents were using baby wipes to clean his hands and hiney then flushing the wipes down the toilet. Bad move. Those wipes aren't meant for the sewer system. It led to a buildup and a backup, which blew the top off the little plumbing pipe on our front lawn, spewing poop and wipes like a sewage Old Faithful. Thankfully, they didn't tell us until we got home.

Still, we had some fun. The beach was warm, the drinks were cold. And there were some hilarious moments, like the night we were at dinner and Bernadette started getting text messages from our oldest daughter Anna, including "Do I need a shower?" and, on another night, "Pop Pop Tom is asking me to watch Jeopardy with him. Do I have to?"

But it was this trip, and that plumbing debacle, which led Bernadette to an obvious conclusion—unless Frederick was significantly more advanced in his potty skills when it came time to travel to Ethiopia, she would have to stay home.

When Christmas came we paid homage to our future son with an extra, empty stocking with no name, while Anna, Frederick and Grace's stockings were stuffed to the top. And as it turned out, so was the Ethiopia adoption waiting list.

When we began looking into an Ethiopian adoption it was a relatively new program with a very fast process. A few years earlier it was possible to go from submitted application to changing diapers in five months. But now, the landscape of adoption had changed. Guatemala was closed and Korea had slowed to a crawl. And many families who were shut out by Guatemala or frustrated with the Korea process were turning to Ethiopia.

To use a funnel analogy, all of the waiting families who were sitting in the Ethiopia adoption funnel suddenly had a lot of company, with couples giving up on those other countries and hopping in with us. Problem was, the neck of the funnel was still the same size because the Ethiopian infrastructure and court system remained the same, so it took all of us longer to get that coveted "match."

In January, the adoption agency officially told its prospective families that the best guess on the wait until referral had grown to 12 months. But we were already six months in, so we felt confident in toasting on New Year's 2009, "This is the year our son comes home!"

The calendar change was also met with Grace coming to terms with Frederick's condition. For years, Anna was the one who struggled with embarrassment, the one who cried and got red cheeks in public when Frederick was dancing with little paper cutouts of his guys. And now Grace, at age 7, was ready to join the Embarrassed Siblings Club. Around that time, we were planning a big playdate with a bunch of her classmates coming over and she asked me if I could take Frederick out for the day. I knew why, but not specifically, so I asked.

"Well," Grace said, as open and innocent as a child could be, "I think he might come down the basement and act silly and talk about Elmo."

At the most recent Christmas Mass, Grace's eyes darted from left to right for the full 90 minutes as Frederick spent the entire service playing with his Sesame characters on the floor. By the look on her face and the hue of her cheeks I think she assumed that every single worshipper packed into that church was watching her brother. Later that night she asked, "Is Frederick gonna act like this when he's older?" And then, I guess worried about catching it someday, as if it could be spread like a cold, she asked, "Do grownups get Autism?"

Our days were once spent waiting (and working) for Frederick to improve, but now we were waiting on his brother to come home. And we waited. And waited. With each passing month, the rate of referrals seemed to get smaller and smaller. The agency changed its official estimate to a 13-month wait. But at least it was springtime, the season of renewal, of life. It would be a wonderful time to receive that overdue referral. Instead, we got the opposite.

Bernadette had four sisters and one brother, Freddy. No one ever said a bad word about him; he was quiet, industrious, the kind of guy who at first glance you could tell would pay his bills on time and edge his lawn and keep the interior of his car uncluttered. Freddy had a good sense of humor—you could bust on him and he would take it. That thick skin was never more needed than the day Grace and Frederick were born. When Bernadette got around to calling Freddy to tell him the names of the twins, his heartfelt response was "Aw, geez Bern, I'm really touched. Really honored." To which Bernadette replied, "Are you serious? He's named after Dad you dope!" then burst out laughing.

Freddy was a non-smoker, very light drinker, and 10K aficionado. So when in late April of 2009 he started feeling bloated and uncomfortable no one in Bernadette's family was terribly worried, even when the first test result came back with elevated liver enzymes. But the family got a little more worried when the CAT scan revealed four nodules on his liver. When they removed three quarts of fluid from his belly the ensuing panic in the family was justified. He began a preposterously rapid decline in which he entered the hospital to begin treatment, and then the next day they realized treatment was futile so he should just be discharged to go home and live out his days, and then the next day he wasn't lucid and the hospital staff simply moved him to the floor below, the Hospice Floor. He died of cancer two days later, leaving behind a wife and two boys, age 14 and 10.

After the funeral, we were sitting at the kitchen table in Bernadette's parents' house. There was awkward small talk, and the even more awkward long silences as an ever-changing cast of people made coffee, served danish, cleared plates, sat down, got up, and sat back down again. At one point I wanted to change the subject of the conversation, which had naturally come back to Freddy's stunningly brief battle with cancer. At that moment, in May 2009, we thought the referral was imminent and we could be traveling in a few months. So with Bernadette in the other room I mentioned that we had yet to figure out what to do about the adoption travel. Should Bernadette stay with Frederick or come with me? Should I ask my mom to go with me? One of my brothers? My buddy Dave? And then Pop Pop Fred said "I've always wanted to see Africa."

Done and done.

Spring turned to summer, and there were rumors about further slowdowns and processing delays in Ethiopia. When Bernadette would post her frustrations on adoption message boards, the response she always got back from moms who had completed the process and whose kids were home with them was always the same thing: don't worry, be patient. You get the child that was meant for you. Always that same mantra: you get the child that was meant for you.

Through it all, our agency was fantastic—and honest—even though honesty meant telling its clients things they didn't want to hear. They even recorded a weekly phone message that updated how many families got a match, how many families passed court, and how many traveled to Ethiopia that week.

On June 15, we called the phone number and listened to the message; only two families were matched in the past week.

On June 22, the number was one.

By the end of summer the rainy season was hitting Ethiopia, closing courts for two months. Because the "back end" of the process was shut down, there was no point in agencies working on the 'matches' of orphans to families; otherwise, the judge would get back to work and find an even larger mountain of cases in the backlog.

On August 3, the number was 0.

We were completely freaked out. We had always been certain that our Ethiopian adoption would happen, but now, who knew? There were rumors that the agency was trying to open a second orphanage in the country. But why? It certainly wasn't necessary to keep up with their caseload of zero referrals per week. Were there improprieties in their orphanage, or in their process? Would Ethiopia be the next Guatemala and shut down? Maybe some unscrupulous agencies were finding women and handing them some money and saying, "Get pregnant. Quick!" Bernadette and I wondered if we would make it before the curtain came down.

The agency then sent out an email to its clients, and part of it read "We are committed to practicing the highest ethical standards in Ethiopia for adopted child and birth family background information." Uh-oh. This smelled to me like a 'get-out-in-front-of-the-story' email. The type of email that begins, "We would like to assure all investors" and ends with "rest assured, Bear Stearns has more than enough liquidity for the next five years."

Aug 24: zero referrals.

Aug 31: zero.

Sep 18: zero.

September 18 also happened to be the night that we accidentally overdosed Frederick. Around 8:30 pm Bernadette said "I gave him his pills." I was lying on the couch and answered, "You don't have to, I gave him his pills." Her tone of voice became more strident. "Dig, I just gave him his pills." I sat bolt upright. "I gave him his pills!"

Bernadette held both hands in the air. "You never give him his pills!"

"I was trying to be helpful!" I said as I sprinted into the kitchen, where Bernadette was holding two prescription bottles.

She shook her head. "It's not helpful if you don't tell me."

"You didn't ask," I said.

"I never ask because you never do it."

We looked like the bungling parents from a sitcom, except for the part when we called Poison Control, who suggested we take him to the ER on the small chance that his heart rate might drop to a dangerously low level. So we called my Mom to come over then drove Frederick to our local ER where they hooked him up and monitored him all night, and when he was stabilized at 3 am they woke me up (Bernadette was too nervous to sleep, whereas I had crawled into the gurney with Frederick and was out cold) and told us he had to be transferred via ambulance to another hospital because their hospital didn't have a pediatric floor. So at 5 a.m. Bernadette sat with him in the ambulance as they drove 30 miles to C.H.O.P. in Philly while I went home to get Anna and Grace ready for school.

And the wait continued. On October 30, there were zero referrals again. The official wait moved to 16-24 months. When we signed up the wait was seven months and now we'd already been on the list for 16 months.

Anytime Dee, our rep at the agency, had called me over the prior few months, she would start the conversation by saying "This isn't the call." But on November 19, 2009, I was sitting in the cafeteria at work when my phone rang with her number on the screen. I said "Hello" and she said "Hi, it's Dee," and then went silent. I paused, and then it hit me. "Is this the call?" I shouted.

"Yes, it's the call," she answered.

Finally, I could put into motion the plan that I had hatched, revised, tweaked and hopefully perfected in the last 16 months.

First I called Bernadette as I was racing to my car, but I didn't spill the beans—I just wanted to know where she was and what her plans were. She was home, and would be there all afternoon.

I drove the 40 minutes home from work in record time. First stop was the flower shop for a nice bouquet. Then I pulled quietly up the driveway and took out the video camera that I had kept in my trunk for months. And then I pulled out my cell and called her from the garage.

"Hey hon, where are you?" I asked.

"Upstairs," she said.

"I think we should talk about something. Do you mind doing it over the phone?"

By that time I was in the house. I hung up the phone and yelled, "Better yet, maybe you should come downstairs."

Right away, she knew. "You come up here."

I was messin' with her now. "No, you come down here."

"No you come up here" she said as she walked down the stairs and saw me. She put her hand to her mouth. "When did you get the call?"

"An hour ago."

"Oh my god!"

I fired up the laptop as we sat down on the couch and then pulled a chair in front of us to setup the video camera. Bernadette protested—"Don't tape this!" But this moment had to be recorded for posterity. I work in production. I own an HD video camera. And this was the moment when Bernadette and I would see a picture of our son for the first time.

When I had spoken to Dee at work, she asked me what email address to send the referral packet. I gave her my work email so Bernadette wouldn't know about it until I got home.

We sat down and opened the email with the subject line: "Here is the referral presentation packet and referral of your son. He is a beautiful boy." The feeling was indescribable.

The email began with a formal cover page, followed by a few pages of background info, then comments from the people at the orphanage describing his experiences and demeanor. We scrolled down slowly, eating up every morsel of information, and the fun part was that each time we were done reading a page and hit "page down," we didn't know if that next page was going to have his picture. Finally, on page 9, there it was: the picture of our son. His name was Fikru.

We screamed out loud in stereo, just blown away by how unbelievably breathtakingly cute he was. He seemed like a cartoon character, with eyes so big they took up half his head. They were gorgeous, gigantic, like two swimming pools of melted chocolate. I wanted to dive in. I wanted to reach through the laptop screen and grab him, just pull him into our home and our hearts right then.

We both cried and giggled and hugged and cried some more. There he was. Our son.

Next, it was time to tell the family. Frederick had a half day so we told him in person when he got home. I wish I could say that he was overjoyed or emotional, but I don't think he really understood it. We printed a full-page picture and said "This is your baby brother. This is your baby brother." He answered, "Yes baby brother. Oh yay!" And he threw his hands up in the air but he was holding Sesame guys so I got the feeling that Grover and Elmo were celebrating, not Frederick.

Our first stop was St. Ignatius, where Grace and Anna went to school. We pulled them out of class, took them outside and showed them the picture. They both erupted in joyous laughter, with Anna adding "I knew that's why you were here. Either that or someone was sick or Grace had lice." Then we piled everyone in the car and went to tell my parents. Grace insisted on running up to the door and making the announcement, but she was talking so fast it sounded like she was saying "We got the Will Ferrell, we got the Will Ferrell!" instead of "We got the referral." As we all studied the picture, my Mom kept saying "look at the big eyes," and we pointed out that he had Anna's lips, Grace's nose and my prominent forehead, so he must be our child. My Dad wasn't home, but later that night I got a voicemail with him screaming, "It's great, it's great, it's great!"

Next we drove down to South Jersey to tell Bernadette's parents. Mom Mom Bernie screamed, "Oh my God, he's so cute! Oh, I love him already." Pop Pop Fred had a typically reserved reaction, just chuckling and saying "Oh will you look at him," or something. But he did add later, "How do you pronounce his name? Fy-kru? Fihk-ru?" We explained it was "Fee-krew" and it meant "my love" in Amharic, the main language of Ethiopia. Pop Pop ignored the emotional impact of the name and honed in on the practical side. "I wouldn't let Frederick try to pronounce it."

It was nearly ten years after we first thought of adopting, more than five years after Frederick's diagnosis, and 17 months after we sent the paperwork. But holding that picture, it was all worth it.

# 25 ALL WILL BE WELL

I had gotten all my shots. I had made a list of what to pack, including copious amounts of power bars and canned nuts in case the Ethiopian cuisine didn't suit me. I was completely ready—or as ready as I'd ever be.

But shortly before we left for Ethiopia in March of 2010, an email from our adoption agency showed up in my inbox. The heading of the email read "new developmental checklists received." There was a .PDF attached, and the body of the message read:

"Currently there is a volunteer medical doctor visiting our partner orphanage in Ethiopia. She has observed a small number of children and is using a developmental check list. We are not aware if this checklist is standardized for other countries, other languages, other living situations or other cultures, so it may be of limited value. Her time in Ethiopia is limited and there are no plans for follow up observations. Because it contains information about your child, we are passing it on to you."

I had to read it twice to understand it, and this was the gist: apparently there was an itinerant doctor who evaluated my son concerning his development, but this evaluation was probably of "limited value," yet it was laying around their office so they sent it to me.

The PDF attachment was a one-page report on our son based on five categories: Communication, Gross Motor, Fine Motor, Problem Solving and Personal-Social. There were six questions (or six types of evaluations) for each category. Unfortunately there was no other paperwork; all I could see were the results. One of three little boxes was checked depending on whether the answer was "Yes," "Sometimes," or "Not Yet."

There was a section called "Scoring the Questionnaire" which stated that a "Yes" was worth 10 points, a "Sometimes" was worth 5 points and a "Not Yet" was worth 0. Sixty was the highest score possible for each. Little Fikru scored a 40 in both Gross and Fine Motor and an impressive 50 in Problem Solving, but I didn't care about those. I knew only two categories counted: in Personal-Social he got a 20, and in

Communication he got a 10. Underneath was the note: "If the child scores below 25, talk with a professional. The child may need further evaluation."

In case you just happened to randomly open this book to this particular page without having read anything prior, let me cut to the chase: this piece of paper was telling me my son in Ethiopia was significantly deficient in Social Skills and Communication, which meant he had a pretty good chance of having Autism.

Oh. My. God.

What. The. Hell.

Can't. Think. Straight.

I immediately emailed our agency, asking what this evaluation meant. They responded quickly, if not clearly, in a follow-up email:

"My understanding is that it was purely random - most likely the little ones not taking naps in the rooms the doctor visited. Please don't read more into it than that... There were a small number of children who got evaluated - the doctor apparently just had a short time and did what she could in a limited amount of time. She then left... Take care."

I called the agency, and spoke to our representative. "You're telling me not to worry about it?" I was nearly hyperventilating. "I know you have a lot of clients but don't you remember me? I'm the guy with the special needs son. I'm the guy who is going to COMPLETELY FREAK OUT when I get something like this in my email!" She tried to assure me that it was nothing to worry about. "I'm sure you're not worried about it," I said to her. "But, to reiterate, I'm the one with the special needs kid at home, so I'm very worried about this." And when she said the evaluation probably didn't mean much in the big picture, I asked what seemed to be the only logical follow-up question: "Then why did you send it?"

I was in total panic mode, but I did my best to calm my fears with some rational thinking. First, it was just a piece of paper. Second, no one could vouch for the bona fides of the person who evaluated Fikru. Third, I overreact to everything. Fourth, it didn't seem to jibe with the social report we had received a month ago describing him as an engaging little kid.

So I did what I always did—went on the Internet, hoping to find some information that would put my mind at ease.

I went on the internet to find a thing called the "Ages & Stages Questionnaire" that had the questions for which I had only seen the answers of "Yes," "Sometimes," and "Not Yet." In the Personal-Social category Fikru earned a "Yes" for the questions, "Does your baby drink water, juice or formula from a cup while you hold it?" and "When you dress him, does your baby push his arm through a sleeve once his arm is started in the hole of the sleeve?" Those "Yes's" didn't inspire much confidence; I would hope a ten-month old did both of those things. The two most concerning "Not Yet's" in this category were, "When you hold out your hand and ask for her toy, does your baby offer it to you even if she doesn't let go of it?" and "When you hold out your hand and ask for her toy, does your baby let go of it into your hand?" Those two seemed like a problem, since they seemed to directly address Theory of Mind.

When I looked at the Communication section, my heart sank.

"Does your baby make sounds like da, ga, ka, and ba?" Not Yet.

"If you copy the sounds your baby makes, does your baby repeat the same sounds back to you?" Not Yet.

"If you ask her to, does your baby play at least one nursery game even if you don't show her the activity yourself ? (e.g. "bye-bye", "Peekaboo", "clap your hands", "So Big") Not Yet.

This paper was giving him failing grades in all the critical areas. It felt like I was living through the C.H.A.T. test at the kitchen table again with Megan, the Early Intervention specialist.

That's it, I thought. My son in Ethiopia has Autism.

And then I proceeded to mentally beat myself up.

I started thinking that I should have been satisfied with Frederick, I never should have considered adopting. I should have listened to the Dayenu poem. Frederick would have been enough. Instead, I flew too close to the sun and got burned; I was about to bring home a special needs baby who would drain precious time and resources from Anna, Grace, and especially Frederick.

I didn't know what to do. Should we back out? Could we back out? Could I live with myself if we backed out? And then I thought back to that meeting with my old high school teacher, the meeting that helped me turn the corner on how I dealt with Frederick's condition. All will be well. Mr. Cornelius blurted out that line and I had clung to it like a life raft. It had saved me. Maybe it could save me again.

I re-read the Julian of Norwich book. I repeated her mantra. "All will be well." I decided then and there that things might not turn out the way I wanted, or planned, but everything would be ok. And I made a suggestion that Bernadette loved: let's name our new son Julian.

# 26  THE ROAD TO HOSANNA

A few weeks later, it was time for our trip to Ethiopia. After a nearly four-hour car ride I sat down with my father-in-law at a restaurant in Dulles Airport outside Washington, DC, for the Ethiopia Airlines direct flight to the capital of Addis Ababa (with a re-fueling stop in Rome.) I was terrified. I knew this was going to be a long trip, but it wasn't until Pop Pop started ordering dinner that I realized exactly how long it would be.

"I'll have the Chicken Florentine," he told the airport waitress. We were at an Italian place right near our gate. The restaurant had white tablecloths but it wasn't exactly Ruth's Chris.

"Although..." he paused, brow furrowed, "is the chicken spicy?" He scrunched up his face in order to convey how much spice he was willing to tolerate. The waitress assured him it was not. "Yeah, but, how spicy is not spicy?" Once that was resolved, he ordered decaf coffee, and then started in again. "But is it fresh? Is it fresh decaf? I don't mind waiting if you have to put a fresh pot on."

Yes, this would be the longest eight days of my life.

At 7 pm on March 4, 2010, we took off.

Sixteen hours later we landed in Addis Ababa in the early evening, and even though I wasn't expecting third-world blight in the airport, I was still pleasantly surprised. The walk from the plane and then through customs was no different than most American airports. And after customs, the airport itself opened up into a friendly area with shops and different food options, with the glass and metal architecture giving it a modern feel.

The agency would place over 250 children from Ethiopia that year, so almost every week they had a contingent of families doing this same routine. We stayed with the other adopting families at the guest house, a three-story structure the agency owned. It had the feel of a bed and breakfast with some tired furniture but freshly painted plaster walls and bright murals in the dining room and common area. Pop Pop and I had a nice size room, maybe 20 x15 with a queen bed and a twin bed, ample closets built into the walls, and a bathroom with toilet and shower.

After a restless night's sleep due to nerves and the six-hour time change, we walked down to the dining room for breakfast.

According to our down-to-the-minute itinerary for the week, we would all gather for family-style meals three times a day in the huge dining area. There were ten couples including us, eight of whom were actual couples and one that was a "convenience couple" like me and Pop Pop—a woman from the Midwest who brought her brother along as she adopted a six-year-old girl.

That first morning we all made our greetings and acquaintances, but you could see it in everyone's eyes—a distant, 'not quite all there' look, because everyone was thinking ahead a few hours to the moment they would meet their child. After breakfast, we piled into the agency's bus, which was a cross between a full-size van and an airport rental-car shuttle, and drove two miles to the orphanage.

Once inside we were led down a massive staircase into a high-ceilinged great room where all of us were asked to sit, and then a woman welcomed us with a short speech that I couldn't pay attention to, knowing my son was somewhere in this house. And then she looked at a list and called out a couple's name and led them into a back room then shut the door.

And there we sat. We were called back one couple at a time. Those with younger kids, maybe two and under, were led down the hallway into that back room. Those who were adopting toddlers and older kids went back up the staircase where the older kids lived.

On it went. Couple by couple the names were called, the people disappeared then came back a few minutes later, some crying, some beaming, all holding their brand new child. Slowly but surely, everyone was called but me and a couple from the East Coast.

Was there a problem? Did they screw something up? Did I screw something up? Was I missing a piece of paper despite scrupulously photocopying a backup of every form? I knew someone had to be last and that, given our experiences over the last few years, it only made sense that one last knife would be inserted in my chest and twisted for the maximum allowable pain, but seriously? It began to feel like the end of the Miss America contest when the two finalists stand there awkwardly, pretending they'd be happy if the other person won. I tried to cut the tension. "Ohhh, I hope you win, you deserve it." The other couple laughed nervously. Pop Pop mentioned it was starting to feel like "The Bachelor." The agency representative came back out. "Liz and

Joel," she said.

That's it. We were last.

I have no recollection of the next few minutes; apparently, that's the medical purpose of going into shock—it numbs and protects the body. Luckily, our agency did a very cool thing in that they filmed the first meeting between the clients and the children and created a commemorative DVD.

I've watched the video dozens of times since and, each time, it strikes me that I can't believe I'm ambulatory. After my name was called I walked through the door, white as a sheet and taking my pulse which, if I remember correctly, felt like it was north of 140, and all the while the cameraman backed his way into the room in front of me, capturing the occasion.

There were at least ten kids in the infant room, along with a few nannies. I scanned the faces of the children and couldn't find him. And then I remembered how much his face had changed between his seven-month referral picture and his next picture, taken at ten months. I tried imagining what he might look like now, given another four-to-six weeks of maturity since that last photo. I looked around the room at the faces of the children—That's not him...that's not him...that's not him. And then out of nowhere a nanny hands me a baby. I grabbed him under the armpits and pulled him up. Oh yeahhhh. That's him. That's my son!

In the video you can see me press him to my face and then I take a big huge breath with my mouth closed and lips tight—I'm inhaling him, hoping in one brief moment to understand who he is and what he's experienced in the first 11 months of his life. And then I pulled a family photo out of my pocket and showed it to him. "That's Mommy and Anna and Grace and Frederick and me. They all love you and can't wait to meet you."

And that was the extent of the mushy stuff. It was time to fire up the radar.

After regaining some internal equilibrium and having my pulse slowly retreat from its near-fatal tachycardia I carried him back out into the common area where all the couples were enjoying their kids.

I was unable to enjoy mine; I had to evaluate him. Despite the fact that he was my son and I wasn't giving him back under any circumstances, I ran him through drills like he was a prospect at the NFL Combine.

I sat him up and waited until he looked away. "Fikru! Fikru!" I said it loud and sharp and he turned his head back immediately.

Responds to his name—check.

I rolled some toys away from him to see which one he liked best. He crawled after a truck. I picked it up and grabbed another toy, holding them both away from him, one in each hand. He reached for the truck. I held it away. He half-pointed, half-pleaded, telling me he wanted that truck.

Theory of Mind—check.

I held him in a rocking chair and every time he heard the shrill voice of a nanny, he turned his head toward the sound, looking for her.

Not sure what that proved, but—check.

I hugged him again. The developmental checklist was wrong. All was well.

**Pop Pop Fred and his grandson in Ethiopia.**

But after the adrenaline rush of meeting my son for the first time and diagnosing him as neurotypical, I came back down to earth and realized I wasn't going home for a while. The agency thought it was best for the new parents and their children to ease into a relationship and have a solid week of transition before going back to America, which, despite my desire to hop on the next plane, made a lot of sense.

They had one big event planned for each day, during which time your child would go back to the orphanage while we went out and explored. We visited the National Museum of Ethiopia where it was humbling to see the display of Lucy, a three-million-year-old partial skeleton that was unearthed in the Awash Valley of Ethiopia. We visited a hospital that the agency supported where we learned that it cost 10 birr to get 14 days of service from the hospital (13 birr is one US dollar) and that women were typically discharged 24 hours after a vaginal birth. We also did some "power-sightseeing," and it was on that trip that I saw the most moving and lasting image of the week (other than the first glimpse of little Fikru.) There were two little boys, maybe four and six, who must have been true orphans. They were picking through trash, finding fruit peels and assorted detritus and placing them in a plastic bag. They were both dressed in what looked like burlap sack tunics, which barely came down to mid-thigh. And that's it—nothing else. No shoes, no socks, no underwear. Potato-sack commando. A dusty film covered them from head to toe.

After giving them a few birr and a power bar I walked back across the street and kept watching them. I suddenly smiled because I noticed that, despite it all, they were still kids. They were messing around, goofing around, pushing each other, and kicking what looked like an empty plastic half-gallon of milk like a soccer ball.

We also had one full-day trip that would take us from Addis Ababa through Tigray, Gurage, Butjara and Werabe before reaching our ultimate destination, a town called "Hosanna." Early in the trip I asked the bus driver about our itinerary.

Me: "What route are we taking?"

Driver: "What do you mean?"

Me: "I mean what roads will we be on? I want to write it in my journal."

Driver: "I don't understand."

Me: "The road. What road are we taking? What's it called? You know, like I-95, the Parkway, the Turnpike. What's the name?"

Driver: "It's called 'the Road to Hosanna.'"

Finally, it was the last day, time for the Goodbye Ceremony. All of us got on the bus to go back to the orphanage. We were led back down to the great room, where several days earlier we had waited to meet our children for the first time.

Occasionally during the week in Addis I'd had what can only be described as out-of-body experiences. I'd be souvenir hunting at a market or lying in my bed at the guest house and it would hit me: What the hell was I doing here?

To recap: I was middle-aged, slightly overweight, with a congenital heart defect and three kids back in America, including a special needs son, I was 7,000 miles from home without my wife, in a country with 5 million orphans and an average median income of $200, and I was here to finalize the adoption of an 11-month-old boy named Fikru, which translates from Amharic as "My love" but would be changed to Julian in honor of a 14th century female Anchorite Nun. But right then, as I sat at the Goodbye Ceremony, the only weird thing was that my father-in-law had gone thirty minutes without complaining about the food.

There was a formality to the whole affair. An agency representative spoke to our group; she was Ethiopian and her English was laced with the beautifully-stilted formalities of the locals that I'd fallen in love with that week. Every word seemed earnest and heartfelt and grateful. "I would like to thank you for coming all the way here to take the responsibility of taking care of this children...Every one of us here have a great attachment to this children."

After the speech, we brought our children up one by one to get their hands dipped in red paint then pressed into a binder, as a forever keepsake for the agency.

And then began the equivalent of Exit Interviews.

It would be the last time we were in the orphanage before returning back to the States and it seemed like we were in the real estate office in *Glengarry Glenn Ross*—all the nannies were "closers." They told the parents that every cough was minor, every kid was a joy, and all their personalities were wonderful. The doctor then came over to me and reviewed Fikru's medical condition. I asked about the three-pack-a-day cough he had. "It's just common cold," the doctor responded. She reminded me to give him his medicine three times a day then handed me the pink liquid—and a giant hypodermic needle.

"What the hell is this?" I burst out.

"It's how we give to him the medicine," she flatly responded.

I was apoplectic. "You injected him? I'm supposed to inject him?"

"No no no," she said with a wave of her hand. She pointed to the needle at the end of the syringe. "This unscrew."

We said our goodbyes, gave hugs and kisses to the nannies and staff, then piled into the agency bus. On the left side were bench seats for two; on the right, single seating. I took a single seat and, with Fikru asleep, I could feel the rattling congestion of his lungs vibrating my own skin. As the bus pulled away and headed toward the guesthouse, I pressed my face against the window and started crying.

But no big deal, right? You're supposed to cry a little bit when you're nearing the end of a two-year transcontinental adoption journey. If you're not shedding a few tears then you've got no pulse.

I glanced around to make sure none of the dads were looking at me. I took a deep breath. Chill, dude. No one died.

But the tears wouldn't stop. I knew I was supposed to be happy, and they felt like tears of joy, but there was something else, something bigger. I squeezed Fikru tighter and began to wonder—what was going on? This was not normal.

At warp speed I went from a steady sob, to crying buckets, to the type of weeping reserved for standing over a casket. My body was convulsing; I was afraid I'd throw my back out. I took another deep breath. This shouldn't be happening. What the hell is going on?

And then it started to make sense. I understood why this wave of emotion had just crashed on me, but I didn't want to admit it.

I tried to shake it off. I thought: Don't go there. Don't even think it.

But the thought wouldn't leave, so I wondered if maybe I was right; maybe it was true.

And then I thought back to six years earlier, when I was leaning against a different car window—not an Ethiopian version of a rental car shuttle but a Toyota Sienna Minivan as Bernadette drove through a steady rain up the Schuylkill Expressway in Philadelphia. On 02-03-04, that car ride led to an appointment with a doctor who made an unbearably sad prediction about my son's future, a prediction that would ultimately come true and change our lives forever.

We got punched in the gut and went down. Hard. But then we shook it off and got back on our feet. We learned to live again. And we realized that living life in full meant being open to everything life offers: the joy and the pain, the sadness and the smiles.

As I sat there on the bus I finally admitted what I was thinking. We went to war against a heartbreaking disease, and even though Frederick would never be cured, we also never gave up. And because we never gave up, I had earned the right to declare victory.

That's right, I thought. We did it. We beat Autism.

# 27  COMING HOME

The flight from Addis Ababa to Rome was scheduled for six hours and took off around midnight local time. Ethiopian Airlines supplied bassinets if you requested bulkhead, which I did, so except for takeoff and landing he slept in a little mini-crib attached to the wall.

If the flight to Rome was the equivalent of a leisurely boat ride on a calm lake, then Rome to Dulles was a white-water rafting adventure. Without a paddle. Or raft. Bernadette later joked that this was my "eight hours of labor and delivery."

It started during takeoff. I guess he was too tired to care on the first flight, but clearly his ears were bothering him as we began the Rome-to-Dulles leg because he screamed and cried like he was lying on a bed of nails. I tried everything—hugging him tight, bouncing him, tickling him, walking him around—but nothing worked.

A flight attendant came around and gestured without a word, as if to say "Give him to me." She calmed him down quickly then handed him back, but it wasn't long before he revved up again. At one point I was standing in line for the bathroom, holding Julian as he cried, and a female passenger in her mid-fifties stood up and gestured to me. What the heck, I figured. It's an airplane; she can't abduct him. I was in and out of the bathroom in under a minute, and when I came out Julian was calm and smiling.

When Julian was really wailing, Pop Pop would offer to help but I always waved him off. I figured he had done enough and been through enough. I guess my experiences with Frederick were paying off once again. I could be out in public or in Church or anywhere with Frederick, and if he was acting really odd and everyone was staring, I had learned to create a shell around me and him. And I did the same thing on the flight home to the U.S. I'm not sure if anyone was giving a disapproving stare, nor did I care. I was here with my son, in the moment, and even if he wasn't behaving—or, more accurately, even if he was behaving like an 11-month-old with congested lungs, a double ear infection, and an intestinal parasite called Giardia—it was fine with me.

When Frederick was bad in public I used to recite a Bible verse in my head, and I did it a few times on the flight: This is my son, with whom I am well pleased.

**The flight home.**

I got considerably less pleased with about 90 minutes left in the flight. Miraculously, Julian had cried himself into exhaustion on my chest and had fallen asleep. I gently put him in the bassinet, watched as he stirred but didn't wake up, and then sighed a long sigh of relief and closed my eyes. And then someone tapped me.

I looked up to see an Ethiopian Airlines flight attendant. "I must collect the bassinet."

My eyes bugged out. "No, no, you can't. No. He just got to sleep. We don't land for an hour and a half."

"I'm sorry, it's FAA regulations when coming into the capital of your country."

"Aww come on," I said, like a kid who just poured his favorite cereal only to see crumbs and dust come out. "Can you at least wait and take his last?"

She smiled. "Sure, sure."

That bought me three minutes.

When the flight attendant returned and took the bassinet, he somehow stayed asleep when I moved him to my chest, and after we landed he didn't make a fuss as we worked our way through customs.

And then it was time for the big moment: meeting Mommy.

I had a digital camera with HD video on the trip, so I got that ready as we walked what seemed like half a mile from customs to baggage claim where Bernadette was waiting.

In my memory, it goes like this: I emerge from a long walk and see Bernadette, then look down at the camera and hit the REC button. I train the camera on her as she sees us, breaks out into a smile bigger than a rainbow, and we meet and embrace and I say "This is mommy" as she pulls Julian from my arms and presses his cheek to hers and weeps quietly and hugs him and takes him into her soul.

But on the video, it's a little different. What I actually recorded was a very long video shot of the Dulles Airport floor during the walk from customs. And then the video shows a fuzzy Bernadette, then the camera autofocuses for a second, then finally shows her crystal clear. And then the video stops. Apparently, my camera was in Record Mode the entire walk from customs to baggage, so when I saw Bernadette and pushed the REC button, I actually stopped the recording.

That's right, I'm a Senior Producer at NFL Films. I've been in the production business for over twenty years. And yet a week spent in Ethiopia with my father-in-law and 16 hours of flight time had rendered me unable to discern the difference between the red light and the green light in a viewfinder.

I didn't have a video of the big moment, but it didn't matter because it happened—we were back in America. It was only then that I realized that the easy part was over. The hard part was still to come.

That's the thought that struck me as I drove our minivan home from Dulles, with Pop Pop riding shotgun, Bernadette in the middle sitting next to her new son, and Mom Mom in the back. We hit some traffic north of Baltimore, and then some more in Delaware, and each time I tapped the brakes it didn't bother me, because it delayed the inevitable. After years of thinking about adoption and two years of going through the process, plus a week in Ethiopia, we were about to drop a complete stranger, age 11 months, into a family situation that was pure chaos. On a good day.

Of course, the main concern was Frederick. Anna was a fantastic big sister and, even though Frederick is her twin, Grace was very much a big sister to him already. But how would Frederick react to this new child? Would he like him? Bond with him? Would he be hostile, or God forbid, violent? I doubted it, but like everything on this rollercoaster ride with Frederick, I wasn't 100% sure.

We had prepped Frederick for weeks, telling him his little brother was coming home. We didn't explain much more because he would not have understood, but we wanted to be very concrete about it. We broke it down into three simple parts: 1) There's a baby who is coming. 2) He will live with us. 3) He is your brother.

"Brothers love" is what we told him. "That's what they do—brothers love."

So when we arrived at home, my mom was watching the kids and I called ahead and asked her to take them upstairs. We walked into a quiet house and sat in the living room. Julian was wide awake. We asked each of his new siblings to come downstairs one at a time.

Anna, who was 12 at the time, came down first. When she saw him she covered her mouth and hunched her shoulders, with her eyes bugging out. I wondered if she was thinking back two years prior when she accidentally discovered the preliminary adoption application that I thought I was hiding well, and then stood almost exactly where she was now, in front of the doors that separate the kitchen from the hallway, and said "I just have two questions—when does he get here and is he older than me?"

I guess she finally had her answers.

Anna walked over and sat down, then spoke quietly, as if not to wake him, although he was wide awake and sitting on Bernadette's lap. "Can I hold him?"

I smiled. "Sure, you can hold your baby brother."

Bernadette transferred him over to Anna and she held him perfectly. His big almond eyes stared up at her. Maybe she was the first redhead he had ever seen.

We called Grace down next. She greeted Julian with the same chipmunk laugh she emitted when she saw his picture for the first time outside of her school. She knelt next to Anna, rubbing Julian's hair. He looked over at her and smiled.

Grace whispered, "I think he likes me."

"Of course he does," Bernadette said. "You're his big sister." Grace flashed a sheepish smile at me then went back to staring at Julian.

And then the moment of truth.

Instead of yelling for him I walked up to the second floor where Frederick was.

"Come on down, buddy." I held his hand as we walked down the steps. "I want you to say hi to your little brother." We turned the corner and into the living room where Julian sat, now back in Bernadette's lap. Frederick pulled away from my hand.

"Mommmmmy!" He ran to her and hugged her. "You home! Mommy's home!" Because our flight landed at 8am at Dulles, and because D.C. is three-and-a-half hours from Yardley, PA, Bernadette had slept in Baltimore the previous night at her niece's house. I had been gone eight days, she had been gone for one night, yet Frederick acted as if Bernadette just came back from two tours of duty.

"Frederick," I said. "This is Julian. Your little brother. He's finally home and he wants to hug you."

Frederick looked down, as if noticing Julian for the first time. He bent awkwardly at the hips and gently put his arms around him. "Awwwww, Frederick's brother." He pulled away and kept looking. Finally, Frederick noticed it: Julian was holding a tiny plush toy. It was Ernie from Sesame Street. It was one of the toys we had sent to the orphanage at Christmas and Julian had bonded with it over there; it had rarely left his hand for most of the past week.

Naturally, Frederick ripped it away from Julian.

"Oh hi Ernie. Hiya Ernie," Frederick shouted to the four-inch-high Ernie that was directly in front of his face. And then Frederick animated Ernie by shaking him up and down quickly and doing the Ernie laugh, which is a cross between a witch's hiss and sizzling bacon.

Julian burst out crying. He was agitated, squirming in Bernadette's arm, dying to get his Ernie back. Frederick kept going with his Kabuki Theater, making Ernie speak lines from *Sesame Street* shows.

"Give that back, its Julian's," Bernadette said. Frederick ignored her.

I tried to grab it gently from his hand. "C'mon buddy, it's your baby brother's. Brothers love. Brothers love." Despite the quiet, sing-song quality, Frederick got fired up.

"Naahayah!" Frederick screamed, which is a long, drawn out "Nooo" when he's frustrated.

Now I was the one getting agitated. Julian was home two minutes and already we had an incident. I took a sterner tack. "Frederick, that is not yours."

Frederick gritted his teeth and bleated another defiant, unintelligible answer.

"Frederick, give me Ernie, now." I held out my hand.

Frederick grimaced and threw Ernie down, hitting Julian in the face. Julian reacted as if a bowling ball fell on him, not a tiny plush toy. He was screaming like a newborn.

"Oh God," I mumbled to Bernadette. "He's been home five minutes." I put Ernie in his arms as Bernadette rocked him. "Shhhhh, it's ok," we both said in unison.

Out of nowhere Frederick flashed in.

For a nanosecond, I was scared. Really scared. Was Frederick just after Ernie again? Was he looking to harm Julian? Frederick had never hit Anna or Grace but would he act different to a boy? Especially a defenseless boy? Time slowed down and then stopped. I was frozen.

Then it happened. An awkward bear hug, all elbows and right angles, enveloped Julian. "Awwww, shorry baby. Shorry baby." Then Frederick looked at me and said "Bwuthers love, Dad, bwuthers love." And then he jumped up, clapping as if it was the happiest moment of his life, and skipped away into the other room.

# 28 THE NEW TWINS

About a year after Julian came home, Frederick learned how to navigate Netflix.

His favorite show to watch was *Kipper*, an animated series that had been out of production for nearly a decade. It was produced in Britain with characters—a dog named Kipper and another dog named Tiger—that speak with a British accent. His favorite episode, "Pools, Parks and Picnics" was made before Anna was born.

Frederick would always fast-forward that episode to a scene where Tiger is being chased by a bull. I'm not sure if the characters were in a park or having a picnic (I know they weren't in a pool), but as they ran away, Tiger would yell, "It's catching me!" and Kipper would yell back for him to "Take off your red coat!" A furious, cartoony bass-line strummed as the two dogs raced across the grass and then climbed a small fence to escape the bull.

Every time—and I mean every single time—Frederick and Julian watched this episode they would race around as if one was Tiger and the other was Kipper. Both of them had the exact timing down; just as Kipper and Tiger would fall to the ground panting, after about 25 seconds of running and yelling to each other, so would Julian and Frederick.

It was moments like these that made me realize we had a new set of twins in the house. At 26 months, Frederick was diagnosed with Autism. At the same age, Julian was bonding with his big brother.

Frederick and Grace were born four minutes apart but that's about as close as they ever were to being on equal footing. Sure, we celebrated the fact that we had twins, and when they were newborns Bern's sisters might ask if we were "bringing the twins to the party?" as if they were a single entity, but by 18 months of age they began to split apart, with Frederick taking tiny developmental steps while Grace "lapped" him, driving 40 miles per hour while Frederick was only going 20, to use Dr. Joplin's memorable metaphor.

We may not dress them in the same outfits but Frederick and Julian, despite their seven-year age difference, are more like twins than Frederick and Grace ever were. At first, Julian slept in a crib in our master bedroom but eventually we moved him into a room with Frederick. At bedtime, Frederick would give Julian a kiss and say "Night-night Julian." He became very protective of his little brother as well; anytime we went swimming at Aunt Carol's pool Frederick would follow behind Julian, making sure he didn't fall in the water. Their favorite show was *Yo Gabba Gabba* on Nickelodeon, and they would do the dances together as they were watching an episode.

**Brothers and buddies from day one.**

It's really hard to comprehend these two competing thoughts: Julian was absolutely meant to be my son, yet had we turned in our application a week earlier or later, he would not be. I'm filled with awe and wonder when I contemplate how he came into our lives, but I always keep in mind something I learned in one of our pre-adoption study classes. The agency made each family attend a full-day seminar, and one instructor said something that stays with me to this day: "Every adoption starts with a loss." A young woman had the selfless courage to bring Julian into this world and allow him the possibility of a better life. I think of her every day. She is my hero.

The transition of bringing Julian into our family had gone well, perhaps better than we reasonably could have expected, but we weren't quite able to put our family life on cruise control. Frederick's "car" may have only been moving at 20 miles per hour but it could still do a lot of damage.

Take our big-screen plasma TV. Seriously, you can have it. Frederick broke it.

Neither Bernadette nor I saw Frederick do it, we just heard him say "I shorry, I shorry" as he walked past us one night, and when we asked him what he did he said, "I throw rock in da river." A few minutes later I discovered the TV didn't work. He had been watching a particular episode of *Kipper* where the characters were skipping stones in the river and we took an educated guess that Frederick mimicked the arm motion of Kipper, causing the hard, metallic AppleTV remote to hit the plasma, creating a spider-web crack in the screen that rendered it dead, according to coroners from the Geek Squad.

He broke the TV during another pharmaceutical experiment. The medication he had been on, in addition to helping him stay calm and be less ritualistic at home, was causing his cholesterol levels to spike. We had to discontinue it, and it took months to cycle through other options. At one point during this trial-and-error phase I jokingly asked the doctor to consider medical marijuana.

The doctor was startled. "On a boy this age?"

"No," I said. "For us." Bernadette just rolled her eyes.

We eventually got him on a medication that allowed him to be at his best, but his best will likely always include limited interests and over-the-top obsessions.

He still liked to control whatever video he was watching, and play it over and over again. Because of that, certain songs and characters were permanently embedded in my brain. I knew the dialogue from multiple scenes of multiple *Kipper* episodes. There was also Ned, a little tow-headed kid from a late 1990's *Teletubbies* episode, who felt like our fifth child from the amount we'd seen him on our TV screen. We heard Ricky Gervais singing the "Letter N" song to Elmo on *Sesame Street* practically every night before bedtime.

But it wasn't always the same stuff. He occasionally found a unique video on YouTube that he became obsessed with for months; one year it was a *Sesame Street* Christmas song that he memorized, word-for-word, and sang out loud quite often. In case I wasn't 100% sure my life had veered into stranger territory than I could have ever imagined, the video was in some Eastern European language, maybe Romanian or Polish, but Frederick sang the whole thing with perfect pronunciation and tempo.

We once let him use a Kindle for a few days, until I saw on my credit card statement that he had racked up over $400 of Amazon video purchases. It seemed that the Kindle was always "signed in" to my account so he was watching dozens of *Sesame Street* videos for a minute or so each before moving on to the next one. Problem was, viewing them for a minute meant he was purchasing them at $9.99 a pop. I called Amazon's customer service number and talked the rep into taking the money off our bill and removing the videos from our library.

Sometimes I felt guilty. Why did I indulge his obsessions? Why did I let him take his little cut-out pictures to bed? (One night, I counted 68 "guys" with him.) Why did I let him watch more videos than he should?

I don't know why. My only excuse or rationalization was this: there's a lot of juggling that needs to be done when you are a special needs parent. There were days when I was busy helping Grace with homework or taking Anna to an after-school activity and I'd let Frederick have his way with the iPad, yet I also questioned myself on those other days when I was dialed-in and giving 100% focus to Frederick because I was never sure if I was doing things exactly right in order to help him reach his full potential. Self-doubt was a constant companion.

I would still get bummed sometimes, but I got better at not beating myself up over it. My son was compromised in a significant way, and I gave myself permission to feel sad about it. I took my nephew to the NFL Draft one year, a very cool perk of working for NFL Films, and the whole time I stood outside Radio City Music Hall I couldn't help but think, "I should be with Frederick." The following winter, I saw that a neighbor who lived down the street had posted a picture on Facebook of her kids ice skating on the pond in Yardley. The boys were both Frederick's age, and I couldn't help get a little jealous, and sad. They would have called and invited Frederick if he didn't have Autism.

But without Autism, we wouldn't have known that there were wonderful people out there whose lives were dedicated to helping the special needs community: all those Early Intervention specialists and therapists and teachers who treated Frederick like he was their own child and poured countless hours into making sure he had the best possible outcome. And we might never have gotten to know a little angel of a girl named Shelby.

We first heard her name when Frederick was in elementary school. He started mentioning her, but when we inquired he could never give us an answer that made sense, so we sent a note into school to ask about this Shelby person: was she a student, a therapist, a teacher, what? We found out she was a kid in one of the "typical" classes at the school, and Frederick's Autism Support class (which numbered only five children) had "specials" like art and gym class with them, as well as being outside at the same time during recess.

Bernadette finally met Shelby at Field Day, the annual outdoor ritual where the school breaks up into teams and has fun competitions. After the events were over the students stayed outside to play, and Bernadette watched as a bunch of girls from the typical class queued up behind Frederick to take turns pushing him on the swing set. Later, he was on top of one of those dome-shaped monkey bars and he was playing it up, saying "I stuck, I stuck" even though Bernadette knew he wasn't. Shelby and her girlfriends stood by, encouraging him. "It's ok, Frederick, you can do it, you can do it."

One recent semester was particularly rough on Frederick; for some reason, a scheduling quirk caused Frederick's class to do specials and recess with the grade below them. Frederick would cry to us at night saying, "I miss Shelby." His teacher noticed how bummed out he was and encouraged him to write a note to her. They sent it home in his backpack one day. It read: "Hi Shelby, I'm sad. I miss you. Have a happy weekend."

Eventually Bernadette friended Shelby's mom on Facebook and we arranged a playdate, which was actually an historic occasion in our house: this was the first scheduled playdate with a typical kid in Frederick's life. She showed up at the door with flowers and Frederick, instead of opening the door, ran around the house at high speed, yelling "Shelby's here! Shelby's here! Oh my! Oh my! Shelby's here." Eventually he calmed down and she drew pictures for him and watched videos with him while Bernadette and Shelby's mom had coffee. I tried to surreptitiously videotape some of it but then decided to sit back and watch, and enjoy.

A few months later Bernadette decided to surprise Shelby on her birthday. She bought flowers and practiced with Frederick on what he would say at her front door. She rehearsed it with him over and over: "Happy Birthday, Shelby! These are for you."

When they pulled into Shelby's driveway, Frederick didn't move. Usually, no matter where he went in the car, he would unbuckle his seat belt as we put the car in "Park" and scrambled out the door before we got the key out of the ignition. But this time he was frozen stiff. Bernadette turned around and said, "Frederick, are you ok?" Frederick scrunched up his face and said, almost out of the side of his mouth, "I'm feeling a little nervous." Bernadette was blown away; it was one of the few "typical-child" moments she had ever witnessed from Frederick. But he knocked on the door, remembered his lines, and they had a nice visit.

At the end of that school year, Shelby did the nicest thing anyone had ever done for Frederick. She showed up, unannounced, after the last day of school and gave Frederick a photo album with pictures of her and her girlfriends who sometimes played with Frederick at recess, because she knew it would be hard on him to go the whole summer without seeing them at school every day.

One night around this time, Bernadette's Mom had surgery, and during their nightly bedtime ritual, there was this exchange:

Bernadette: "And let's pray for Mom Mom Bernie…"

Frederick: "And Shelby."

Bernadette: "…who's in the hospital tonight…"

Frederick: "And Shelby."

Bernadette: "…and needs to get surgery tomorrow.…"

Frederick: "And Shelby."

Bernadette: "Yes, ok…and Shelby."

I knew that one girl caring about Frederick wasn't going to change the world, but it changed me. It's people like Shelby that gave me faith in the future, a belief that Frederick will be ok because there are enough decent people in the world.

Kids like Shelby help take the edge off of being a special needs dad. If I got angry every time I had a pretty good reason to be angry then I might not be happy very often. But if I pay attention to the little things, then the big picture gets easier.

So at night, I would stand outside the boys' bedroom door and listen to what passed as conversation between them. Julian might be getting crazy and yelling things like "ahoy" from his favorite pirate cartoon and Frederick would crack up laughing; other nights Frederick was the wild one and Julian would yell, "Calm down Frederick!" They are the new twins, but Julian will someday, probably sooner than I think, zip past Frederick in his development and won't want a kiss goodnight from his big brother, and Frederick will have to go back to mimicking Kipper by himself.

But that's ok. I often think back to when we were waiting for the referral. When our adoption journey began, the referral time for Ethiopia was seven months. It more than doubled before Julian came home. In fact, it took so long that several of the documents we had submitted had expired, and we had to get them notarized and re-submitted. Don't get me wrong, it was a lot easier than battling Autism but it was still incredibly frustrating, and there were moments of despair where we didn't think the adoption would ever happen. In those down moments, the only thought you have is "My child should have been home by now!" And then the people from the adoption agency or the friends my wife made on the adoption blogs would reassure us with that pithy little saying: "Don't worry. You get the child that was meant for you."

Julian was meant for us, but I think that's true of all our children.

# EPILOGUE

If you are a parent, you probably remember a time when you were out in public and lost your child for thirty seconds or a minute. Even though it likely turned out fine, you didn't know it would turn out fine, so for that short time-span your heart was racing, your senses were on high alert, and you were so stiff from head-to-toe you felt like you could snap in two. That's the same feeling a special needs parent has every moment of every day.

And you can probably recount some very specific details from that time of terror—what you were wearing, what your child was wearing, the smells, the sounds, the look on people's faces.

That's how I was able to write this book. I didn't start keeping notes the day Early Intervention arrived, and I certainly didn't have time to "journal" when we were racing from one quack doctor to another. I didn't think about writing a book until Frederick was at least seven years old, and I didn't start collecting notes or committing things to paper for some time after that. But I remember every detail from those first few years because I was scared, every moment, every day.

But we made it.

I have to admit I'm not "good" with everything. Whatever hopes we had of mainstream schools and blending in with typical peers is gone. My oldest son Frederick has Autism and a degree of Mental Retardation. He will not live an independent life. I don't like to admit those things out loud. Yes, I did think we had won after we adopted Julian, but there was a little "Dewey Defeats Truman" in that pronouncement. I still have anger. I still want to know why my son can't have a normal conversation or be in a regular classroom. I want someone to give me a reason. I want to know why I can't fix it. And I want somebody to stand up and announce to the nation and to the world that the "Aupocalypse" is coming—a generation of children on the Autism Spectrum about to hit adulthood. Where will they go? How will they be cared for? In a culture where nonsense and trivia are re-packaged as momentous and consequential, these are the questions that need to be asked and answered.

But I don't want to think about those things every minute, every hour. I have a life to live and kids to raise, so I've come up with a way to deal with our situation without getting devoured by it: me and Autism have come to an understanding. You could call it an out-of-court-settlement if you want. I'm not saying I agree with what has happened, I'm not stipulating that I'm ok with it, but the record is sealed and I'm just trying to get through the day.

Before Frederick's diagnosis, I was a different person entirely. When my best friend Dave got married, Frederick and Grace were not even one-year-olds. We didn't have Autism in our family, or in our vocabulary, and Bernadette and I were just a young-ish couple with three kids who had a babysitter and a night out. We were at his wedding reception in some old mansion that was separated into a dozen different rooms. One room had the band and a dance floor, another had the dessert, another had the bar. The reason I remember the layout was that this night would be the first time I was in the same place as Mr. and Mrs. Kelly, friends of my parents who had lost their son in the North Tower on 9-11. For me, the goal that night was to avoid the Kellys. I told myself it was better this way because if I saw them I'd have to give my condolences and they certainly wouldn't want to be reminded of their son's death on such a happy occasion. But the real reason was selfish: I didn't have the courage to extend my condolences. I preferred to hide than to say something. This was pre-Autism, and I was gutless.

Fast-forward a few years. My mom was having a Christmas cocktail party and she asked me to stop in and bring Frederick because some of her friends hadn't seen him in a while, and a few only knew him as "Joan's grandson with the Autism," and my mom wanted to show him off. And, lo and behold, Mrs. Kelly was there. I made small talk with the ladies and they all marveled on how well Frederick was doing because that's what people say, whether he's doing well or not. And as I was leaving I said goodbye and hustled Frederick out, and then I stopped. I realized that I always liked it when people asked me how Frederick was doing, I mean really asked, wanting the unvarnished truth. When they would ask, it was like they were telling me they understood it wasn't easy, that they knew it must be hard to be the parent of a special needs child. So I marched back in the house and waved Mrs. Kelly over. I paused for a moment, and then blurted out, "Mrs. Kelly, I just want you to know that I think about Billy a lot and how hard it must be for you and Mr. Kelly, and I've told my oldest daughter his story and we remember him every September 11th."

She put her hand to her mouth as if she had the wind knocked out of her. Oh great, I thought, I just ruined her night.

She gathered herself and said "Dennis, thank you so much for saying that. I can't tell you how much it means to me." Then we hugged, wished each other a Merry Christmas, and Frederick and I drove away.

The two takeaways from that moment were 1] some of my mom's friends will never be comfortable calling me Digger and 2] people want to know that you know.

Mrs. Kelly's biggest fear is that people will forget her son Billy. They will forget that he ever existed. He may be gone, but she wants people to know he was once here. And I want everyone to know that Frederick exists, that there are thousands of Fredericks out there, and they have moms and dads, and we want you to know it's not easy, and we want you to acknowledge that. Sorry, but we do.

I didn't know that before I had Frederick.

I've learned many other things as well. I've learned that everyone's worst problem is a catastrophe to them, and that's fine, even when I want to scream "How can you act like it's the end of the world just because your kid needs some extra help in math? Do you know how good you have it?"

I've also learned one of the great contradictions of life: if you don't have a special needs kid, then you don't know what it's like to have a neurotypical kid. Let me repeat that: if all of your kids have no disabilities and do at least ok in school and have at least a few friends, then you really don't know what it's like to have a normal child, even though that's all you have.

Your mind is blown, right? You can't wrap your head around this concept. That's ok. Just realize that it's only when you see a child struggle every day to communicate and interact that you can have the feeling I've had seeing Frederick's twin sister Grace talk to kids in the school yard and decide on a game to play, then see a few kids break off from that pack and watch Grace decide on which ones to follow, and with a few words be right in the mix with them. That social dance is not a given; that understanding of how to navigate people, and the world, is not automatic. It's something to treasure.

In addition to being occasionally angry and occasionally at peace, I also have many jumbled, contradictory thoughts.

I miss someone I've never met. I mourn for something that never occurred. I want Frederick back, but I'm not sure I ever had him. And I realize, as I'm writing the last of this book, that Frederick will never have a meaningful career but has already been more successful than almost everyone I know because he makes people better. Everyone is better for knowing Frederick.

If you think you've come to the end here, you're wrong. It's just the pages running out. I wish there was a Hollywood ending to this story but there isn't, mainly because it doesn't end. The day ends, the calendar flips, but the whole thing keeps going.

One more thing: if you're ever out shopping or at the park or at your child's soccer game and you see a kid who looks like he's misbehaving, hit the pause button before you react. Don't automatically think he's a spoiled rotten brat or that his parents let him play too many video games. It may be true, but if you don't really know, then don't assume. There may be something more going on than you think. And whatever you do, don't point. If that kid can't, you shouldn't either.

# ACKNOWLEDGMENTS

There are many people to thank, but the combined acknowledgements to them would pale in comparison to the love and appreciation I have for my wife, Bernadette. She is without a doubt the most selfless and giving person I've ever met, with unending patience and a high tolerance for all of my shortcomings, although she will not abide one particular thing: a sequel to this book. All four of my children—Anna, Frederick, Grace, and Julian—had to sacrifice a little here and there to allow me to finish this project. I am so proud to be their Dad. Special thanks also go to my mother and father, Joan and Tom O'Brien, my brothers Kevin and Michael and sister Colleen, as well as the entire Repsik family.

A project like this, which had no plan and no deadline, needs a lot of good fortune to be realized, and I was blessed to stumble upon Marla Miller, an outstanding editor whose revisions and suggestions made this book far better than it would have been. Eric Lupfer is a great agent and better person who never wavered in his commitment, and Naomi Rosenblatt saw something in this work that many publishers did not.

Thanks also to a family friend, Carolyn Hagan, who looked at the pages I wrote and told me they had a distinct voice, and to Keith Cossrow and Paul Camarata, two gifted filmmakers at work who gave me their extraordinarily helpful notes after reading the first draft. And to the most gifted storyteller of them all, Steve Sabol, who taught us to have a good beginning, a good ending, and to place them as close together as possible. To all the friends along the way, especially Dave and the Yardley gang and the entire SMC/ND crew; you are part of this story whether you know it or not. Special thanks to the teachers, aides, bus drivers, therapists, Jeffrey, and anyone who has ever worked with Frederick, formally or informally—yours is the greatest gift.

# AUTHOR BIO

Digger O'Brien was born and raised in the suburbs of Philadelphia. He graduated from the University of Notre Dame, was a volunteer teacher at Cardinal Hayes High School in the Bronx, and has won five Emmy Awards as a Writer, Producer, and Director for NFL Films. He and his wife Bernadette rarely find time to watch TV after putting the kids to bed but when they do, it's the social highlight of their week. You can reach the author at DiggerOB@gmail.com

CPSIA information can be obtained
at www.ICGtesting.com
Printed in the USA
BVOW03s1621280317
479663BV00013B/6/P